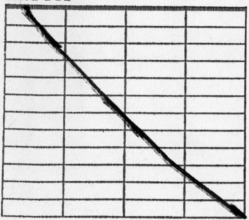

Personal Liberty and Education

Monroe D. Cohen, Editor

Alliance of Associations for the Advancement of Education

Citation Press   New York   1976

Grateful acknowledgment is made to Harcourt Brace Jovanovich, Inc. for permission to reprint "ygUDuh" by E.E. Cummings, copyright 1944 by E.E. Cummings, renewed 1972 by Nancy Andrews. Reprinted from COMPLETE POEMS 1913–1962.

LIBRARY OF CONGRESS CATALOGING IN PUBLICATION DATA
Main entry under title:
Personal liberty and education.

Includes bibliographical references.
1. High school students—United States—Political activity—Addresses, essays, lectures. 2. Liberty of speech—United States—Addresses, essays, lectures. 3. Education and state—United States—Addresses, essays, lectures. 4. College and school journalism—Addresses, essays, lectures. I. Cohen, Monroe D., 1924- II. Alliance of Associations for the Advancement of Education.
LA229.P42   373.1'81'0973   76–2511
ISBN 0–590–07462–8 (hdcr.)

ISBN 0–590–09406–8 (pbk.)

Copyright © 1976 by Alliance of Associations for the Advancement of Education
3615 Wisconsin Avenue, N.W., Washington, D.C. 20016
Published by Citation Press, General Book Publishing Division, Scholastic Magazines, Inc.
Editorial Office: 50 West 44th Street, New York, New York 10036
Library of Congress Catalog Card Number: 76–2511
Printed in the U.S.A.

1 2 3 4 5   80   79   78   77   76

Cover design by Constance Ftera

Acknowledgments

The following articles were written expressly for this volume:

"Personal Liberty and Education: A Commentary" by Nat Hentoff

"Art's Essential Meaninglessness" by Harlan Hoffa

"Mathematics: Road to Intellectual Freedom" by Marguerite Brydegaard and James E. Inskeep, Jr.

"Interlocking Rights and Responsibilities" by Marjorie Blaufarb

The following articles are reprinted from publications issued by member or cooperating associations of the Alliance of Associations for the Advancement of Education; grateful acknowledgment is made to:

"Relating and Responding" (from *Childhood Education*, Feb. 1972), copyright © 1972 by the Association for Childhood Education International.

"The Human Imperative" (from *The Music Educators Journal*, May 1973), copyright © 1973 by the Music Educators National Conference.

"Open Up the Well of Feelings" (from the Sept. 1971 issue of *The Music Educators Journal*), copyright © 1971 by the Music Educators National Conference.

"English as a Passionate Language: A Reminiscence" (from *The Reading Teacher*, May 1974), copyright © 1974 by the International Reading Association.

"Intellectual Freedom and the Rights of Children" (from *The School Media Quarterly*, Winter 1973), copyright © 1973 by the American Association of School Librarians.

"Is Tomorrow a Four-Letter Word?" (from *The School Media Quarterly*, Winter 1973), copyright © 1973 by the American Association of School Librarians.

Acknowledgments

"Freedom of Speech for Public School Students" (from *The Speech Teacher*, Jan. 1971), copyright © 1971 by the Speech Communication Association.

"Freedom of Speech" (from *The English Journal*, Oct. 1974, Jan. 1975, March 1975, and May 1975), copyright © 1974 and 1975 by the National Council of Teachers of English and prepared by the Speech Communication Association.

"Censorship and the Values of Fiction" (from *The English Journal*, March 1964), copyright © 1964 by the National Council of Teachers of English.

"Children's Rights and the School Counselor" (from *Elementary School Guidance and Counseling*, May 1975), copyright © 1975 by the American Personnel and Guidance Association.

"Assessing the Alternatives" (from *Childhood Education*, Feb. 1971), copyright © 1971 by the Association for Childhood Education International.

"The What, Why, and Where of the Alternatives Movement" (from *The National Elementary Principal*, April 1973, Vol. LII, No. 6, pp. 14–22), copyright © 1973 by the National Association of Elementary School Principals.

"The Helping System: Fostering Autonomy in Adolescents" was originally titled "The Education of Disadvantaged Adolescents" (from *The Educational Forum*, May 1974), copyright © 1974 by Kappa Delta Pi.

"Are Students Involved in Deciding Crucial Issues?" (from *NASSP Bulletin*, Oct. 1974), copyright © 1974 by the National Association of Secondary School Principals.

"The Antiachiever: Rebel Without a Future" (from *The School Counselor*, May 1975), copyright © 1972 by the University Center, Inc. and reprinted with permission.

"Walkabout: Searching for the Right Passage from Childhood and School (from the *Phi Delta Kappan*, May 1974), copyright © 1974 by Maurice Gibbons.

ALLIANCE OF ASSOCIATIONS
FOR THE ADVANCEMENT OF EDUCATION
3615 Wisconsin Avenue, N.W.
Washington, D.C. 20016
Elvie Lou Luetge, Executive Secretary

MEMBER ASSOCIATIONS

American Alliance for Health, Physical Education, and Recreation
1201 Sixteenth Street, N.W.
Washington, D.C. 20036
George F. Anderson, Executive Secretary-Treasurer

American Association of School Librarians
50 East Huron Street
Chicago, Illinois 60611
Alice Fite, Executive Secretary

American Personnel and Guidance Association
1607 New Hampshire Avenue, N.W.
Washington, D.C. 20009
Charles L. Lewis, Executive Vice-President

American School Counselors Association
1607 New Hampshire Avenue, N.W.
Washington, D.C. 20009
Donald W. Severson, President

Association for Childhood Education International
3615 Wisconsin Avenue, N.W.
Washington, D.C. 20016
Alberta L. Meyer, Executive Secretary

Home Economics Education Association
1201 Sixteenth Street, N.W.
Washington, D.C. 20036
Catherine A. Leisher, Executive Secretary

International Reading Association
800 Barksdale Road
Newark, Delaware 19711
Ralph C. Staiger, Executive Director

Music Educators National Conference
1902 Association Drive
Reston, Virginia 22091
Gene Morlan, Acting Executive Secretary

National Council of Teachers of Mathematics
1906 Association Drive
Reston, Virginia 22091
James D. Gates, Executive Secretary

Speech Communication Association
5205 Leesburg Pike
Falls Church, Virginia 22041
William Work, Executive Secretary

COOPERATING ASSOCIATIONS

Kappa Delta Pi
Box A, West Lafayette, Indiana 47906
J. Richard McElheny, Executive Secretary

National Art Education Association
1916 Association Drive
Reston, Virginia 22091
John Mahlmann, Executive Secretary

National Association of Elementary School Principals
1801 North Moore Street
Arlington, Virginia 22209
William L. Pharis, Executive Director

National Association of Secondary School Principals
1904 Association Drive
Reston, Virginia 22091
Owen B. Kiernan, Executive Secretary

National Council of Teachers of English
1111 Kenyon Road
Urbana, Illinois 61801
Robert F. Hogan, Executive Secretary

Phi Delta Kappa
Eighth and Union Avenues
Bloomington, Indiana 47401
Lowell C. Rose, Executive Secretary

CONTENTS

Foreword   xiii

Personal Liberty and Education: A Commentary
    Nat Hentoff   1

FREEDOM TO BE

Relating and Responding: The Adult
    Karl W. Deutsch   15

The Human Imperative
    Fred G. Burke   29

Open Up the Well of Feelings
    Asahel D. Woodruff   37

Art's Essential Meaninglessness
    Harlan Hoffa   45

English As a Passionate Language:
A Reminiscence
    Marian Ronan   55

Mathematics: Road to Intellectual Freedom
      Marguerite Brydegaard and
      James E. Inskeep, Jr.   65

Interlocking Rights and Responsibilities
      Marjorie Blaufarb   72

FREEDOM TO SPEAK, WRITE, AND READ

Intellectual Freedom and the Rights
of Children
      Judith F. Krug   79

Is Tomorrow a Four-Letter Word?
      Jean Karl   86

Freedom of Speech for Public School Students
      Peter E. Kane   96

Freedom of Speech
      Thomas L. Tedford and Ruth McGaffey   109

Censorship and the Values of Fiction
      Wayne C. Booth   127

Children's Rights and the School Counselor
      William H. Van Hoose   143

FREEDOM TO CHOOSE

Assessing the Alternatives
      Charles H. Rathbone   155

The What, Why, and Where of the
Alternatives Movement
      Mario D. Fantini   161

The Helping System: Fostering Autonomy
in Adolescents
      Moshe Smilansky and Donald P. Sanders   176

Are Students Involved in Deciding
Crucial Issues?
      James E. Calkins   205

The Antiachiever: Rebel Without a Future
      Stanley R. Sherman, David Zuckerman,
      and Alan B. Sostek   219

Walkabout: Search for the Right Passage
from Childhood and School
      Maurice Gibbons   236

About the Contributors   254

Because we exist within the context of a pluralistic society, the Alliance of Associations for the Advancement of Education recommends that the education of children and youth incorporate activities involving ethical decision-making and aesthetic discrimination.

Because the Alliance of Associations for the Advancement of Education supports the constitutional rights of all persons to their individual and collective freedom to express views and feelings which have also been recognized by the courts of this nation; and because the United States Congress has enacted into law protection of the rights and privacy of parents and students, particularly relating to the school records maintained on each student (PL 93-380); and because our children and youth need specific interpretation related to the constitutional and lawful rights related to the rights to which present and former students (and parents) are entitled, the Alliance of Associations for the Advancement of Education formally supports the Constitution of the United States of America, in particular the first and fourteenth amendments as related to this position statement, and Public Law 93-380: and AAAE is thereby committed to be actively involved in assuring that students be treated as citizens of the United States of America with all due rights, privileges, and responsibilities; and AAAE supports legislation and court actions which will insure rights of students as citizens of the United States of America.

FOREWORD

What better recognition of the Bicentennial could educators make than to reaffirm Jefferson's faith in democracy and dedicate themselves to his pledge of "hostility against every form of tyranny over the mind of man!"

The organizations in the Alliance of Associations for the Advancement of Education (AAAE) represent, by and large, teachers who share Jefferson's faith. The Alliance was formed in 1970, partly to fill a void left by the demise of the Education Policies Commission. The member associations exist to serve the cause of American education rather than for the individual benefit of their members.

A prime concern of the Alliance has been the need to re-establish public faith in the schools. The Constitution of AAAE states: "It shall be the purpose of the Alliance to improve the quality of education in America. . . ."

The two resolutions on the opposite page, adopted by the Alliance as policy positions, are specifically concerned with decision-making and with the responsibility of the schools in a democratic society for preparing citizens to make informed choices.

The governing body of AAAE voted unanimously to prepare a volume that would serve as a public statement of its support of the civil liberties of both students and school personnel in a trying time. Each member association of the Alliance was asked to contribute an original piece or pertinent material from its own publications, and an invitation to select appropriate articles was also extended to several cooperating organizations.

Warm appreciation is extended to Monroe D. Cohen of the Association for Childhood Education International for his many contributions as editor.

Charles L. Gary
Former Executive Secretary, Music
Educators National Conference

President, Alliance of
Associations for the Advancement
of Education, 1974–75

A frequent writer on events involving civil liberties surveys highlights of the articles in this volume and points out some ramifications of the issues of freedom in education to society at large.

Personal Liberty and Education: A Commentary

NAT HENTOFF

Two years after *Tinker* v. *Des Moines Independent School District* (1969)—a key Supreme Court decision resoundingly reaffirming the fundamental Constitutional rights and liberties of students — the American Civil Liberties Union asked me to engage in a national survey of Tinker's effects on secondary schools.

It was a dismaying journey. Some schools, to be sure, had come to discover that their responsibility, in a democracy, was to enable their students to learn how to be independent citizens. Most schools, however, considered student nonconformity to be at best eccentric and in any case, culpable. What particularly saddened me was that most students appeared to concur in that judgment or did not think about the matter of their liberties at all.

There were exceptions among students, and there continue to

1

be, but I do not expect that a similar investigative journey around the country during the Bicentennial Year would reveal significantly different results—except for the fact that more civil liberties groups have directed their attention to supporting those bold young citizens who insist on confronting teachers and principals with the United States Constitution (from which some of the latter recoil as if it had been written by Lenin). There was a high school student in South Carolina, for instance, who, when running for school office, was suddenly expunged from the ballot by the principal because he had written an article critical of the administration in the school paper. The young man informed the principal that his name could *not* be removed from the ballot. "That's unconstitutional!" the student emphasized.

The principal shuddered. "The constitution of this school," he instructed the student, "takes precedence over the United States Constitution."

FREEDOM TO SPEAK—AND TO WRITE

In 1974, three years after my hegira, *The Report of the Commission of Inquiry into High School Journalism*, convened by the Robert F. Kennedy Memorial, was published by Schocken under the title *Captive Voices*. The Commission, composed of high school students, teachers, journalists, school administrators, and community organizers, had held hearings on the freedom of the student press in various parts of the country. It concluded that, Supreme Court decisions notwithstanding:

> Censorship and the systematic lack of freedom to engage in open, responsible journalism characterize high school journalism. Unconstitutional and arbitrary restraints are so deeply embedded in high school journalism as to overshadow its achievement.

Censorship, of course, ineluctably leads to self-censorship, and, the Commission continued:

> Self-censorship, the result of years of unconstitutional administrative and faculty censorship, has created passivity among students and made them cynical about the guarantees of a free press under the First Amendment.

A California student, Janice Fuhrman, told the Commission that

2

as editor of her high school newspaper, she had been suspended by the principal for writing critically of his censorship of another publication. Tom Paine would have admired that kind of spirit, but her principal considered such doughty independence dangerous to the other students. With the help of a civil liberties attorney, Ms. Fuhrman was reinstated but did not feel particularly triumphant because, as she told the Commission, "This may sound zany, but I don't think the majority of kids in our school care that much about individuals expressing themselves."

"Zany" is not quite the word. What kinds of citizens will these high school students and their counterparts throughout the country become? How wide-ranging a freedom to read, to inquire, will they want *their* children to have?

In the article in this present book, "Freedom of Speech," Thomas Tedford and Ruth McGaffey provide some evidence of how denotatively ignorant many Americans are of what the First Amendment means and was meant to mean. I can add all too many equally grim illustrations from other surveys of the populace. For example, a 1974 Gallup poll of high school juniors and seniors asked the question: "Would the nation be better off, in your opinion, if every news article sent out of Washington was checked by a government agency to see that the facts are correct?"

Sixty-three percent of the polled youngsters did indeed believe the government should have a look at all news copy coming from Washington before it is printed.

As is indicated, with specifics, in several articles that follow, censorship is far from an extinct force in the United States. Within a relatively brief period of time in 1975, for further illustration, school boards and libraries in Wisconsin alone banned *The Godfather, Bury My Heart at Wounded Knee, The Exorcist, The Last Whole Earth Catalogue*, and that venerable but still hardy target of suppressors, *Catcher in the Rye*. How less censorious are the children of these censors likely to be?

LIVING THE FIRST AMENDMENT

The material in this book on censorship, and on students' rights to freedom of speech and freedom to read ought to be discussed

3

in classrooms, all kinds of classrooms, with passion and historical example, and in debates so students can get a sense of how urgent an issue this is and always has been in American history. If more students did get caught up in the high excitement of both free inquiry and of battling against those who would squash it, the abstractness of "freedom"-of-the-word-on-the-page would fall away and they would begin to know it as an active state of being.

I have seen a number of such students *living* the First Amendment, bringing their glowering principals into court and reclaiming their patrimony with the help of branches of the American Civil Liberties Union. Theirs has been, in a most durable way, a decidedly invigorating educational experience. One young woman in New York, Priscilla Marco, wrote an article on student rights for her high school paper, and it was instantly suppressed by the school's authoritarian principal who for years had kept out of the paper any of the myriad ideas with which he did not agree. Ms. Marco went to the New York Civil Liberties Union which, in turn, forced the Board of Education to have a special issue of her school paper printed with her article in it. The last paragraph read:

> It is illegal for us not to be informed as to what our rights are. This cannot be allowed to continue. We are human beings, we have rights—they must not be ignored. Students, arise and demand your rights, because that's the only way you're going to get them!

In my view, Priscilla Marco is already well-educated in being a sturdily independent citizen. If I were superintendent of a school system, I would invite her to give workshops in free expression for principals and teachers.

LEARNING TO FEEL ADEQUATE

Just as palpable knowledge of one's liberties and rights as a "person under the Constitution" cannot be acquired passively, so a sense of one's other capabilities as a free citizen is most keenly learned by testing oneself in action. Consider James Calkins' article, "Are Students Involved in Deciding Crucial Issues?", a description and analysis of how students at Staples High School (Westport, Connecticut) have really become part of its decision-making process. There are still few such high schools, and for that matter, I know of not many more colleges at which students have actual, not cosmetic, responsibility for making and sharing in decisions for whose consequences they have to be responsible.

Despite all the school "reform" furor and "radical" alternatives of the 1960s, most students continue to go from kindergarten through graduate school with scant chance to learn how to be independent, to take risks, to stretch themselves, to surprise themselves, to begin to imagine their potential. It is difficult, to use Paul Goodman's phrase, for *people rather than personnel* to emerge from so many spirit-constricting years.

A while ago, Noel McInnis, teaching at a two-year college in Evanston, Illinois, wrote:

> My greatest challenge as a teacher of college freshmen and sophomores is the large number of students I encounter who feel that they are inadequate human beings. My greatest problem is convincing them they are not. It is not difficult to understand why so many students feel personally inferior and why it is so hard for somebody in my position to convince them otherwise. Very simply put, their previous teachers have contributed greatly to their feelings of personal inadequacy, and they now find it hard to believe a teacher who treats them as competent persons.

"WILL THAT BE ON THE EXAM?"

My own experience as a sometime teacher of college students has been similar. An itinerant adjunct, I teach education, criticism, investigative journalism, and First Amendment case law for non-lawyers. In each course the grade is based on an independent project of substance and seriousness. At the beginning of each course, many students proclaim fearfully that they are utterly incapable of engaging in a sizeable undertaking on their own. But to their surprise, they turn out, with some prodding, to be capable. That alone, aside from what they've learned about the subject of the undertaking, is of initially stunning educational value to them.

I've also taught, the same way, in graduate schools, where I am considered peculiar by some colleagues because, they say, I expect too much initiative of students. Many of *their* students, however, I find suffering from the same debility described by a commission of five graduate students in a report for the American Political Science Association on graduate education in that field. That report says in part:

> Fear is the dominant motif in the life of the graduate student.
> . . . Much of graduate education is an obstacle to, rather than a
> means of . . . learning and development. . . . The real goals—
> education, learning, and enlightenment—get subsumed by the
> more obvious criteria like grades, exams, and the degree itself.
> . . . Too high a value is placed on answering questions posed by
> others rather than the posing of one's own questions, which is so
> important to original research.

It sounds like junior high school all over again! The ultimate effects of this kind of teaching and "learning," which started, of course, well before junior high school, have been distilled in one of G.B. Trudeau's *Doonesbury* cartoon strips. A law school professor says to his class: "Let me put it to you all, then—What should a knowledge of the law tempered with a sense of morality produce?"

There is silence from the assembled students until the professor, exasperated, answers his own question: "Why, JUSTICE of course!"

Finally, one student reacts, asking, "Will that be on the exam?"

"No," the professor's head sinks into his fist, "of course, not."

AUTO-ANESTHESIA

Doonesbury came to mind while I was reading a question posed in this volume by Fred Burke in "The Human Imperative:"

> Is there not a message somewhere in the fact that half a century
> of humanistic instruction in our schools and colleges preceded
> My Lai? In the American response to our policies in East Asia?
> In the persistence of racism and in the frightening brutality of our
> cities? In the almost sadistic maiming of our environment? In
> the parochial and selfish insensitivity of our complacent suburbs?
> Has the teaching of music, art, drama, philosophy and literature
> contributed *anything* to soothing the savage breast, to mitigating
> the violence of men?

What is there, moreover, about the way in which this knowledge has been learned that has nurtured not only violence but the enormous capacity of our educated citizenry to remain passive in the face of violence committed abroad in its name and in the face of violence, psychic and physical, done to the insulted and injured in its own country?

When education has been a largely passive process, when education has not actively involved and tested the self, the result of all those schooling years is a citizenry afflicted with what Joseph Lyford has characterized as auto-anesthesia:

> The first step in auto-anesthesia is to turn one's eyes away from the object or act of cruelty itself. It is not necessary to ignore the object or act completely, but it is necessary to consider it only in the abstract—in photographs, television, books, speeches, conversations, etc.; then the mind, which is naturally intolerant of pain, can erase a great deal of the shock and guilt.

Judging by years of school completed, ours is a quite highly educated populace, but it is so anesthetized that for one of the more glaring examples, health care for millions of the poor remains abysmal, with infant mortality rates still much higher in ghettos than in middle-class enclaves while the defense expenditures exceed $90-billion a year.

This is an educated populace that does not care that in 1974 *each* of the ten largest American cities had a higher murder rate than Northern Ireland. This body count, law professor Franklin Zmiring has pointed out in the *Wall Street Journal*, has been "adjusted" to because it mostly consists of "faceless young black males."

TOWARD SELF-TESTING LEARNING

How to root out auto-anesthesia? How to prevent it from taking root? In considering these questions, Maurice Gibbons' "Walkabout: Searching for the Right Passage from Childhood and School" in the last section of this book is especially provocative. I find too many of his models of complementary self-education by the young too upper-middle class, but he does get at some of the fundamentals of what education in a democracy ought to be:

The school—and concerned adult—can have no higher aspiration for young people than assisting them to develop a profound sense of their own worth and identity. . . .

The major challenge for young people in our society is making decisions. . . . Yet, in most schools, students make few decisions of any importance and receive no training in decision making or in the implementation and reassessment cycle which constitutes the basic growth pattern. . . . The test . . . of life is not what [the student] can do under a teacher's direction, but what the teacher has enabled him to decide and to do on his own.

Youngsters who do develop a sense of their own worth and identity are much more likely, obviously, to be immune to auto-anesthesia and to grow up—instead of sideways. They are more likely to respect the individuality (however diverse) and the potential of others because of their security in themselves and their undiminished curiosity about themselves. And if they have been able to test their abilities, while young, to make decisions on their own, they are more likely to be risk-takers, in terms of imagination as well as action, for the rest of their lives.

But I would expand the "Walkabout" concept, involving students at earlier ages in outside-the-school independent learning, and incorporating some of the ideas in "The Helping System: Fostering Autonomy in Adolescents" by Moshe Smilansky and Donald P. Sanders.

In the past, when schooling time was shorter, many more of the young than now were already ordinarily engaged in non-school activities that, by the natural order of things, quickened their sense of self-worth. As workers, they had, as James S. Coleman has pointed out in *Youth: Transition to Adulthood, Report of the Panel on Youth of the President's Science Advisory Committee* (The University of Chicago Press, 1974):

important roles involving productive activity: helping with child care, working at home, in the store, on the farm, at the shop. . . . These were roles in which [the youngster] was not a student but a young person with responsibilities affecting other people's welfare.

The young then were more able than now to experience what "becoming adult" means "in matters other than gaining cognitive skills."

Now, as then, all kinds of kids, not only the "disadvantaged," need to experience different ways and contexts of self-testing learning, outside as well as inside schools. The Panel suggests that youngsters, starting in high school, be able to alternate their time between school and jobs for which they would receive learning credits. Jobs out there in "the world of work," as certain educators like to say, where the young would have a chance "to be enlarged by experience with persons differing in social class, subculture, and in age."

In another suggestion, not likely to be applauded by teachers' unions and administrators, the Panel proposes that educational vouchers be provided directly to students:

> For the period following compulsory education [from age 16], rather than direct subsidy to high schools and colleges from governments. Such vouchers, perhaps equivalent in value to the average cost of education through four years of college, would be given to the young at age 16, to be used at their discretion for schooling and other skill acquisition at any subsequent time of their life. That is, they should have a wide range of use and they should not lose their value if not used in continuous sequence.

If what we want to quicken in the young is the capacity for self-discovery, that's one way to help. Another way is to enable students to *experience* the arts from the inside, to create and not just appreciate. This, in part, is the cheerful gravamen of the papers here on the various arts in the first section. It can be extraordinarily important for youngsters to know that what they most feel the need to express can find a form—their form—and thereby actually connect with other people's emotions. I have never, for instance, heard my young daughter more exhilarated than when one afternoon, after some years of piano study, she called to shout, "I can improvise! I can improvise!" In one quite vital way, she had found a new dimension of herself.

TEACHING AND LEARNING THAT RESPOND

It takes more than knowing one's field, as a teacher, to be the kind of adult who can respond, through teaching, to the self-

9

improvising that is endemic, painfully and exhilaratingly, to grow-ing up. Some of what it does take is discussed in Karl W. Deutsch's "Relating and Responding: The Adult." To that article I would add a note by Jonathan Kozol, which relates to how auto-anesthesia can be transmitted in classrooms by adults who do not respond:

> The secret curriculum is in the teacher's own lived values and convictions, in the lineaments of his face, and in the biography of passion (or self-exile) that is written in his eyes. The . . . teacher who appears to children to be vague or indirect in the face of human pain, infant death, or malnutrition may not teach children anything at all about pain, death, or hunger, but he will be teaching a great deal about the capability of an acceptable adult to abdicate the consequences of his own perception and, as it were, to vacate his own soul. By denying his convictions dur-ing class discussion, he does not teach objectivity, he gives, at the very least, a precedent for nonconviction.

There was much adult nonconviction, as the young saw, during the Vietnam war, and it was the young who eventually had to lead the opposition to that war. One of the relatively few independent adult decision-makers early in that war was Dennis Brasket, who had designed munitions for Honeywell but then stopped, refusing to work any longer on military projects because he considered them immoral.

Brasket once said to his co-workers: "If the government decides it needs a rack to interrogate children, you'll sit down and design that rack. One of you will propose to get chimpanzees for a test program. Someone else will do the structural analysis. None of you will make a value judgment about what is, after all, just a piece of equipment."

To an interviewer, Brasket added, "I've been in this industry for 17 years, and I've never found an engineer or a secretary who ever stopped to question, 'Maybe we shouldn't be building this piece of lethal equipment.'"

Those people, the non-questioners, had, in the most fundamental sense of the word, been badly educated in terms of their potential as private and public citizens. What on earth had they learned—aside from the skills that got them their Honeywell jobs—in school?

THE EDUCATION OF DAN ELLSBERG

Thinking of the title of this book, *Personal Liberty and Education*, I remembered, along with Brasket, the education of Dan Ellsberg. I don't mean his formal education, which had taken place in thoroughly prestigious institutions along with the rest of the best and brightest. I mean what Ellsberg learned in releasing the Pentagon Papers. Having worked for years in the Pentagon and at the Rand Corporation with many people whom he considered good and even close friends, he waited for their reactions once his name was revealed as the perpetrator of the unprecedentedly rebellious act that was the surfacing of the Pentagon Papers.

"Not one of them," Ellsberg recalled months later, "has sent me a postcard or phoned or tried to contact me in any way. A lot of them see me, I think, with a kind of horror—not just anger, but with an awe of the sort that you'd have for an astronaut who stepped out of that capsule and cut his umbilical cord and just floated off into space and had become weightless, drifting in a black void, because he had cut himself off from the capsule and from NASA, and the United States government, and the United States budget that supports that entire system. No salary, no mama, no papa. He's become part of a vast nothingness.

"As *I* see it though," Ellsberg concluded, "I've become free. I've grown up."

The abiding question, though, for those searching for connections between personal liberty and education, is why the Ellsbergs and Braskets are so rare and the citizens who will construct a rack for the interrogation of children are so many.

FREEDOM TO BE

*An eminent political scientist
analyzes "What it is to be an adult"
amidst today's whirl of cognitive
dissonance. For there to be a
"new birth of freedom" in this
nation and for the world, there
must be a new form of relating and
responding between the young and old.*

Relating and Responding: The Adult

KARL W. DEUTSCH
Professor of Government
Harvard University

R ecently I was riding in a car with two old friends, people who had been study-colleagues of mine years ago. We had all been young student activists in the 1930s and now we were discovering we had all become parents, concerned parents of the young, and in the last three years had become grandparents. We were adult indeed and our children were adults. And the question formed in my mind, "What is it to be an adult?" What had become of us? In what way were we different from what we had been thirty-five and forty years ago?

CHARACTERISTICS OF ADULTHOOD

Perhaps the first sign of an adult is to have met some test of *action*. It is to remember that sometimes when something had to be done one has done it, that in the memories of one's life there are a few deeds one can remember, and not only promises. One cannot be a promising young man or a promising young woman for two or three decades.

The second, related to the first, is to have met the test of *endurance*. To be adult means to have stood up somehow to a hundred pressures coming day after day, year after year. To be adult is to know that it takes more of a man or more of a woman not merely to beget children but to raise them through the long years when they need help; to have been there when needed; to have stood by them; to have been available to them; to have functioned for them when the going got tough and not to have avoided it.

To be adult means to have met a test of *judgment*, to have some sense of reality, a judgment as to what can and cannot be done right here and now in a particular time and place. It is to know from experience how many things and how many people must be taken into account; to know what things must not be forgotten, overlooked or simplified away just in order to make a declamatory phrase or educational appeal sound a little prettier. We know as adults how many different people, how many different problems, moods or feelings of other human beings must be listened to, attended to and understood. You cannot be adult if you do not learn sometimes to listen.

The fourth test is the test of *experience*. It is the capacity to retain rich and deep memories of many past experiences and to combine it with continuing openness to new expressions. This continuing balance of old and new experiences is desperately difficult, for the older we get, the more experiences we accumulate and the more their cumulative bulk will tend to outweigh any new information we might still acquire. When we go from our first year to our second, the time we live is equal to 100 percent of the time we have lived from the time we were born. But the time from the second to the third is only 50 percent of our previous experiences. Our eleventh adds less than 10 percent to our past experience. I shudder to think how few percent of our experiences every new year adds by the time we have reached the age of forty or fifty. That is to say, our new experiences each year necessarily tend to form a diminishing portion of the experiences we already have. We have a built-in risk, a built-in danger of overvaluing the past and giving less and less attention to the new experiences of the present.

If we should try to balance the accounts by selective amnesia, however, by forgetting simply what we learned, we would not be doing any better. We would then just be drifting with the environment. There is no easy way out of this predicament, of having more and more memories that will tend to threaten or outweigh anything new that might happen. And at the same time we must not throw away these memories if we are not to drift with every new trend of fashion, sartorial or political. We need a depth of understanding if we are to be adult, a way to manage both the things that we remember and the new that are just happening and the imperfect, partial but significant repetitions of some of the things that happened before.

To be adult means to be able to manage *cognitive dissonance,* to tolerate ambiguity, to cope with the illogic of the world. Sometimes I wonder if our university has not been designed with fiendish ingenuity to drive young people almost out of their minds. We collect the most sensitive, the most gifted, the most curious, the most active youngsters we can find, and we put them together by the hundreds of thousands on large campuses. By the time they come on the campus they have watched 15,000 hours of television, they have seen the whole world, they have heard presidents describing peace, and they may have seen marines putting zippo lighters to huts of Asian peasants. They have heard about military honor and they may have glanced at the headlines describing the activities of Lt. Calley at My lai. And they may have seen the photograph of a southern governor shaking the somewhat sticky hand of that lieutenant. They have seen so much and by the time they come they see more and more and we teach them more. We bring together all the information we can and put it before them. There is information in the laboratory, in the classrooms, in student discussions, in campus newspapers and in the ceaseless stream of mass media. And we are putting all this vast amount of incongruous, dissonant, contradictory information before young people who are in their most sensitive, open-minded years, the least equipped to cope with cognitive dissonance, to handle contradictions, to tolerate a world that does not quite make sense. Sometimes I am astonished at how well our young people do under these conditions, how many of them manage to keep their heads, and how many manage not to blow their tops and then try to blow the tops of buildings by way of symmetry.

It is difficult to stay sane in a world whose sanity is so precarious. A traffic jam in an insane traffic pattern composed of sane motorists, and you can see it every day at 5 p.m. If a traffic jam is the collective insanity of sane individuals, what are we to say of a foreign policy? What are we to say of international politics? We find again that relatively rational individuals, in groups acting together in a system bigger than one they can comprehend or control, produce an almost insane outcome; and young people are somehow to cope with it. To be adult means to have reached the point where we know that the rationality of the world as a whole is very doubtful, that the world is terribly dangerous, that we cannot expect it to make more sense than at the moment it does, and that if eventually it makes more sense it will be because of something we do about it. But we will then know, when we are truly adults, that we cannot expect the world to have much sanity, that we have to have it, that we have to develop the responses and responsibilities that are needed.

To be adult also means to have *knowledge of one's limits* as well as of one's assets: to know that one is not all-powerful and yet to know at the same time that one is never negligible. Perhaps the strongest point here is to have acquired the *stability of motivation,* to know why one does something and have good cause for doing it. The mother who brings up a child will look after the child every morning, not just because she happens to be in the mood or because she is "turned on" to being a mother that morning. Very few babies would survive if it were a matter of the mood of their parents. None of us would be alive if caring for us had been mainly a matter of mood, if those caring for us when we were helpless and small had not acquired stability of motivation. What is true of raising children is true of keeping a marriage going; it is true of getting any major amount of work done, of producing any sustained effort at creation, building an organization or institution. We have learned to stick with it; we have learned to some extent to turn inspirations into habits, to keep going, to keep plugging, to keep doing the work that has to be done.

All this is necessary. We need steadfast habits and an objective cast of mind—a mind that can think in terms of consequences and results—in order to cope with a world of facts and deeds. But here again we are dealing with a difficult and dangerous balance in our own minds and lives. To become adults means that we eventually integrate our habits into our personality and we begin to think of ourselves no longer quite so much as being what we feel, and we try to persuade ourselves that we are what we do. At this point we are running a mounting risk, often without being aware of it. We no longer think of ourselves as people who are moved by a sunset; rather we are thinking of ourselves as people who are enjoying teaching or whatever occupation we may have. It is the things outside ourselves that become more visible to us than the things inside ourselves, and the risk is that what used to be inside ourselves becomes pale, gray and shadowy, forgotten while the things outside ourselves keep on until we become an emotional vacuum propped up by a gray flannel suit.

LIABILITIES OF ADULTHOOD

To know our limits and assets is to know more about how we learn. Years ago the Canadian psychologist D. O. Hebb performed experiments on animals which then permitted him to develop a concept of two kinds of learning. He called them infant-type learning and adult-type learning. An infant learns in very small units, although he learns very fast. He can build up tiny bits of routines. An infant learns to build up a house brick by brick; and if none of your ingredients are bigger than single bricks, you can build up an amazing variety of different houses. The adult learns in a way similar to building a house from prefabricated eight-foot panels. The adult has fairly large sub-routines which he can quickly move around. If you see a dubious book advertised, or a contraption that promises muscles like Atlas, and if you are experienced, then you know immediately what kind of a dubious promise this is and you snap the eight-foot panel into place, "Don't believe this nonsense," and turn the page. The youngster still would probably read this advertisement with great credulity and thus keep the advertiser in business. But the adult who learns so quickly to cope with certain situations that frequently occur because he can put into place his pre-learned and prefabricated sub-routines of behavior, who is therefore so much faster, so much more competent than the child or adolescent, is also so much poorer in learning. All adults are in danger of becoming prisoners of the too big sub-routines we have learned.

The New Testament describes a sound piece of psychology when it says "unless you become like little children, you shall not enter the kingdom." We shall not become fully human, the New Testament suggests, and we shall not enter fully into our heritage as children of God, unless we recover some of the learning capacity of the child, some of the ability of breaking up these rigid sub-routines, some of the capacity of breaking up the stereotypes of sub-assemblies and start learning again in small amounts, in smaller units, more precisely fitted, more responsive to the new situation and new programs.

These are some of the liabilities of being an adult—the tendency toward rigidity, the tendency toward incomprehension, the trained incapacity to understand, the trained incapacity to see what is in front of us, because we are so busy with attending to what is already in our heads and is already there prefabricated and put into place.

Studies of intelligence organizations and international politics show that governments hardly ever fail because they didn't have agents listening at the right keyhole. Usually they had had their agents there. What the trade calls "intelligence production" is relatively easy, and indeed with the new marvels of electronics we may have far too many ears and far too many keyholes already. The intelligence failures occur typically in the failure to understand what one has heard. The great errors of World War II, and later, occurred not because of any lack of data in the intelligence reports, but because those who read them could not understand what was staring them in the face. If space permitted, I could give quite a number of thrilling case histories on this. The Nazis got the Allies' plans of the invasion of Normandy but they couldn't believe them.

The Allies got information of the Rundstedt offensive but they couldn't believe it. And I wonder how often in human relations and in education we have the information, but what we don't have is the ability to recognize it.

But if there is this rigidity, this inability to respond, what do we do when the prefabricated routine of the response, of the stereotype, doesn't work? Isn't it likely we will be tempted to say, "If I don't know what to do with the underbrush, why not bulldoze my way through? Why not call upon authority? Why not call upon power? Why not call upon violence as the ultimate damage control?" When you get entangled in brambles or prickly bushes somewhere in the woods and you don't have the coordination or the patience to get the thorns out of your coat or your jacket, you tear yourself free. Violence is always the last damage control after a failure of coordination, a failure of control. As the failures of coordination and control increase in our society predictably, this is when violence enters. The less we can steer our lives, the more we would like to bulldoze our way through—while running into similar bulldozing tactics of our neighbors. Incompetence and violence are twins, and they escalate together.

This risk of an escalation of incompetence and violence is made worse by another liability, that of communication-overload and decision-overload. Our society is competitive; for every first-level job there is only one second-level job. For every ten workers there is one foreman; for every ten foremen their is one engineer. Have you ever tried to figure out how many bank clerks there are for one bank vice-president or bank director? You begin to see the steepness of the pyramid, the slipperiness of the greasy pole up which people are scrambling, trying to make it to that world of comfort and importance the advertisements and television commercials promise all of us.

We are trying, it takes our attention, and there is too much else for which there is no time left over. So husbands spend all their time on their careers and have no time to listen to their wives. And wives try to help their husbands so that when the boss comes to dinner the family can present the right social image. Both may not have time to listen very much to their children. And the children are trying to be popular in class or make the football team or the glee club or the class presidency, and they don't have much time to listen to themselves or each other. Communication-overload, decision-overload, decline of attention—flight into routine and stereotyping are becoming common characteristics of life in all industrial nations; and east of the Iron Curtain, the problem is not much easier. It is much the same—the red flannel suit, so to speak, is no more humane or satisfying than the gray one.

And at the same time that there is no time for change, changes are happening faster. As the biophysicist John Platt has put it, "Change has fallen like a knife between the generations." So long as changes occurred slowly, we could consider the society and environment as given and the individual as changing. The Greek poets speak of the generations of man succeeding each other like grass every spring, but all the world around them seemed stable like the rocks and mountains. But today societies are changing faster than people in very many ways. Many occupations become obsolete in twenty years—think of the craftsmen who used to make propellers for airplanes—and our working lives are still forty years. Many people are now in our schools who will have to change their professions at least once, possibly twice, and the best thing they could learn would be to learn how to learn. What we are teaching them will be obsolete long before their working years are up; at least some of the technical subject matter will. Some of the values I hope will not be obsolete.

To this change, this "future shock," we have two responses, equally convenient and equally misleading—to idolize the past and to idolize normality. In the days of World War I, people thought the America of President Taft had been normal, the America in which Jack London wrote *The Iron Heel* or the America of the Homestead Massacre of the 1890s. In the 1930s the people thought the 1920s had been normal, the America of Scott Fitzgerald, the hip flask, Al Capone and prohibition. In the 50s and 60s people began to wonder if the 1930s hadn't been normal, and the Arms Race and the beginning Nuclear Weapons Race were normal. Strange images of normality, when you come to think of them. The other response is to say that nothing is normal, that everything will change, that we can live lives of grim cynicism and despair, that we can go along with everything, believing in nothing.

And finally there is the failure of deeds, the failure to back our judgment by action, the ability to say "yes, we would like to respond but somehow we do not have the depth, the strength, the courage to change a structure, to change a daily practice," so that our response becomes more than a gesture or a good intention.

I have talked about the problems of adults; how they are similar in some ways and different in others, from the transitional, the late adolescent, the people on their way from late adolescence to young adulthood, whether they are in our colleges or outside of them. They, too, have their self-doubts as to whether their promises will ever turn into deeds. And they have perhaps still greater doubts about the promises of the elders around them. They have doubts about their own endurance, their own judgment, their experience; doubts about their own ability to make sense of the world around them, to understand what is going on. They have doubts about their own stability of motivation; they are embarrassed or angry when well-meaning parents ask them what would you like to study, what would you like to specialize in, what would you like to become? Because their own motivations aren't there yet; they have not set into a stable pattern yet; and some of them would like to think they are a new kind of people whose existence would be their accomplishment.

RELATING TO THE WORLD

The need then is here for relating and responding between the young and the old. And at the same time this task cannot be fulfilled, I believe, without relating and responding to the world we have made, the world none of us has made individually, but the world all of us are making every day, together, whether we notice it or not. Politics today is inseparable from morality, from our values, from our priorities. An expert can tell you that it is very important to have an automated library or a computer-assisted research center at the university campus. Whether this computer is more important or less important than a day care center for young children of women students and faculty is something the computer cannot tell you. It is something you must decide. But if you throw away hopes for full intellectual and emotional development of one-half of all the able people in this country because one-half are women (I suspect it might be a little more than half), if you think of what happens on the one hand to the women and their marriages and what is happening to the small children on the other, I wonder why it is we have at my own university a splendid department for studying Assyrian inscriptions, but we had a demonstration because we didn't have a day care center for young children of the hundreds of women working at this great university (such a center is now open).

Perhaps behind these strident cries and overstatements there is a cry for attention, a cry for listening, a cry for new priorities. When an adolescent cries out, "Fascist, racist pig" or a young lady says, "Sexist male chauvinist," behind the overstatement, nonsense and rhetoric, aren't we being told in small but legible print, "Please listen to me for at least five seconds!" And shouldn't there be a better way of getting five seconds of attention for those who need it? This, it seems to me, is the occupational disease of adulthood and the problem of the goals of education. We take the motives, the values, the priorities we acquired for granted; we assume the priorities are simply there. The priorities are there for the department of Assyrian inscriptions and against the day care center for the small children. There is a priority for the umpteenth super-highway, the six-lanes for the automobiles and the 487 cubic inches of engine that will give the tired executive a surging feeling of power as he sits on top of it, probably in a traffic jam moving at five miles per hour; but there is no particular priority for low-rent housing. The priorities are always there with us. As somebody said, we are well on the way to becoming the country with the dirtiest air, the filthiest water, and the cleanest shirts in history. But we cannot breathe our shirts.

The priorities are always with us, and to be adult means to be in danger of becoming the slave to a set of priorities that happened by accident, were inherited from the past, that are put together by people whose names we have forgotten but whose chains we cannot break. To be an adult, then, means to understand this, to notice there is not much gain in a wonderful career if your marriage goes to pieces, there isn't much to gain if your child wins a fellowship by driving himself so hard that the first thing he does on the new college campus is to go urgently to the mental health department. And they come by the dozens and the hundreds, and those are the lucky ones. Those who don't come sometimes end up in worse shape.

The quiet destruction, the cost behind our current blind priorities are all around us. We have all seen the pictures of combat that the photographer brought back from the village of My Lai, the dead bodies, the dead women, the dead children; but there are invisible pictures of carnage and havoc all around us in our civilization that looks so orderly on the outside and has so much utter disorder within. We move from overload and overcommitment to habits, to prejudices, to routine, to doing the things that take the least thought, the least emotional readjustment. And we end up with the type of social work, the type of medicine, the type of education that seem to me to be best expressed by the image of veterinary medicine. A veterinarian is a physician whose patients do not talk. And he wouldn't like them to talk either. Haven't you met sometimes a doctor who seems to you one of the most competent veterinarians you have seen? And haven't you sometimes wondered whether we are moving toward veterinary public administration, veterinary social work, veterinary education? It saves time if the patients don't talk, if one doesn't have to listen to children, if one doesn't have to pay painstaking attention to other persons; but a veterinary pattern of human relations ends up with an invertebrate pattern of personality.

You may remember from science classes what an invertebrate is. It is a shellfish—hard, tough outside and soft, defenseless mush within. How many invertebrate personalities, how many invertebrate institutions do you know? Consider how they have to work. Their surface hardness must be defended because the surface hardness is all they have. These are the hardliners of all times, of all places, of all ideologies. There were fewer of them in the sixteenth century; but it was the hardliners, the Catholic hardliners, who killed Protestants in the Netherlands, as the Duke of Alba did, and there were Protestant hardliners who burned Catholics in England. In those days the hardliners burned people for differences of opinion about the nature of God. Today we slaughter people for differences of opinion about the management and ownership of factories. I do not think it is a nobler reason for killing people, nor is it the better way of settling the question.

The hardliners are around us in our own personalities all the time. Hardlining leads to a fear of children ("If you give an inch, they will take a foot"); a fear of other nations ("Negotiate from strength"—we've tried that one for over twenty years); the domino theory ("If we don't do such and such, all other nations will topple over like dominoes"). And the fear becomes greater and greater. We fear our black fellow-citizens, and we strengthen the fear with the fantasy of the vast biological urges that we project on our black neighbors. We fear women. We have given them legal equal rights and now those insatiable greedy types want to be hired, they want to be promoted, they actually want to be paid equally for equal work. Where is this going to end? They actually want to be equal!

We are afraid of students. They may want to have a share in deciding how they are to spend their next four years. We are afraid of labor. The newspapers used to say fifty years ago unions were usually run by the IWW—bombthrowing anarchists. Today we are afraid of women, and we think when they feel their husbands should help with the dishes, they are probably lesbians. Actually, if all husbands helped with the dishes, it would stimulate the sale of electric dishwashers.

An occupational disease of adulthood is fear. We have a fear of peace; we are afraid of neo-isolationism, fear of withdrawal from the world. Do you notice how much these things have in common? In each case a bogeyman is erected, a caricature is made; and the purpose of the protective caricature is to save us from changing an old habit, an old institution. And if there is some financial incentive, a war contract to be gained, if there is employment or career privilege to be defended, then the good old mechanics of reinforcement learning will be put into service of maintaining the prejudice. The effects of prejudices, apart from their short-run reinforcement, disagree with the traditional Marxist view. Prejudices often do not serve the long-run interests of prejudiced persons and groups, neither do they damage or ruin them. Why then are they effective? It is not so much the advantages people get from their prejudices, it is rather that prejudices save them much emotional effort and intellectual effort.

To be able to relate and respond, therefore, we must be able to learn. And to learn means to change our inner structure; it means ·to relocate some important resources of one's own personality from one of us to the other. There must be some inner structure for relocation to be meaningful. Somebody who has no inner structure can't learn anything, because nothing he learned would stick. But if the inner structure becomes rigid, nothing can be learned either. These priorities in a structure of morality, in a structure of a sense of what is right and wrong, can be put together again. We can go on with the old routines, keeping our minorities in their places, the Spanish-speaking Americans and the black Americans; keeping the poorer nations in their places and keeping Latin America in its place; keeping the Cold War in its place; and producing bigger and faster airplanes for no reason in particular and bigger and better bombs to wipe us all out in the end. Or else we can learn. We can learn that this nation, as was said more than one hundred years ago, will have a new birth of freedom and that this could be a new birth of freedom for the world.

TWO CONTRASTING ETHICS

More than seventy years ago, in 1899, an American economist, Thorstein Veblen, wrote in his book *Theory of the Leisure Class* that there were two kinds of ethics in the world. The ethics of the New Testament, he said, had slowly been driven back until only one refuge was left for them, and that was the kindergarten. In the kindergarten children were taught to share their toys; they were taught not to escalate their conflicts, not to hit back but rather to be willing to make up, to be conciliatory. The rest of society of 1899, Veblen said, had been taken over by the ethics of the jungle and the stock exchange, the ethics of dog-eat-dog and the bigger one eating the smaller. But Veblen did not leave the matter there. He said that the future of the world would be decided by a large contest as to what in the end would prevail—the ethics of the jungle or the ethics of the kindergarten.

And, having discussed what it means to be an adult, I must say that to be a true adult will also include the ability to recover the openness, the joy of life, the sharing and cooperating of the kindergarten. We do not know yet which of the two kinds of ethics will prevail. The decision is not yet in whether the radioactive jungle is the future of mankind, or whether once again people can work together with the openness of children but with the forbearance, the help and the mutual love of an ethic that is thousands of years old.

In a world of technological and biological advances, what is the role of the humanities and humanism in education? "Education at its best is always concerned with values."

The Human Imperative

FRED G. BURKE
Commissioner of Education
for the State of Rhode Island

By 1980 it is virtually certain that a chemical means of predetermining the sex of children—and perhaps even the means of predetermining certain emotional or physical characteristics—will be readily available for human use. Whether we will by then have developed a moral and decisional capability that will enable us to use this chemical technology responsibly is most problematic.

Incredible advances in the prolongation of life are being achieved in our laboratories. Whether we will develop the aesthetic and emphatic capabilities that will make that life worthwhile and meaningful is most problematic.

The ability to produce children by "cloning" rather than sexual reproduction (that is, the ability to produce perfect genetic duplicates of any individual) will almost certainly arrive within our lifetime. Whether we will also develop a moral philosophy that will allow us to cope publicly and privately with questions concerning the essence of our being is problematic.

The biological revolution that is underway will give men the ability to achieve enormous control over the living and growing processes of all organisms, including man himself. This revolution is bound to alter the shape of our lives even more than the industrial revolution of the nineteenth century did.

MORAL CONSIDERATIONS OF THE FUTURE

The serious moral questions about the very definitions of life and death raised by the development of heart-transplant techniques will pale when compared with the questions that will demand our attention in the future. I am not speaking of some never-never land over the rainbow. I'm speaking of the very near future, a future in which we—and our children—are going to have to make incredible decisions. Our ability to control the very processes of life and death will make the question "what is man?" more than a mere philosophic or semantic game. I am convinced that the fundamental issue of our time will be our ability to find answers to this question that are adequate to face the challenges of a world that seems to defy comprehension.

What are we, as educators, doing to prepare children—and ourselves—for a world in which new technological and biological advances are going to require enormous moral courage? At a time when our traditional morality is characterized by atrophy, how are we going to find the courage and the will to prepare our sons and daughters for an Orwellian future that is here today? Through the ages, man has been bedeviled by impossible attempts to achieve harmony with other men. In our time, this human imperative has taken on cataclysmic proportions. A highly developed humanistic philosophy (embedded in all of man's major religions) is not a luxury for scholars, but a fundamental challenge for all men.

In the barbaric days before the scientific revolution and before the knowledge explosion, man's inhumanity was, in part, excusable. Indeed, it was even ennobled in saga and art. Parochial ignorance and chauvinism allowed cruel struggles to be employed as a technique for survival. But today we kill and maim, we wound and destroy psyche and body for reasons having little to do with our personal survival. And as man's control over every phase of his environment increases to a degree that staggers the imagination, the question of his inhumanity will also increase—with all its frightening significance. The Hobbesian war of one against all and all against one is tolerable when it is believed that personal survival is at stake and when the weapons are only human cunning and bows and arrows. But, be it in American streets or Asian rice paddies, dehumanized anarchy in an age of mace, death rays, plastiques, napalm, and the ultimate bomb is not survival, but apocalypse.

The next logical question is, how are we going to develop a definition of man that is adequate to meet the needs of the twenty-first century? What institutions will organize man's collective intelligence and focus it on these problems? What institution will employ the accumulated essence of three thousand years of civilization to organize and mobilize man's ultimate means, his intelligence, to work toward a solution for these problems—problems that are eternal, but so altered in form and so rapidly changing in character that they make history, institutions, and ideologies seem inadequate? If we in the public education system will turn our attention to these matters, we will not only fulfill our responsibilities to the future, but we also will revitalize ourselves in the process. One West African tribe expresses this concept very clearly in a proverb: "If the left hand washes the right, both hands become clean."

Where do we turn now to find relevant definitions of man? To conventional theology, whose essential definition of man is that he is a child of God? To Darwin, who defines man on an evolutionary scale? To Marx, who defines man as a victim of economic necessity? To Freud, who defines man as the sum of his neurological connections? Or must we turn instead to the humanities to search for definitions that defy oversimplification?

FAILURES OF HUMANISTIC INSTITUTIONS

For a wide variety of reasons, modern man is largely cut off from his cultural heritage. We have lost touch with the vitality of the traditions of art and music and philosophy. The loss has oc-curred not because this heritage is inadequate or irrelevant, but because we have been unable to transmit the heritage in a relevant and adequate manner. The modern emphasis on science and tech-nology has made American humanists overly defensive. This de-fensive posture leads backward to a reliance on the unassailable, prescientific traditions of our aesthetic culture, and in the process, art becomes art history, literature becomes chronology, and music is lost in cultural history. In times like these, we cling to the past— to Plato, Shakespeare, Beethoven, and Michelangelo.

As we retreat, however, we become so concerned with defensive strategy that we lose sight of the purpose and the goals of the enterprise. Humanism is the vehicle for transmitting the laboriously and painfully acquired values of Western civilization—those per-spectives, beliefs, and emotions that distinguish Western man's highest thought. Often these purposes are forgotten, and we con-centrate on form and overlook essence.

Is there not a message somewhere in the fact that half a cen-tury of humanistic instruction in our schools and colleges preceded My Lai? In the American response to our policies in East Asia? In the persistence of racism and in the frightening brutality of our cities? In the almost sadistic maiming of our environment? In the parochial and selfish insensitivity of our complacent suburbs? Has the teaching of music, art, drama, philosophy, and literature con-tributed *anything* to soothing the savage breast, to mitigating the violence of men?

The real test of humanistic institutions is their ability to transmit values as well as ideas. By this test, I'm afraid we have failed. Not only have we concentrated more on form and less on purpose, but we have tended to make the implicit assumption that these values were somehow transmitted automatically through the meticulous study of the masterpieces of Western culture.

So long as fear—fear of hunger, of future depression, of pain, of punitive reaction—shaped the adolescent mind, it was possible to impose the strictest of these ancient values and to demonstrate their legitimacy through mandatory study of the relevant scriptures. But today's youth are uniquely free. Science and technology have created new media, and the concomitant creation of twentieth-century values has lessened the restrictive nature of the books and cultural documents that, in times past, tied the young to the dictates of their elders. Our images of American life shaped by Mark Twain, Frederic Remington, Winslow Homer, and Henry James are giving way to images shaped primarily by television, Mickey Mouse, *Gunsmoke*, and *Sesame Street*. By the time he reaches kindergarten, the average child in America has spent more time in front of a television set than a college graduate has spent in the university classroom.

The failure of education in the humanities in contemporary twentieth-century life is more than just an academic issue because we are in such desperate need of a humanistic morality, of an accepted and acceptable code of right and wrong, good and evil, ugly and beautiful. Not only has relative social freedom excused the young from the lessons of tradition, but twentieth-century science has proudly increased the vitality of social change. History is less important because it no longer takes many years for fundamental changes to occur. Today's young person is aware not only that he is observing, but that he is also making more history in a year than his father did in fifty.

Humanists must seek to relate increasingly to the here and now. The computer, mechanized visual art, electronic sound, and psychedelic imagery should not be ridiculed or resisted as bad dreams or bad trips. Instead, they should be embraced as the very stuff of modern humanity and, if possible, reconciled with our best traditional values.

An education in the humanities has been regarded as the essential veneer applied by civilization to distinguish its aristocrats from its peasants, but our egalitarian ideologies and scriptures and our economic abundance have made us all "potential gentlemen." Because ours is economically a people's era—a people's culture—our students are primarily the sons and daughters of peasants, and they find less relevance to contemporary life in the way humanities are traditionally taught. But I feel, almost instinctively, that we have sensed what we have lost and have begun to rethink some of our most cherished concepts of how we educate humanity.

REINTRODUCING AESTHETIC VALUES
AND ENJOYMENT

Where do art and music belong in the schools today? Off in some corner of the building where we won't be disturbed by them? One of the things that encourages me most these days is to see some of the fantastic work being done in many of our schools in encouraging and developing the creativity and growth of each child through various kinds of exercises related to the arts. There is no better way, it seems to me, to stress the worth of the individual than through artistic expression. In the past, many teachers in the humanities have felt a sense of envy for the certainties of the hard sciences; now I see a real appreciation for the very inability of the humanities to be simplified or even closely defined.

I do have some concrete suggestions about what I think might be done to move toward some of the goals I have mentioned. Some European education systems offer imperfect models in this area. Italian elementary school students learn about their artistic patrimony during their earliest years of school. Michelangelo, Botticelli, and Leonardo are still strong and vital influences on Italian youth; they remain a vital part of life. They are not the moldy antiques that we have allowed them to become in this country.

But I am not suggesting that we pull these men out of the closet for our grade school children. Rather, I would like to suggest that we seek to develop an aesthetics strongly linked to our own American heritage. This is not a new idea; it has been a principal theme in American art and literature from Hawthorne to Hemingway. Let's teach our children to discriminate between the beautiful and the ugly in our immediate environment. The distinction traditionally drawn by intellectuals between high art and low art, between "serious" art and "popular" art, has been a dysfunctional dichotomy. It has not led to a positive attitude toward the arts; rather it has made the arts less accessible and in doing so has been of profound disservice to man. Let's teach our children to appreciate and make aesthetic judgments about all aspects of the environment—from television commercials to the lines of a handsome automobile to the appreciation of a glass of pure water. Let's

begin to erase the false and damaging divisions between art and life
—and between "serious" art and "popular" art.

We have created the idea that art is a leisure activity, a pastime,
an interlude outside the *real* activity of men within the economic
world. This narrow conception fails to take cognizance of man's
real needs and aspirations. It is also an element in the generation
gap, because there is a very real difference in the conceptions of
work and play held by the younger generation and the older generation. Those of us scarred by the aftermath of the Depression and
the dark days of World War II tend to think of work as our primary purpose in life; a man is valued according to the amount of
work he does. Children of affluence are applying different standards. (And what was the creation of this affluence for, if not to
enable our children to have broader vision than our own?) Today
a man is also judged according to his play. Life is defined as play,
and it is the work of man to perform all of his endeavors as creatively and imaginatively—as playfully—as possible. And this emphasis on creativity and imagination is not seen as icing on the
cake, but rather as the essential activity of man.

All of the people I know in the field of education are working
to make our schools more responsive to individual needs. It's a
difficult task because the regimented institutions of the past have
provided few models to guide us. We're in a very primitive stage
in the educative process; we're still learning how to be teachers.
If schools are going to become more humanistic, the teaching of
the humanities will have to be strengthened in our schools. We're
going to have to utilize all the arts to help our young people understand themselves, their communities, and their world. Here is the
real relevance of the humanities, of the artistic vision. If the central
problem of this age is man's inability to get along with his fellow
man, we must become acquainted with the spiritual roots of man
through his arts.

Education is a failure if its sole reason for being is the mere
transferral of ideas and information. Education at its best is always
concerned with values. For many years, the emphasis has been
placed on discipline (sometimes to the point of regimentation),
conformity, and order. In fact, these values are sometimes seen as

ends in themselves. It is the responsibility and challenge of the humanities today to reemphasize the equally positive values of spontaneity, creativity, and joy. The notion of the perfectibility of man—perhaps our most utopian of ideas—is man's final hope and highest dream.

Education has not affected the out-of-school behaviors of students because most of what they do in school is an academic game, never played out of school. . . .
The educator's task is to stimulate the student to construct his own ideals.

Open Up the Well of Feelings

ASAHEL D. WOODRUFF
Professor of Psychology
University of Utah

There are many victims of inhumanity in our world. Minorities are suffering from infringement on their rights and their opportunities. Idealistic young people are suffering from the hypocrisy of society. Disgusted students are suffering from an indoctrinating school system that is miserably failing to cope with their concerns. These and other victims of inhumanity are asserting themselves with increasing vigor.

Society is responding in a number of ways, but it seems that the most significant change is the humanizing of life. It is not moving very fast, nor is it progressing evenly and smoothly. It is marked by disruption, disagreement, destruction, and frustration. It is being fought for by some, and opposed in a variety of ways by others. In spite of these difficulties it is occurring.

WHAT HUMANIZATION IS

To humanize means to enable people to enjoy being alive. Humane is defined as "characterized by tenderness and compassion for the suffering or distressed." The terms "suffering" and "distressed" describe many students and probably many teachers. The goal of humanization in education is to reduce the suffering of students and teachers and to cultivate large amounts of "keen and lively pleasure, exultant satisfaction, great gladness, and delight," which the dictionary equates with joy.

Humanizing does not require charity or patronage. It is not something you *do to* people; it is what you make it possible for them to do for themselves. There are two conditions required for a humane life. The first consists of respect for the feelings and values of all other persons, so that there are no arbitrary or imposed barriers to freedom of choice or to freedom of opportunity. It will be a long time before this condition exists either in our society or in our schools.

The second consists of the opportunity, above all other forms of opportunity, to learn how to feel good, and to learn how to cultivate conditions that enhance good feelings in all aspects of life. It is not enough that some people in the society know about this. It is necessary that every person achieve these learnings.

This is no simplistic pursuit; its pitfalls have been pointed out by one thinker after another. The difficulties are great, but they are only the difficulties inherent in clarity of thought about life and in the hard work of self-development.

If the search for good feelings is conceived as a search for fun and comfort, it will prove to be a destructive and bitterly disappointing search. If it is conceived as a selfless devotion to impersonal truths and values held before us by others, it will prove to be tiresome and empty of personal meaning.

To yield joy consistently and forever, the search for good feelings must be the pursuit of ideals that are conceived by a person out of his own experiences as better conditions for enjoying life than exist at that given moment. It must be conceived as the struggle to produce those conditions, continuing throughout his life. But it must also be seen as a struggle liberally sprinkled with enjoyment along the way. The joy a person realizes at any moment in time will be some combination of a sense of success in his efforts to build those conditions and a taste of a new level of pleasure that his last achievement has just made possible. These two elements make up a rare and powerful combination, for when the struggle for better conditions ends, the pleasure derived from enjoying that which already exists soon begins to fade. One concludes that keeping happy is hard work. The alternative, however, is unbearable.

JOYS OF SELF-DEVELOPMENT

This state of affairs is of no arbitrary nature. It is the way the human being is by virtue of his mind and his feelings. The only hope of substantial joy in life lies in a path of continual self-development, which makes the educator vital to the humane condition. His task is to stimulate the student to construct his own ideals, whether they be about home life, dress, social affairs, economic conditions, music, or anything else, and then to help him learn how to pursue those ideals effectively.

The central problem in education today is relevance. Relevance is defined in the dictionary as "close logical relationship with, and importance to, the matter under consideration." The matter under consideration is how each person can learn how to feel good, and also learn how to cultivate conditions that enhance good feelings in all aspects of his life.

How can music education become relevant to the goal of humanizing life? What rationale can be developed out of the available facts and how can it be put into operation? Certain facts about human behavior are of prime importance in such an effort.

Every human act consists in part of the expression of some feeling because cognition and affect operate inseparably. A person's feelings determine what he will try to do, and his concepts and skills determine how he will go about it. Humans acquire affective and cognitive abilities in a slow cumulative manner from a constant flow of specific encounters in life. Each encounter leaves lodged in the brain its bit of residual meaning. Concepts are nothing more than these accumulated meanings. This kind of growth does not start with generalizations that are learned verbally and that gradually distill out into specific actions. The reverse is true. Generalizations are meaningful to a person when they grow out of his own specific experiences and are formed by himself. Unfortunately, syllabuses are usually constructed around the generalizations of a given discipline, and the school seldom supplies the inductive experience students need to give meaning to those generalizations.

No "learning" experience can affect a person's life in any significant way unless it occurs as a result of direct engagement in activities that are, or are becoming, a regular part of his life (not just a part of his in-school activities). Education has not affected the out-of-school behaviors of students because most of what they do in school is an academic game that is never played outside of school. For example, the acquisition of verbal information about music or about musicians has very little effect on the musical behavior of the learner. There is almost a cleavage in music education between training in musical performance, which is highly successful in producing specific performance skills, and the cognitive study of information about music, which has a dismal record of impact on human life. Unfortunately, even performance often fails to humanize music education when it overemphasizes the ability to play music composed by other persons and underemphasizes the expression of the learner's own musical feelings and understandings.

The objects that make up the student's environment become involved in his behavior as processes that do something to him or for him. A guitar proves to be a process he can use over and over for personal enjoyment, but a band is a process he cannot use after he leaves school. When the student encounters musical objects and events in this transactional relationship, he conceives them as processes that are usable or unusable for his own purposes, and they become functional parts of his behavior patterns to the extent they have this personal usefulness. If he encounters them only in nonfunctional and verbalistic ways, as he is likely to do in many classes in music history, their process natures are never discovered or utilized.

Education today is often irrelevant to life because teachers ignore these facts about human behavior, thus creating a critical discrepancy between what happens in school and the potent forces outside of school that shape most human behavioral patterns. Awareness of these aspects of behavior can help music educators make their courses relevant. Such courses would involve students in music within their own life structures, rather than in talking about music in the life of a composer, a performer, or any other person. They would engage students in musical behaviors that are, and can increasingly become, part of their daily lives in or out of school. Charlotte Du Bois was given a letter from a young girl to her teacher who was using guitars in the classroom. The girl said, "This is the first time anything good has happened to me in school." All good things have beginnings. Who knows where students can go if educators respect their motives and needs, and help them build on them.

A second change that will make music education more relevant is the presentation of the literal phenomena of music in the curriculum rather than abstractions. Students must do more than just talk about music. Their attention should be focused on the musical experience itself, with comprehension and concept development growing out of it, not preceding it. "Information" is then subordinated to those musical experiences.

Finally, music education will become relevant when it enables learners to live with and to enjoy their own aesthetic feelings. To keep cognition and affect constantly associated, it is necessary for the central thrust of music education to involve the expression by the learner of his own musical feelings. Cognitive processes and performance skills will then grow out of that thrust by contributing to its fulfillment. When a learner is focused on his own musical feelings and their expression, his cognitive and motor facilities are engaged as supporting elements. Cognition and affect work together.

When a student is asked to focus his attention on music as an external entity, as for example in so many ensemble rehearsals, there is no way in which his own affect can be tightly wedded to what he is doing. Fine ensemble performances do serve the development of a performer, but they do it best when they emerge out of his own search for aesthetic satisfaction. This means that the first priority for music education must be to make music serve students, and to let the great mass performances and the intellectual grasps of our musical heritage be the products of musical growth and personal comprehension and expression.

THREE APPROACHES TO EDUCATION

This approach can have value for every subject matter field, in slightly different specific forms. Its status in education today can be seen in the model suggested by Jon Davis, a social scientist and social studies educator. Davis describes three distinct educational positions that are clearly visible in classrooms today and in curriculum literature.

One can be called *discipline-oriented*. It consists of training in fact-finding and information-organizing, which are the processes for developing a given subject matter field, and of learning the information already assembled by other researchers. Emphasis is generally put on having students engage in two processes: inquiry or search for data and the organization of the data into some logical system. This approach is very prominent in the new social *science* proposals, and is patterned on the structure of the physical sciences. There is a component of this "social science approach" in music education. Most of what is called concept teaching today falls within this position—namely, transmitting the main verbal concepts of the literature about music to students.

Another position can be called *person-oriented*. It consists of engaging students in a continuing series of in-life behaviors of exactly the same kind as will constitute their daily lives when school is over. Emphasis is on the making of personal decisions by students as to what they will do in one situation or another, and in carrying out their decisions effectively. Inquiry and the interpretation of discovered facts play a contributing role in this daily living process, but they are always subservient to decision-making and decision-executing behaviors. Davis calls this the social *studies* approach. Concept learning falls within this position when it consists of perceiving and manipulating actual musical objects and events and forming concepts from this activity. Concrete and viable approaches to this kind of education, which produce large amounts of very basic learning, have been developed.

A third position can be called *institution-oriented*. It consists of indoctrinating students in normative behavior so they will become good members of the society and so that social institutions will function smoothly. This is called the institutional support approach, and examples abound in all fields. Persuading students to like the classics and forsake rock, admonishing students in order to forestall deviant choices rather than living openly with diversity and controversy, and using students to stage entertainments for parents or to win trophies for the school are examples of this approach.

It is Davis' contention that many curriculum planners today strongly advocate the first position. In spite of its visibility in the literature, this approach is seldom employed in classrooms. At least this is true in some fields.

He also contends that there is strong advocacy among other curriculum planners for the second approach, although there is a serious lack of instructional guides and materials for engaging in it. In this case, too, there are very few classrooms in which it is being practiced.

There is almost no support for the third position among thoughtful educators, but Davis feels that it is by far the most common approach in the schools. There is heavy stress on the norms in our society in the form of devotion to the American political heritage, use of the white upper-class version of the English language, insistence on the dress codes of the present adult generation, veneration of the music of the masters, participation in contests, putting on cultural events, and so on.

FEELINGS ARE MOST EFFECTIVE MOTIVATORS

A teacher who was sensitive to the inner motives of young people received in one of his classes a young girl who had almost withdrawn from communication with teachers through a long record of failure and disinterest. One day after patient effort to draw her out, she entered the room quietly and left a piece of paper on the teacher's desk. On it was a short verse that expressed her appreciation of a teacher who did not use the institutional support approach:

> This man will listen
> He will not grudge
> This man's opinionated
> Yet he will not judge
> And what he offers is sound advice
> In other words, this man is nice.

The life of a human being revolves around his feelings, which are the core of all his motives. His cognitive and motor resources enable him to become wise and effective in the pursuit of joy, both for himself and for others. Music is one form of expression of aesthetic feelings, and along with dance, it is probably one of the most intimately personal. Music, therefore, is intensely relevant to life. It has both exhilarative and therapeutic values.

The expression of personal feelings is always a creative act, never an imitative act. One may borrow mechanisms of expression from others for his own use, but those that best express his own feelings are likely to be those of his own origin and choice. As a person matures, he becomes aware of both his feelings and his means of expression, and he will learn important things about both as a direct result of perceiving what he does and how well it satisfies him. If he discovers that his musical expressions are enjoyed by others, he is likely to become responsive to a teacher who can help him learn how to be increasingly effective.

If in any manner a teacher closes off the well of his students' musical feelings and subverts their overt musical behaviors to the service of any other cause, however socially acceptable it may be, he thereby stops their personal aesthetic development, and puts an end to the relevance of both music and music education to their personal lives.

Every form of musical comprehension, creativity, and artistic ability is more likely to be achieved when the learner is driven by, and trying to serve, his own aesthetic feelings. Creativity and democracy are really just two facets of one concept of life. It is the responsibility of teachers to put them together in American education.

A past president of the National Art Education Association argues the case for personal choice *and* personal reward *as unique avenues to personal freedom.*

Art's Essential Meaninglessness

HARLAN HOFFA
Head, Department of Art Education
Pennsylvania State University

The first Sunday in the new year was not exactly auspicious. The sky was grey, the news was grey, and my mood was grey. Maybe it was all a result of lingering jet lag, post-vacation blues, and a head cold that couldn't make up its mind whether to leave me wet-nosed or dry. If so, however, those psychophysical maladies were firmly reinforced by the elements because the weather, like my mucous membranes, seemed incapable of settling on wetness or dryness. The sky was absolutely colorless, the remnants of the last snow turned darker by the hour as melting exposed successive layers of grit, and even the evergreens in the woods behind the house seemed determined to be ever-grey instead.

LIFE AND THE TIMES

And the state of the world, at least insofar as it was revealed by the Sunday *New York Times,* was even more grim than my mood or the weather. If no news is good news, as the adage says, it must be equally true that good news is no news because that two-pound 200-page edition of the *Times* contained column after column, page after page, and section after section of "all the news that's fit to print" — most of which was bad. Inflation, unemployment, famine, overpopulation, energy crises, environmental pillaging, parochialism disguised as nationalism, violence on the streets, corruption in high office, abuse of the political mandate, boycotts, highjackings, global economic dislocations, and on and on it went. Each successive headline seemed more grim than the last, and each seemed to further demonstrate mankind's inability to govern his affairs with any freedom of choice, any significant ethical considerations, or any aesthetic merit.

It seemed as though all sense of individual existence had vanished and, as an art educator, I felt frustrated and impotent. Do children who are starving in Bangladesh still paint pictures, I wondered? When inner-city unemployment runs to forty percent, do the disenfranchised catch up on their museum-going? When the land is deformed and deflowered by strip mines and carbon monoxide, what is the value in landscape painting — or in earthworks for that matter?

In utter frustration I turned to the magazine section of the *Times,* knowing that even if its contents were equally disheartening, at least its format might be more colorful. And it was. Somehow the familiar ads for butcher-block tabletops and summer camps for fat kids and dollar-chic furniture and condominiums and wrinkle-free neckties were mildly reassuring. The dental-perfect, skinny-hipped models who smiled out from the four-color ads showed no concern for the rest of the news; and for a brief, through-the-looking-glass moment their faces, with their $100-an-hour smiles and their determined anonymity, were more real than were those of the troubled leaders of the troubled world that appeared on page one. Which, I wondered, is more unbelievable, Alice in

Wonderland or Dr. Strangelove? Then I made the mistake of turning away from pictures and I started to read.

First, I read an article relating to triage and the prospects of world-wide famine. Triage was a system devised by the French army during World War I to determine who would receive the limited medical attention then available: those who would probably die regardless of what was done for them, those who would probably recover even though nothing was done for them, and those who could be expected to survive only if they received prompt medical attention. Needless to say, only the latter group was provided for under the triage system. The article suggested that triage might represent a model for best determining the allocation of food resources among the starving peoples of the world.

After digesting triage (with some discomfort) I turned to the next article, a sci-fi projection of a world in which mankind becomes utterly dependent upon an omniscient, omnipotent, omnipresent techno-system in which individual freedom is totally abrogated to the need for efficiency and security.

Two additional articles, one on the abuses of television in dealing with young audiences and one exposing the seamier side of high-level diplomacy, did little to make the day seem brighter. As I ruminated on the sorry shape of the world around me, I couldn't help but wonder once again about the significance of art education in a world that seemed well on its way to hell in a handcart. I did not want to think that my profession was totally irrelevant in the face of such traumas; but, in all honesty, neither could I believe that art education would contribute very much to their resolution. In a world where life is real and life is earnest I wondered what role the arts could play and what contribution they might make to the betterment of the human condition. Clearly, they could neither feed the hungry nor clothe the naked nor employ the jobless nor house the homeless. Nor have the arts much of a track record in protecting the environment or in cleansing the political system or in provoking greater love for fellow man. At best they might represent the difference between making a living and making life worth the living — between seeking riches and being enriched.

No, that first Sunday in the new year was not very auspicious. But, as I pondered the role of the arts in human affairs more deeply, a half-forgotten event that had taken place long ago came to mind; and I felt a little better, if not about the state of the world in general, at least about art education and its purposes.

THE BROKER WHO COULDN'T PAINT

Years before, when I was a very junior instructor at Buffalo State College, I faced one of life's sterner but more persistent realities: my expenses exceeded my income. So I moonlighted. Two nights a week I taught in the adult-education program of a suburban school system; most of my students were youngish housewives who arrived late, left early, and took long coffee breaks. They were generally bright, well-educated, and modestly blessed with the trappings of the good life as they saw it — two kids, two cars, a big dog, and a big mortgage — and, almost incidentally, they painted surprisingly well. Predictably, they were also a most forgettable group; but, among them was one student the memory of whom lingereth provokingly long.

He arrived early, he stayed until the very end of each three-hour session, he never took a break, he rarely spoke to anyone else in the class, he painted with a dogged determination — and his painting was God-awful. I probably spent more time and effort with him than with anyone else in the class, and though he seemed to understand and even accept my suggestions, he never improved. His painting was as inept at the end of the semester as it had been at the beginning; but he seemed pleased enough with it and, strangely, he seemed to be not in the least discouraged.

Late on the last day of classes he called me over and, to my great surprise, he apologized for being such a poor student. He said he knew that he did not paint well but that he was not unhappy with the class and he hoped that I was not disappointed with him. He went on to explain that he was a broker and that, as such, he had to make daily decisions about how his clients' funds were invested. Any wrong decision, he said, could cost them thousands of dollars, for which he would be liable, and he worked very hard to represent their interests responsibly.

48

Then came the clincher! He said that he could come to the painting class on these evenings to be free from this burden of responsibility because he knew that, if he made a mistake while painting, it would have no particular consequences. It would not matter. I was dumbfounded because I had assumed all along that he came to class to learn to paint. Clearly, he had his own reasons for enrolling in that class which were unknown to me but which satisfied his personal needs and I was very pleased that he felt he could share them with me.

I also learned something about art and art education from that long ago experience that I believe is critically important. Each artist — whether child or adult, student, amateur, or professional, sophisticated or naive — confronts his work absolutely alone and on his own personal and idiosyncratic terms. Between the artist and his work there are no intervening variables — which is not to say that there are no external influences upon the artist. Rather, those influences that may come to bear do so once removed from the moment at which the artist confronts his work. That is a private moment at which the artist is alone and at which he is solely responsible for what happens. I have often used this example with art teachers-in-training to illustrate the point that no teacher can ever fully know, fully control, or fully predict what a student will do or why.

"WHAT GOOD IS IT?"

As I turned this recollection over in my mind for the umpteenth time, I also recognized another moral in the story, one perhaps not altogether compatible with much that has been axiomatic in art education. One of art education's most persistent and perhaps most fundamental canons is that the art experience has meaningful consequences in human behavior. Almost every argument in behalf of art education is based on that premise. In short, we say that art education is valuable because it is meaningful and that its value is directly a function of its ability to enhance specific (though ever-changing) components of the good life — however they may be defined.

It is understandable (and perhaps inevitable) that a pragmatic

society such as ours should demand a return on its every investment, including its art, and the "what good is it?" question is so
deeply ingrained in the culture that it rarely needs to be asked.
The answer, more often than not, precedes the question, and if
we art educators sometimes bend over backwards to proclaim that
art does, indeed, contribute significantly to the individual and collective well-being, it may be because we have a gut feeling that art
is deemed to be nonproductive and, therefore, nonessential by the
great unwashed public. But I have begun to wonder whether this is
really true or whether we might, for all this time, have been whis-
tling the wrong tune. Does art really have consequences or is it a
meaningless activity that has value precisely because it *is* meaningless?

During half a lifetime and a quarter of a century in art education
I had heard both sides of the argument many times; but, more
often than not, the apologia for art education was that it was instrumental to some purpose beyond itself — hand-eye training, the
social graces, therapy, creativity, or perceptual acuity to name but
a few. Yet the issue was far from clear in my mind; neither, I
suspect, is it clear in the minds of most of my colleagues in art
education. If one argues that art is intrinsically valuable, the logic
often degenerates into a vapid nineteenth century "art for art's
sake" rationale. If, on the other hand, art education must always
serve some purpose other than art, it is invariably reduced to a
commodity, to a vehicle, to a genteel pandering. On some occasions, those who have most loudly trumpeted the instrumental
values of art may have been jumping mindlessly onto every band-
wagon that came down the road, regardless of the tune it was
playing.

THE AHP PROGRAM

During the Camelot days of the mid-1960s when the U.S. Office
of Education's Arts and Humanities Program (AHP) was in full
swing, a number of vigorous (if not rigorous) discussions took
place regarding the best ways to get and keep a solid base of support for the arts — and for the Program. The argument was that
federal funds expended for the arts must always be justified in

terms that non-artists would understand and support. Some argued that since Congressmen, our fellow bureaucrats, and educational leadership in general knew little and cared less about the arts and since the AHP was small and vulnerable, it was necessary to curry their favor by making the goals of the Program compatible with purposes these others maintained as their own. In other words, we had to build the case for the arts in deference to the interests of others who were the more powerful makers and shakers.

It was, undoubtedly, a politically astute move because, as long as it prevailed, so did the AHP budget for supporting educational research in the arts. At the same time, however, it sometimes had a musky aroma, and none of us who were so involved could avoid an occasional twinge of doubt. The issue bore, once again, upon that question of the consequences of art and whether art remained art when it was subordinated to other purposes, however noble or worthy or socially relevant they might be.

In some ways I can not help but feel that the approach to art my broker student had demonstrated twenty years before in Buffalo was much more pertinent to our problems and lifestyle in the 1970s than was that taken in Washington a decade earlier by a group of supposedly knowledgeable professionals. For him the art experience was valuable though meaningless. In the Arts and Humanities Program in the 1960s art education was self-consciously purposeful but it also seemed strangely without value in its own right.

The decisions my erstwhile student made were entirely his own and, for better or worse, he felt freed from every social, economic, political, and (I hesitate to say) even aesthetic fetter while he was in that painting class. More to the point, the exercise of that freedom was obviously pleasurable, exhilarating, and fairly unique in a lifestyle that was otherwise bound up with prescriptions, proscriptions, rules, regulations, and responsibilities.

It is even more interesting to note that in a strange way, the decision-making processes that dominated the activities of the Arts and Humanities Program in Washington were permeated and subsequently attentuated by precisely the same sort of restrictions that affected my student in his workday life. He dealt with money (other's money, not his own) even as art teachers must often deal with art (their student's art, not their own) as a medium of exchange that is instrumental but has no intrinsic worth and that must be carefully invested lest it fail to accomplish its intended purposes. The difference is that he was able to turn to his art (awful as it was by every known aesthetic standard) as an essentially meaningless activity by which he refreshed and rediscovered himself again.

"ALL IN THE BACKSEAT"

I am reminded of an old chestnut in which a policeman asks the obviously drunken occupants of a demolished car, "Who was driving?" They reply, "There was no one driving, officer. We was all in the backseat." The punchline may not be such a thigh-slapper when it is so easy to believe that the world's leaders are "all in the backseat" too, but it is illustrative of our confused and confusing times.

When the news and the prevailing public mood make it difficult to retain a sense of control over our own destinies and when global economic and political storms crackle about like summer lightning, erosions of our individual freedom of choice and sense of personal responsibility may be inevitable. When we get the feeling that, regardless of whatever we might do, the consequences will be the same, the impetus to do anything at all soon fades away, and with it the awareness of our worth as individuals fades as well. Because of this danger to the endogenous delights of individualism, personally reinforcing activities — even if they are socially non-consequential — become all the more important. At the risk of overstating the case, I would even say that the less socially consequential such activities are, the more personally rewarding they can become.

The need is not, of course, for the sort of "bread and circuses" that distracted Roman citizenry from the decay of their empire but rather for participatory outlets through which the potency of the individual as an individual may be maintained — providing only that one not threaten the general welfare of others. Given this need, there are few alternatives except the arts, and we arts educators need only shake ourselves loose from our marketplace mentality in order to discover a whole new world as our oyster. In the jargon of the TV commercial, we are hooked on the idea that art is "good for you" — though, as every parent knows, such arguments have little pervasive power.

ART AS AVENUE TO PERSONAL FREEDOM

Whether the arts do or do not embody all of the panaceas ascribed to them is not, however, the point at issue. The more fundamental question is whether by relying almost exclusively upon the instrumental values of art in our rationalizations we may not be losing sight of the most compelling arguments of all — namely that the arts give pleasure and that the overwhelming majority of art works produced since Altamura and Lascaux have had no social consequences nor, in fact, were they intended to have. Most of the painting and sculpture that adorn our homes and offices and classrooms and studios, and even our museums, are valued because of the pleasure their presence provides and, indeed, their very production was, in most instances, undertaken for exactly those reasons — for the pleasure of its making.

If the only purpose of art is to provide pleasure to the maker, which may almost incidentally be shared by viewers after the fact, it is no small wonder that our puritanical and pragmatic forebearers looked upon art as a useless, if not a sinful, activity. Nor can we easily escape the long and gloomy shadows such attitudes have cast upon the present. Were we to admit that art has no consequences except to the individual and that it represents a unique avenue to personal freedom unlikely to exist in other aspects of our complex social life, its value becomes more clearly apparent. Where but in the arts is the opportunity for personal choice and personal reward so readily accessible and where else can they be obtained without affecting the rights and privileges of others? Where else in our pragmatic world can something be useless but still valuable?

The maintenance of a sense of individual responsibility (which I assume to be a self-evident good) obviously requires the exercise of individual choice somewhere in the social fabric. As the areas where an individual can be free to make choices are slowly diminished, it becomes increasingly important to recognize, to maintain, and to nurture those few areas where individual privilege does not interfere with the welfare of the society as a whole. One such area is clearly in the arts. Contrary to the tradition of art's instrumental uses, which has built up in art education in recent decades, it is art's essential meaninglessness that gives it renewed validity in a world where social demands tend, increasingly, to blot out areas of individual initiative.

*In this open, deeply personal
autobiographical account of a
teacher-as-learner, "ethical
decision-making and aesthetic
discrimination" come vividly alive.*

English As a
Passionate Language:
A Reminiscence

MARIAN RONAN
Graduate Student in Elementary Education
University of Pennsylvania

Proust had his Madeleine and I, it seems, have this year of teacher training. What a hemorrhage of recollection the past week of classes has caused me. By the end of Dr. Botel's first lecture, a frozen stream of personal history had melted and was trickling down from the lost places of my childhood.

There I am, a fat little girl with pigtails, sitting underneath the forsythia bush by the side of a gray stucco house. Inside the house my mother is trying to listen to "Wendy Warren and the News," while my grandmother plays "Beautiful Dreamer" on the piano. Daddy is at the electric company earning the money to send me to college. And Joseph, my brother, is in the playpen, wearing a pair of authentic Mickey Mouse.ears.

In 1953 Collingdale, our suburb, managed to partake of the last tip-touch of small town America. I remember with genuine relish, for example, the mixture of patriotism and penny-scramble that was the Fourth of July celebration, and the shivering glow of neighborhood Christmas caroling. I remember, too, our first telephone, my mother dialing in pantomime to make me guess what the surprise was. And "Big John and Sparky" on the radio, before any neighbor kid even had a television set for us to go and watch.

Precious little of my early years at school remains with me. Oh, of course I can smell the furnace at St. Joseph's on the first cold autumn day and taste the pretzels with mustard in the forbidden candy store on Bartram Avenue. And I'll probably never lose the glorious fantasy about swinging from the hanging lights in the first grade classroom to stab my teacher with a yardstick. Remembering little else is, I suspect, a great mercy.

The parish school we attended was staggering under the weight of the postwar baby boom. There were one hundred and eight children in the first grade, with one young nun. The first time I faced my own class of children, twenty-one of them, I thought of that nun and wondered if she'd been an archangel in disguise.

ENGLISH CLASS

Perhaps I taught myself to read. Who knows? All reading lessons have slipped from my memory, except for an incident with an old nun who punished me for not taking my reader home at night. Why, I wondered, did we spend a whole year reading it out loud, when one could read the whole thing in a night? But I was a very good little girl and carried the book home ever after.

What I do remember, in technicolor, is poetry class. Poetry, to Catholic children, was a subject unto itself, having nothing to do with reading. Every fall we received a thin, soft-covered volume full of tolerable line drawings and a mixed bag of verses. *That* I carried home, partly out of terror, because in the course of the year we memorized a large chunk of that book, reciting our lesson, one by one, every day after lunch. And God help the child who was "unprepared."

Appropriating those poems was one of the most intense emotional experiences of my childhood. How I came to love them! To this day I consider the pedagogical technique of memorizing poems to have been one of the happiest crimes the Catholic schools ever perpetrated on me. Doubtless ten children were alienated for every one that fell in love, and perhaps the experience would have been far richer for me without fear. But when, years later, I got to Wallace Stevens and Theodore Roethke, I knew them for who they were: descendants of the Longfellow and Whitman and (heaven help us) John Bannister Tabb of my school days. When I myself manage to teach children anything at all, they tend to come away thinking poetry is as important as recess.

To do justice to that awful Catholic school, there was one nun, long since dead, who knew a few important things. Sister Nazarius, who probably wasn't as huge as she seemed, had the fiercest temper I'd ever encountered. She was given to banging children's heads on the blackboard and bellowing, "I'm going to knock you into the middle of next week." No doubt she was frustrated almost to madness by the sheer numbers of us. Yet she was the only teacher there who had much sense of beauty. I remember best the Marguerite De Angeli books Sister read to us before we went home at night; *Thee Hannah* is still one of the world's great wonders to me. We had art lessons too, in a crude fashion, and singing: "There'll Be Bluebirds Over the White Cliffs of Dover" and "White Christmas." And it was in that class that I learned the poem I can't get rid of:

> Will there ever be a morning?
> Is there such a thing as day?
> Could I see it from the mountains
> If I were as tall as they?
> Has it feet like water lilies?
> Has it feathers like a bird?
> Does it come from far off countries
> Of which I have never heard?
> O some soldier, O some scholar,
> O some wise man from the skies,

Please to tell a little pilgrim
Where the place called morning lies.

I've forgotten the name of the author (two points off in the June exam), but Sister Nazarius can't possibly mind. I've recited the poem almost every day for years.

Poetry was not the limit of my passion; there were comic books too. My mother forbade them, but could never enforce the dictum. Poor dear, how could she, with my father and grandmother bringing them home by the wagonload? Eventually we worked out a compromise, and Mom began buying "Classics Illustrated," which I obligingly read, along with *Superman* and *Archie*. They, together with *Ladies' Home Journal, Redbook*, and the *Reader's Digest,* constituted the intellectual fare of my early days. But comic books were really the heart of the matter, and I give them to my students now, along with anything else they'll fall for.

I once read of a Jewish community in Poland during the Middle Ages. They introduced their children to the word of God by pouring honey over a plaque bearing the first few words of the Torah. The children licked off the honey and commenced their studies. My mother knew nothing about Polish Jews, but she intuited the basic principle. As I was growing up there was a drugstore catty-corner from the white frame public library, and I can still taste the delicious books of my childhood, followed by huge ice cream cones on the way home.

There weren't very many books in that library, and most of what was there was hardly worth reading. I suppose the Bobbsey Twins didn't do me any harm, though, and standing out like silence after a pneumatic drill was all of Greek mythology and *The Wind in the Willows* and *The Secret Garden*. Fortunately, the volunteer librarians didn't know enough to forbid us the use of the adult collection, so there was all of that, too, in time.

Toward the end of grade school I began to write horrendous poems that rhymed perfectly; they make me blush even yet. It was a mercy, I think, that nobody knew enough to tell me how awful those poems were. A standard, college-educated English teacher might have squashed what was the beginning of an intensely personal experience of creation. As it was, I sailed on, expecting to become a great poet fairly soon.

HIGH SCHOOL DAYS

The high school I attended, Notre Dame, is in Rose Valley, and I remember it as the loveliest place on earth. I was happy there in the way that precocious children are happy the first time they find friends. Susan Donahue and Helen Sweeney and Kate Dougherty and Mary Ann Sullivan. . . . What an immensity of confidence our secure little world instilled in me! What a splendid mythology to emerge from!

The nuns at Notre Dame come just behind those silly, infinitely innocent Irish girls in my warmest recollections. They were the first genuinely educated adults I ever knew, and few encounters since then have equalled those long, late afternoon conversations at Notre Dame for richness and excitement.

In *The Seven Storey Mountain* Thomas Merton writes that the first time he learned about the important things in life was in Mark Van Doren's classes in Shakespeare. Van Doren, he says, asked questions, good questions, and "if you tried to answer them intelligently, you found yourself saying excellent things that you did not know, and that, in fact, you had not known before." My first English teacher at Notre Dame was a bit like that. Probably what made her (Sister Maura was her name) was that she was no English teacher at all. Her competence was French, but in those days nobody cared whàt one knew; both my biology and my algebra teachers had degrees in English, so why should my English teacher have had one?

What Maura did have was a passionate sense of the language, a passion as contagious as cholera. I know that that English class never covered the prescribed curriculum, and probably a few grammatical errors went unmended, but as for me, I read, and wrote, and tasted the shape of the language as I never have since.

She really had no sense, Maura, but perhaps a touch of genius. She taught us what she liked. Early on she began to copy hunks of Gerard Manley Hopkins onto the board; by the end of the year

I had memorized most of it. "I caught this morning morning's minion, kingdom of daylight's dauphin, dapple dawn drawn falcon, in his riding. . . ." She read prayers to us. She read Chesterton, and Thurber, and Caryl Houselander. She brought books to the classroom and auctioned them off. And gave writing assignments that unlocked our experience for us: "Pretend you are lying on a hill, on your back, looking up through the branches of a tree. . . ." "How do you know, when you first wake up in the morning, if there's been a snowstorm?"

And me, Maura gave me poetry — my own, in exchange for all the Longfellow and Tennyson I'd been trying to imitate. I can't remember when I first showed her my poems, but she wrote a note asking for more, and before long we had a regular correspondence going. Don't try to rhyme, she'd say, and don't write "o'er" and "e'en" — write the way you talk. The notes got to be more than poems from me and more than criticism from her, and a whole world of literature and culture and sensibility exploded in my consciousness. Oh, what a year that was! And when Sister Maura went away for the summer, she left me a shopping bag full of books, harvested, no doubt, from convent corners: Shaw, Moss Hart, James Stephens, Dickens, C. S. Lewis, and on, and on.

After that the only feeling I ever had for English classes was scorn. The three nuns who succeeded Maura endeavored to teach literary criticism and the finer points of grammar while I read novels tucked inside my textbooks, planning all the while to return to that school some day and teach English as it was meant to be taught.

In college, however, it became apparent that *nobody* was teaching English as I felt it should be taught, and I concluded that four years of linguistics and dissection would make me loathe literature. So I took up philosophy, acquiring a little rigor thereby and losing what muse I'd ever had in the process. But my passion for the language survived and flourished.

It was in my senior year, I believe, that Joseph Featherstone published a series of articles on the British Infant School. No doubt those articles influenced a great many potential teachers;

in any case, they initiated a revolution in my sense of the possible. After Featherstone I discovered Sylvia Ashton-Warner and John Holt, Caleb Gattegno and Herbert Kohl. Finally I stumbled upon what was the ultimate enticement to teaching, *In the Early World,* a beautiful, little-known work by an Australian teacher, in which all the aesthetic possibilities of elementary education stood up and shouted at me.

FIRST TEACHING YEAR IN A FOURTH GRADE

Fools, I suppose, rush in just as I did to the fourth grade of a little Catholic school on 39th Street. The Catholic practice of having virtually no requirements for teachers was clearly to my advantage, if not to the children's, and the powers-that-be did me one of the greatest favors any school can—they left me alone. Considering the salary they were paying, perhaps St. Leonard's hadn't the nerve to make many demands. In any case, I was quite certain I knew exactly what was important to teach children. And when those twenty-one dear, gentle, sensitive kids wandered in, I set out to do it.

Now the truth is, I didn't know anything about skills education at all. The kids taught *me* phonics. (I was lucky, they had learned it all before.) Modern math I puzzled out one lesson ahead of my students, and science we kept to an incompetent minimum. On the few occasions when I did an experiment that succeeded, the kids clapped and cheered, it was such a novelty. And the social studies curriculum I junked entirely; it was dull and, for the most part, untrue. A few periods a week I followed the teacher's guide to the basal reader, dozing off in the middle of a lesson, much to the children's delight; they were bored, too.

The rest of the time I taught the kids English as a passionate language. First of all, I read to them, because I enjoy reading and because the school lacked multiple copies of some of the more desirable children's literature. We began with the *Narnia* tales and a splendid children's Bible; by the end of the year the children were reading out loud to each other. At the same time I began using only those stories in the reader that interested me, figuring that dullness is something that one acquires an immunity to over the years; if I found a story boring, my students would, no doubt, be maddened by it.

In October the class began keeping journals, and what fine, thoughtful things they wrote. I cajoled the children into reading a mountain of books, hauling them up from the library by armloads and losing a great many en route. A prize was offered, at one point, to the child who could read the largest number of books by Christmas. With a less ingenuous group of children this might have been a disaster, but I watched them devour the books. Christopher, far from the best reader in the group, blushed with pleasure when he won.

That was the year that Kenneth Koch published *Wishes, Lies, and Dreams*, and I stole ideas from him with joy, as he had obviously intended. The kids began to write delicious poems, which got read right back to them, along with others from Koch's book, and *Reflections on a Gift of Watermelon Pickle*, and my own rag-tag memory store. At the same time I reproduced, in cheerful oblivion of the copyright laws, a great hunk of a sample language arts text that I found in the closet. Besides being full of excellent ideas for writing, it was based on the history of the language, so we were able to learn "social studies" from it, too. By the time we got from the Romans to Chaucer, we were going, with great glee, on field trips to the medieval wing of the museum, building castles, making Viking boats, and writing stories, essays, and poems about those ancient people. It was splendid.

At Christmastime we put out a newspaper, "The Supercycle," and oh, the elation that paper engendered. The haiku, cartoons, sketches, and pieces of out and out opinion in that paper make me laugh with delight even yet. As the year went on, the kids' writing got better, and they began working in other areas as well — pottery, printmaking, dramatics. In the spring we invited a poet who teaches at Rosemont College to do a poetry reading for our class. That reading was one of the peak experiences of my life; not only did Sister Mary Anthony read her poems to the children, they read theirs to her and illustrated them all while listening, referring to her ever after as "our poet." One of the kids recently mentioned to me that Sister Anthony had visited four or five times, an exaggeration which indicates as well as anything I can think of the intensity of the experience.

Several aspects of the year weren't great. The SRA scores were lower than some people had wished. A few children took reading problems with them to the fifth grade, because I knew precious little about teaching reading to kids who were pre-literate. And the principal was never really thrilled by my approach, enamored as she was of learning centers and programed individualization. The buzzing, booming confusion of children writing on the floor and shouting out ideas didn't really fulfill her expectations. About the poems in *Wishes, Lies and Dreams* she said, "They're really nothing but a lot of run-on sentences," and about me, "I think you have the kind of gift that would be better appreciated on a higher level." So I didn't go back there the next year, which is perhaps too bad, because I know something unique and important happened in that fourth grade.

THE SECOND YEAR—DISAPPOINTINGLY DIFFERENT

Would that I could end this tale right here. There is, however, a brief, painful epilogue. I taught a second year in a Black, parent-controlled community school in Harlem. But I was unable to teach out of the passionate experience of my past. I taught, rather, out of the reader and hated it as much as the children did.

When I ask myself why, I realize that I thought one couldn't afford to "play" with deprived ghetto kids; that they needed "skills" too badly. I just hadn't the wisdom to recognize that those bruised innocents needed play most of all.

One thing that made the teaching difficult was that many of our Black parents didn't trust play. They thought that education had to look serious to be serious, and I had neither the skill nor the belief in my own convictions needed to bring off a deception. And then, too, I'd taught the children at St. Leonard's out of an intuition of a culture that we shared, and I had no such intuition in Harlem. I was an alien. Somehow, beneath all the retrospective analysis about play, and phonics, and non-standard dialect, I have to admit that the thing just never really worked. The imagination of those children was always beyond my reach, so every day of every month was a struggle.

Sometimes I wonder which of those two teaching experiences to trust. Sometimes I bat like a shuttlecock from hope to anxiety. At its very worst, I don't want to teach at all anymore, preferring to read books about education or write autobiographies. But there's something about the memory of that first year — something, too, about the immeasurable riches of my own schooling that draws me past the anxiety in anticipation of another group of children. And that's all one can ask for, I suppose.

Two distinguished mathematics educators present an eloquent case for the values of their discipline in enabling the learner "to free himself and act wisely for nearly every aspect of his life."

Mathematics: Road to Intellectual Freedom

MARGUERITE BRYDEGAARD and
JAMES E. INSKEEP, JR.
Professors of Education
San Diego State University

M athematics, as a part of our intellectual repertoire, is often classed with the automobile and the paring knife. The art of "mathematicking" is commonly held to be an ability to balance a checkbook and develop facility with sums. As the automobile becomes merely a vehicle of convenience, so many regard mathematics as a tool of expediency. As the knife serves to cut and prepare victuals, so the art of "mathematicking" is but a means to a prosaic end. Conversely, many feel that the discipline of mathematics is reserved for very intellectual, divinely inspired individuals who closet themselves and think big thoughts — thoughts incomprehensible to the man in the marketplace. Neither of these analogies is genuinely representative of the true worth of mathematics.

CONTENT AND PROCESSES

Not just a tool nor the sole possession of an intellectual elite, mathematics is a way of personal development for everyman. *Mathematics is a road to intellectual freedom.*

The road is complex. There are byways — such as the mundane and yet important acts of reckoning and computing. There are waystops — intuitive geometry and measurement for instance. There are freeways and highways that give a regal air to our road — the development of logical processes, the examination of alternatives in a systematic manner, the classification of the environment to serve society. The flow of traffic is stimulated through a dynamic union of inspired teachers and motivated learners. This combination completes and gives meaning to mathematics as a road to intellectual freedom.

The highways of mathematics are actually tollways since they require something of the one who would travel them. The ability to reason and develop logical choices, the art of categorizing and organizing the environment, and the systematic development of knowledge are not without cost. Few persons come to the study of mathematics with well-developed knowledge. As a man-made discipline, mathematics must be learned; and when well learned, it enables the learner to free himself to think and act wisely for nearly every aspect of his life.

Logical processes are the domain of the philosopher, but thinking in an ordered and systematic manner is a possibility for all learners. For thousands of years, philosophers have argued "logically" in complex dialogue. Today, the study of mathematics allows a learner to reason with a greater accuracy than even Socrates or Plato. In simple form, children are taught to use symbols for abstractions that follow a classic two-valued logic. They are taught to develop precise thinking patterns and to categorize much of their learning. The older pupil uses a form of logical symbolism that frees him to reason in much the same manner as shorthand frees the stenographer to record.

The child well educated in mathematics will be able to transfer his power of reasoning to cut through the endless ambiguities of modern mass media: "Brand X is better!" Brand X is better than what? "Dentists advise the use of Supershine toothpaste." All of the dentists? Some of them? It makes a difference! With some basic learning in mathematical logic, an individual is freed to cut through the multitude of half-truths and partial statements that confront and insult him. He is freed to think for himself.

Alternatives for personal action imply the defining and interpreting of choices. Mathematical models have been used to describe nearly every natural and most human systems. The descriptions give precision to the organization of our world. The child who can systematically explore an algorithm through flow-charting is helped to see meaning in his computation. The young adult who sees beauty in his study of the universe is freed to explore by the mathematical models of Einstein and Newton. A multitude of man-made inventions lend themselves to such mathematical models. An individual who uses mathematical models for his study of the world and his part in it, is freed to make wise choices of alternatives for action.

Classification of the environment begins early. Children are taught to separate objects by color, shape, and size. They learn that selected attributes serve to define their immediate universe and give order where there appears to be randomness. Scientists continue to classify findings and the environment. Without this mathematical approach, many modern medical and technological advances would not have been developed. All men should be freed to classify and order their worlds.

THE TEACHER

There is a source of wonder in the study of mathematics that leads to intellectual freedom. It is rooted and described through the dynamic of teacher-stimulated learners. It is a freedom to teach and an equally free opportunity to learn. Where mathematics serves as a road to intellectual freedom, we find an inspired knowledgeable teacher and a motivated learner complementing one another. Thus we have the vehicle and flow of traffic that gives the road its meaning.

Freedom to teach and freedom to learn go hand in hand. Therefore, teachers should be provided with many opportunities to gain freedom in teaching mathematics. Teachers should experience learning situations that are desirable for them to use in their own classes.

There are many attributes that characterize the freedom of a teacher. Let us consider some of these:

1. The teacher appreciates the beauty and power of mathematics because he experiences it himself. He is an observer, an explorer, a discoverer of mathematical patterns in his own environment; and he shares his observations, his explorations, and his discoveries with his students. Teacher and student note that the leaves of grass and of lilies are parallel-veined; they see that the petals and sepals of the lily family are in multiples of three. The gears of a motorcycle attract their attention, and they note that gears are like wheels with teeth cut into their outer edges, and that when two gears are meshed together, one gear can turn the other. They observe the turning and know that if one gear turns clockwise, the other turns counterclockwise.

The teacher observes patterns of constancy and variability and uses the ideas to interpret mathematical systems. He finds that in the decimal system, only ten digits are used to express number values as great and as small as he wishes. Each digit has a constant value (digit value). Each also has a variable value based on its position within a numeral (place value). Thus in 44, each of the 4s is constant in digit value but variable in place value. The 4 at the left represents 40 or ten 4s (10×4) and the 4 at the right represents one 4 (1×4). The idea of constant and positional arrangements also operates with the alphabet — an almost infinite number of new words can be created from twenty-six symbols. But there are twenty-six symbols in the English alphabet compared with only ten for the decimal system. The "sound" values for some alphabetical symbols vary with little reason or system. The place and digit values for numerals are accurately predictable. There is even greater genius in the invention of the numerical system than in the creation of the letters of the alphabet.

The visual symbols used to express the language of mathematics, of music, of harbor markings, of road signs, and of science contribute greatly to communication. The symbols of mathematics are especially notable in their simplicity. The simplicity lends itself to facile recognition and to precise systematization. For example, consider the following:

Mathematical	English
$3 \times 18 = 54$	eighteen multiplied by three equals fifty-four
$21 + 84 < 11 + 95$	twenty-one plus eighty-four is less than eleven plus ninety-five
3,624,494.7	three million, six hundred twenty-four thousand, four hundred ninety-four and seven-tenths

The teacher truly appreciates the spark of genius in the creation of visual symbols and in the systems for interpreting mathematical ideas.

2.   The teacher understands in depth the mathematics that goes far beyond the things that he teaches. He understands the concepts underlying measurement, spaceometry (study of space including geometry), number systems, numerical computation, probability, and other topics. The understanding leads to knowing *what* questions to ask, *when* to ask them, and *how* to help the learner discover the concepts for himself. During discussion periods, laboratory sessions, and work times, the teacher, by questioning, guides the direction and level of thinking achieved by the individual child and by groups of children. The teacher realizes that as long as he teaches he needs to continue his personal learning of mathematics. And, in the learning, the teacher receives good dividends — a continuous education that is tuition free.

3.   The teacher identifies the specific ideas and skills essential to the topics he teaches. Since the symbols for mathematics facilitate systematization, it is relatively simple to identify and analyze types of examples that occur with various units of instruction. The teacher develops expedient procedures for analyzing pupil error with the concepts and skills that he teaches. He diagnoses pupil needs and prescribes appropriate learning activities to meet the needs. And he continuously evaluates pupil growth and knows what comes next in the learning sequence.

4.   A successful teacher gives devoted attention to individual differences and the individual needs of his pupils. He realizes that

each child is a unique person — a special creation of God. He believes that each person has special worth and knows that with some children he will need to search to find the unique qualities that should be cultivated.

Cultivation of the "hidden spark" in each learner is essential for excellence in teaching. Mathematics offers fine kindling for creative, individualized thinking. Frequently, the pupil who receives the mark of excellence for computational prowess is not the pupil who has keen insight into problems and how to solve them. Even the learner who is called "very capable" is often imprisoned by his unquestioning acceptance of memorized rules and his expectation of excellence in his class. His experimenting, testing of ideas, and formulating hypotheses may not be at a high level of achievement. Conversely, the so-called low achiever may be very capable in seeing how gears turn and in sensing the how and why of practical applications of mathematics, and may be potentially a fine mathematician who has been undiscovered by his teacher.

Teaching has no meaning apart from the learner. If our road to freedom is based on the content of mathematics and made plausible by an effective teacher, it becomes real and genuine when translated into student behavior. Latent energy in the quest for intellectual freedom becomes positive dynamic force in the developing behavior of the learner.

THE LEARNER

The young learner is drawn to mathematics as iron filings are drawn to a magnet. His world is full of wonder, and much of his wondering is with mathematical ideas. He explores his universe, and he thinks about quantitative ideas: How big? How small? How far? How fast? Which is bigger? What holds more? Who is taller? Are they the same? How many? The young learner is self-propelled. If he is fortunate, his direction is guided by loving parents and others who care. He is commended for his "mathematicking." He is a special child who is praised for his worth.

The young learner is personally involved in finding out, and his learning keeps pace with his involvement. When Joey, a six-year-old, was provided with rubber bands and sticks of doweling that were 3 feet long and ¼ inch in diameter, he was challenged to experiment by building things and telling about what he built. Joey built buildings, rocket cones, and rockets and in the experience, he learned about geometric shapes; he found out about the rigidity of triangles and about symmetry of figures. He came upon problems and he was free to solve them. He practiced his language skills when he wrote about what he did and then read his story.*

Through active involvement in doing things with materials that represent and illustrate mathematical ideas, children develop a base of experience that frees them for further learning. As the learner grows older, the tasks that he is expected to do may be more prescribed, but there are many teachers who help the learner continue a spirit of self-propelled learning. The wonder is kept. Discovery-making, inventing, experimenting, and finding out continue and become even more powerful tools for learning.

From simple beginnings, great ideas grow. When doors are left open for wondering, appreciating, and growing, each learner interprets mathematical ideas and masters skills needed to blaze his own trail. Each year he grows in his analytical power and intellectual freedom.

The world is full of wondrous things, most of which may be described, categorized, and at times numbered. Literature, science, language, and art lend themselves to the learner's "mathematicking." Income tax forms, newspaper advertisements, and batting averages involve mathematics. All experiences in life have their mathematical component. The behavior of a learner, whether child or adult, gives vibrant meaning to mathematics. When children are freed to think and wonder, when teachers are free to express and channel this wonder, and when mathematics is more than just computation, it truly becomes a road to intellectual freedom.

---

*Scott, Joseph. "With Sticks and Rubber Bands," *The Arithmetic Teacher*, February 1970, pp. 147–50.

Educators in the areas of health, physical education, and recreation should respect the rights of all students, regardless of sex or race, to participate in programs that will contribute to their well-being and enjoyment of physical activities and athletic competition.

Interlocking Rights and Responsibilities

MARJORIE BLAUFARB
Managing Editor
Update

W hen the American Alliance for Health, Physical Education and Recreation (AAHPER) Task Force on Equal Opportunity and Human Rights was preparing a position statement, implicit in all our discussions was the realization that denial of opportunity to one section of the educational community results in infringement on the rights of others. As we attempted to formulate a position on the rights of women teachers and coaches, we found ourselves talking about denial of opportunities to female students. In talking of the problems of minority coaches, we could not escape the fact that coaches' problems interlocked with those of their students.

72

LACK OF RESPECT

Successful coaches are reputed to be authoritarian, and many are. They tend to put the general good, which they perceive as fielding a winning team, ahead of the immediate good of the individual. We physical educators, whose programs lead up to athletic activities and who are often coaches ourselves, sometimes display the same characteristic. We must set both goals and limits, but trouble arises when, in setting them, we do not respect individual rights of students.

How does lack of respect display itself? One way is when we coast along with a poor, outdated program because physical education is a required subject for graduation. Not keeping up with new knowledge and methods deprives both ourselves and our students.

Lack of respect is evident when we accept and act without reflection on old shibboleths and sex or race stereotypes: "Girls (or intellectuals) are poor sports," for instance, or "Women physical education teachers (or male dancers) are homosexuals"; or when we equate conformity to an arbitrary team standard as being synonymous with patriotism and Americanism.

As professionals, we deny ourselves and our students the right to the best education if we accept stereotyped ideas of ourselves as "dumb jocks" or assume a spurious intellectuality because we have ambivalent feelings about being part of a discipline associated with movement and sweaty action.

CLARIFYING RIGHTS

In recent writings about the "new physical education" and in programs exemplifying it, great stress has been laid on the fact that a good program allows children to develop at their own rate and to choose activities they like. The old-fashioned physical training program in which children in classes of sixty to one hundred went into a gymnasium and did "gymnastics" by rote was no more stultifying than the modern equivalent of spending every activity period playing round-games in elementary school or milling around shooting baskets at the junior high or high school level.

73

Whether designated "new" or "movement-based" or "elective/ selective," a student-oriented program respects the right of young people to receive training in activities that will contribute to their health and well-being for the remainder of their lives in addition to having opportunities for appropriate competition. In elementary schools, the aware physical education specialist respects the right of the young child to be exposed to programs that focus on individual coordination and that sets individual goals. Every child then achieves a measure of success.

Congress recently enacted legislation stating that: "No person shall, on the basis of sex, be excluded from participation in, or be denied the benefits of, or be subjected to discrimination under any education program or activity receiving federal financial assistance."* This law has had some interesting repercussions because what Congress and the Office of Civil Rights of the Department of Health, Education and Welfare perceive as the rights of students conflicts with what many physical educators and coaches consider to be their rights. The conflict seems to emanate from the assumption by faculties that the programs they teach or administer, and in which they have a vested interest, are unchangeably theirs.

ISSUES OF SEXISM

Because physical education classes and athletics have traditionally been sex-segregated, there is now resistance in some areas to the regulation requiring classes to be coeducational. This reluctance to integrate, even at the elementary school level, is based on several factors. One is the desire to protect children from injury—about which more later. A deeper fear is economic. Departments that formerly were separate may now be integrated, thereby eliminating one top job and possibly other positions too. Then there is the personal pride of teachers who consider "their" programs superior and unique. In vocalizing these fears, little thought is given to the rights of students to take part in physical activities in which both sexes mingle — a pattern based on what happens in the family and the community.

---

*Title IX of the Education Amendments Act of 1972.

74

Similarly, the traditional pattern in athletics, which offers varied programs of competitive sports for male high school students and a much curtailed program for high school females, was based on assumptions that denied the rights of the female adolescent student to enjoy the same athletic opportunities accorded to their male classmates. Again, this arrangement has come about partly because of a mistaken desire to protect young females and partly because of community pressure to retain the traditional image of women. But the result has been a denial of student rights. And now that things are changing, the male athletic director is still sometimes heard to say, "But what about *my* program?"

A more subtle infringement of the rights of students is the assumption that any youngster of either sex who displays athletic ability naturally wants to be a competitor. Of course many do; but when the rights of an individual to be different are respected, children will not be forced into a competitive role before they are ready for it.

PROTECTION AND OVERPROTECTION

To return to the idea of protecting children from injury — in discussions of Title IX and the regulation stating that one may not discriminate against students because of possible pregnancy-related conditions, almost always somebody says, "If we can't keep them from playing, how can we protect them from harm?"

This innocent, even benevolent-sounding question goes to the heart of one of a young person's most significant rights — the right to experience even possibly dangerous activities such as skiing — the right not to be overprotected. Under the guise of safeguarding a young woman, a teacher cannot make arbitrary decisions on whether or not she should engage in activities because of later pregnancy. There is often no physical reason why a healthy female cannot engage in activities that, in fact, may be good for her health. It is her right to make that decision and one hopes she consults her family and doctor.

This desire to protect students comes up in many contexts and many guises, but people generally deplore overprotectiveness in a nonschool environment. A mother or babysitter shielding a young child from the ordinary rough-and-tumble of play is a stock figure of comic literature. And fortunately, the fragile, breakable female weakling is also becoming a farcical idea observed more in comic strips and jokes than in fact. Why should the school or recreation environment be different?

RIGHTS OF TEACHERS

More has been said about the responsibilities of teachers toward students than about the rights of teachers. It must be remembered that students have responsibilities too, and that they infringe on the rights of teachers from time to time. But a good teacher has control in the school environment and the backing of authority, which an unruly, disrespectful student does not have.

We who work in the areas of health, physical education, athletics, and recreation pride ourselves on the fact that we touch the total school population. We justly pride ourselves on being successful in motivating young people to greater responsibility and achievement not only in athletic competition but also academically. We have an important place in school life as instructors in strategic areas of education and human endeavor. Attention to and acknowledgment of some of the rights of students mentioned here can only strengthen an already strong discipline.

FREEDOM TO SPEAK, WRITE, AND READ

*The U.S. Supreme Court has laid
to rest the concept of* in loco
parentis *as it relates to the mind.
The Constitution and the Bill of
Rights apply to all citizens
regardless of age.*

Intellectual
Freedom and
the Rights of
Children

JUDITH F. KRUG
Director of the Office for Intellectual Freedom
American Library Association
Executive Director
Freedom to Read Foundation

In the controversy over the use of *Slaughterhouse Five* in the
Rochester Community Schools, all substantive actions and maneu-
verings were initiated, developed, and resolved by adults. The students, whose accessibility to the novel was at stake, never directly
participated. This situation is not unusual. Almost all requests for
removal of curriculum and library materials are generated by
adults. Attacks are based on the doctrine of *in loco parentis*, meaning, in broad interpretation, that parents or other adults, such as
teachers, librarians, and clergy, designated by parents, have complete responsibility for — and control over — children, including
their minds. The *in loco parentis* concept, however, conflicts directly with the intellectual freedom concept, which provides for
free choice, regardless of age, in matters concerning the mind.

This basic conflict has reached new proportions in recent years because of the U.S. Supreme Court's recognition of youths' rights in the First Amendment area.

The *in loco parentis* doctrine has been recognized in Western civilization from about the sixteenth century, resulting in an unusual, and in many ways incongruous, situation today. The term "children," in a legal sense, covers all individuals up to age twenty-one. In general, but with a few exceptions, "children" can be drafted and taxed, are subject to corporal punishment by the family, are subject to dictates of school authorities and to juvenile curfews, and can be sent to adult prisons. But, again with a few exceptions, children cannot sign a binding contract or hold and dispose of property, work in many occupations, represent themselves in divorce or will proceedings, sit on a grand jury or jury, run for elected office, be appointed to state agencies, marry or travel without parental consent, purchase liquor or cigarettes, attend certain movies, or read certain books. It is, indeed, an incongruous situation.

The incongruity was accentuated by the Twenty-sixth Amendment to the United States Constitution granting a portion of the "children," the eighteen to twenty-one-year-olds, the right to vote. Adoption of the Twenty-sixth Amendment made clear a new direction for the nation in regard to children's rights, the advocacy of which began nearly one hundred years ago. Over the years, other plateaus such as Child Labor Laws and the juvenile court system were reached. But, it was not until the 1967 *in re Gault* case that the courts recognized children's rights.

GAULT AND THE RIGHT TO DUE PROCESS

To understand the *Gault* decision, one must look at another milestone of juvenile rights — the juvenile court system. Created at the turn of the century, the juvenile court stresses that a child be examined and treated, not punished. This humane concept was verbalized by one of its original architects who, in 1909, wrote:

> Seated at a desk, with the child at his side, where he can on occasion put his arm around his shoulder and draw the lad to him, the judge . . . will gain immensely in the effectiveness of his work.

Unfortunately, the system didn't quite work that way. Among the juvenile court's more visible shortcomings *was* its rather blatant disregard for the concept of due process. To a large extent, juvenile courts seemed to believe that due process safeguards were irrelevant or unnecessary.

In 1967, however, the *Gault* case, focusing on due process in regard to juveniles, came before the U.S. Supreme Court. Fifteen-year-old Gerald Gault had been found guilty of making an obscene phone call. He was not notified of the charges against him, was not told of his rights against self-incrimination, was not represented by counsel, and, for an offense carrying a maximum sentence of *two months* for an adult, was declared a delinquent and subjected to institutionalization until age twenty-one — *six years later.* In its opinion, the Supreme Court asserted that a juvenile like Gerald Gault had a right to a timely notice of charges and that notice at the first hearing was not timely. It also said he had a right to counsel or appointed counsel if indigent, a right to be informed about self-incrimination, and a right to cross-examine the witnesses testifying against him. In the majority opinion, Mr. Justice Black wrote that children are entitled to these rights "because they are specifically and unequivocally granted by provisions of the Fifth and Sixth Amendments, which the Fourteenth Amendment makes applicable to the states." In other words, the Bill of Rights to the United States Constitution applies to all citizens regardless of age.

TINKER AND RIGHT TO FREEDOM OF EXPRESSION

If the *Gault* case marked the turning point, the *Tinker* case of 1969 was not only a giant step in the right direction, but is even more pertinent to the conflict between adults and children. In *Tinker vs. Des Moines Independent Community School District,* the U.S. Supreme Court held, in February 1969, that the First Amendment protects the rights of public school children to express their political and social views during school hours. The decision held, further, that school officials may not place arbitrary curbs on student speech in the public schools. It is particularly interesting to note that, while many individuals had taken for granted that school children did have First Amendment rights of free speech, the Supreme Court had never directly said so prior to this case.

The *Tinker* case arose when a group of students decided to publicize their objection to the Vietnam war and their support for a truce by wearing black armbands in school during the 1967 holiday season. Principals of the Des Moines schools announced that any students refusing to remove the armband would be suspended.

A number of students, among them John and Mary Beth Tinker and Christopher Eckhardt (ages fifteen, thirteen, and sixteen, respectively) persisted in wearing the armbands to school. There was no disturbance or disruption of normal school activities but, nevertheless, the students were told to remove their armbands. When they refused, they were ordered to leave school. They returned two weeks later, without armbands but, in the meantime, had filed suit in federal court.

The students lost their case at both the district court level and in the U.S. Court of Appeals. The Supreme Court, however, reversed these decisions. In the majority opinion, Justice Abe Fortas pointed out that neither students nor teachers "shed their Constitutional right to freedom of speech or expression at the schoolhouse gate." He said:

> School officials do not possess absolute authority over their students. Students in school as well as out of school are "persons" under our Constitution. . . . In our system, students may not be regarded as closed circuit recipients of only that which the state chooses to communicate. They may not be confined to the expression of those sentiments that are officially approved. In the absence of a specific showing of *Constitutionally valid reasons* to regulate their speech, students are entitled to freedom of expression of their views. (Emphasis added.)

As Justice Fortas saw it, the First Amendment was designed to insure toleration of dissent even where dissent may cause social discomfort or dispute. Accordingly, student expression in the schools may not be prohibited unless it "materially and substantially interfere[s] with the requirements of appropriate discipline in the operation of the school."

The *Tinker* case is a definite affirmation of students' or children's

First Amendment rights. Also, upholding the right of the students to express their views by wearing armbands in school, the court said that such a form of expression "is exactly the type of symbolic act that is within the free speech clause of the First Amendment." *Tinker* thus makes it clear that symbolic forms of speech will continue to be protected by the court as long as the symbolic conduct does not interfere with legitimate and substantial state interests. *Tinker* has been tested several times in recent years and it is now fairly evident that in order to curb students' First Amendment rights, disruption must have occurred. If disruption has *not* occurred, the courts have generally — but not always — found in favor of students' rights.

INTELLECTUAL FREEDOM AND
LIBRARY BILL OF RIGHTS

How, then, do these newly acknowledged rights of children fit into the concept of intellectual freedom? To answer that question, one must first define "intellectual freedom." In its broadest sense, it means that any person may believe what he wants to on any subject and may express his beliefs orally or graphically, publicly or privately, as *he* deems appropriate. The ability to express opinions, however, through whatever mode of communication suits you, does not mean much if there is no one to hear what you say, to read what you write, or to view what you produce through other methods. The definition of intellectual freedom, therefore, has a second integral part — total and complete freedom of access to all information and ideas regardless of the media of communication. This, in turn, gives a man something to think about, to consider, and to weigh prior to coming to his own opinions and decisions. Then he, too, is free to express his beliefs. The definition is circular, and the circle breaks if either the ability to produce or access to the production is stifled.

It is in relation to access that librarians perform their unique role on behalf of intellectual freedom. Through libraries, librarians have assumed a responsibility to provide materials presenting all points of view on all questions and issues of our times and, in addition, to make these ideas and opinions available to all patrons who need or want them, regardless of age, race, religion, national origins or social or political views.

These words are taken from the *Library Bill of Rights*, the profession's interpretation of the First Amendment to the U.S. Constitution and its embodiment of the "intellectual freedom" concept. Articles II and V of the *Library Bill of Rights* specifically state:

II. Libraries should provide books and other materials presenting all points of view concerning the problems and issues of our times; no library material should be proscribed or removed from libraries because of partisan or doctrinal disapproval.

V. The rights of an individual to the use of a library should not be denied or abridged because of his age, race, religion, national origins or social or political views.

The word "age" was not always included in the *Library Bill of Rights,* but was added to the document on June 27, 1967, about one-and-a-half years before the *Tinker* case. The addition resulted from a Preconference, sponsored jointly by the ALA Intellectual Freedom Committee and the ALA Young Adult Services Division, entitled "Intellectual Freedom and the Teenager." The pertinent recommendation of the Preconference read: ". . . (3) that *free access* to *all* books in a library collection be granted to *young* people." (Emphasis added.)

This revision of the *Library Bill of Rights* caused a few stirrings in 1967, but there was certainly no loud outcry, either pro or con. There was, however, some concern as to what exactly this addition to the *Library Bill of Rights* meant.

In mid-1968, ALA's stand was verbalized. Its position in regard to "protecting children" from materials that some individuals or groups may deem questionable is that *it is the parents' — and only the parents' — right and responsibility to guide his child — and only his child — in appropriate reading materials.* Once and for all, the general pervading concept of *in loco parentis* was cast aside, and responsibility placed solely and squarely on a parent for his child. This does *not* mean, however, that librarians are no longer to serve as librarians — to help individuals, regardless of age, to verbalize their needs or wants and to help them find appropriate fulfillment. It does mean that librarians should not tell patrons what they *ought* to want, the "ought" being based on some preconceived notions of age, or hair style, or height, or other equally unreasonable factors. It is a strong stand, but with two precedent-setting decisions by the U.S. Supreme Court, librarians cannot act *in loco parentis.*

During the last several hundred years of Western civilization, adults have made determinations as to what children may or may not read, listen to, and view. This is changing, and the change will continue. The U.S. Supreme Court has laid to rest the concept of *in loco parentis* as it relates to the mind. The Constitution and Bill of Rights apply to all citizens regardless of age. The conflict will continue only as long as adults force it to.

A noted children's book editor
justifies "books for the time" and
looks to the not-too-distant future.

Is
Tomorrow
a Four-Letter
Word?

JEAN KARL
Vice-President and
Editor of Children's Books
Atheneum Publishers

Billy and Bobbin and big bouncing Ben
Could eat more meat
than four-score men;
Bill ate a cow, Bob ate a calf,
Bill ate a church, Bob ate the steeple.
Ben ate the priest and all the people.

This rather hearty bit of verse, accompanied by a suitable three-color picture showing Bill holding the church and eating it. Bob's hands holding the steeple, and Ben's hands gathering up the people, comes not from the distant past, when we might expect more earthy rhyme, nor from our much talked of modern approach to realism, but from a book published in 1929, designed as a text-book to teach the ABCs. *Jingling ABC's* also has charming verses on trains, geese, umbrellas, seaside bathing, and, in general, rather gentle pastimes. Yet there are Bill and Bobbin and Ben. We are not the only ones to have dealt in horror in one way or another. Yet sometimes there are those who think that "realism" and other "horrors" have been invented only in the last five years.

REALITY IN BOOKS OF THE PAST

Those who wrote children's books in the past were fully aware of the realities of life, perhaps more so than the author of *Jingling ABC's*. In a book of short rather preachy stories published in 1826, a young boy whose father is interested in chemistry hears a discussion on the make-up of gunpowder. Soon the boy is busy making gunpowder, only, eventually to create an explosion and nearly kill himself. Remember *The Poor Little Rich Girl?* Her story might not have been typical. But for some, the realities of life at Miss Minchin's establishment once one had fallen from grace may not have been far from the truth in the lives of a number of children. In *David Copperfield*, long read by children and young adults, Dickens recounts some of the horrors of his own childhood. E. Nesbitt's *Railway Children* have a father who is sent to jail — an innocent victim — but nevertheless in jail. Coming down to the present, such books as *Linnet on the Threshold* drew a realistic picture of depression life for children of the 1930s. Linnet's father and mother separate for a while in the course of the book. Linnet has to leave school to get a job, working for $8 a week. Though the ending is happy enough, the tale is true to many lives. The Moffets are not rich and neither is the heroine of *The Hundred Dresses*.

Though these books may seem commonplace, accepted in our time, or passé because their time is past, they did hold up to the eyes of their readers in the day they were written, the more unpleasant things, as well as some of the good things of life at that time. They may not have quite the bite of our books today, but if that is true, it is true because the thinking of people was different then, too. Authors live and write in a specific time, and their books contain, in essence if not in fact, the spirit of their times. The means by which books accomplish this differ. Historical fiction will not reflect the present in the same way science fiction does and neither of these will speak in the same way as realistic fiction. To say this may seem to repeat the obvious. Most people recognize this when they look to the past. But too many forget it when they look to our own time. Or else they wear rose-colored glasses when they look out at the world around them. They refuse to admit that what they see is what is really there. But children who have not lived in any other time see it quite clearly.

REALITIES OF TODAY'S WORLD

Our world is not a pretty one. Take a look at your local daily newspaper. In one day in a Knoxville, Tennessee, paper a few years ago the following headlines appeared: Depot in Flames After Raid Near Haiphong; Three British Soldiers Slain in Erin Riots; Four Tots Die In Fire; Our Time Running Out on Nuclear Clock. In the same issue of the paper, Steve Canyon (in the comic strip) gets a letter from his first wife. He and his current wife are talking. "Steve," she says, "this was a break. When we return to the suite — where the microphone can hear — I'll make a big row because you still hear from your first wife. Then I will throw you out — so I may get on with my spy job!" By coincidence, probably, Ann Landers writes to a man who asks what he should do when his wife beats him up. Should he fight back? "No," says Miss Landers, "just leave." Finally a column talks about the night club act of a man named Alice Cooper and his troupe. They chop up baby dolls, stage a mock hanging of Alice, work hard to get their audience stirred up, and are consistently drunk when they go on stage. This is one paper for one day and is only a part of what was there. Furthermore, it is not one of the nation's large city newspapers.

At about the time those articles were appearing in the one issue of the Knoxville newspaper, the magazine section of *The New York Times* carried an essay called, *An Eighteen Year Old Looks Back on Life*. An eighteen-year-old girl, obviously very bright, a freshman at Yale, one of the first women admitted, discussed TV (I watch in earnest. How could I do anything else? Five thousand hours of my life have gone into this box). She was not bothered by repetition or dull, banal programs. "Boring repetition is itself a rhythm." In fact she confesses the world is so full of absurdities, of nonsequiturs, that it is impossible to take anything too seriously. The things that seemed to have made the most impression on her were the realization of the power of the atom bomb and pictures of unborn fetuses in a *Life* magazine. The church she turned to in eighth grade soon disappointed her. She did not smoke pot or take drugs, but had come to understand peer group pressure in another area — "the embarrassment of virginity." Her dreams of the future? "As some people prepare for their old age, so I prepare for my 20s. A little home, a comfortable chair, peace and quiet — retirement sounds tempting."

This young woman may be retiring before she's begun to live, but one who in her childhood coped with death and the atom bomb, unborn fetuses, the boredom of repetition, the pressure of sex, and the problem of eluding drugs, and who has searched and found no meaningful pattern in life, is not about to be wooed into life by *Elsie Dinsmore.* She did not read much, she confessed. There was little encouragement to do so. True, books may not have made her twenties more attractive to her. They may not have penetrated the gray sameness of her days. But there again, the right book might have.

"BOOKS FOR THE TIME"

A book like *Henry 3* perhaps. That girl would have understood Henry's preoccupation with keeping his intelligence a secret in order to stay one of the crowd. And she might possibly have been moved enough by Henry's unique problems to understand his breaking out of the crowd when life demanded it; she might then have come to share his concern with peace, with the meaning of life, and with human values. Precisely because it is a shocking book in places for some, but a book with enough reality to speak to the repetitious horrors of reality children find every day in their newspapers, on TV, and in school, it might have given life a more coherent pattern for her.

Or take *A Nice Fire and Some Moonpennies*, a not very gentle spoof of drugs, sex, and the whole "with it" culture. Decidedly shocking. Also terribly funny. And real enough to meet Steve Canyon, Ann Landers, and the daily headlines head on.

For children who can pick up a magazine and see photographs of fetuses, why should *In the Night Kitchen* be a shock? Nudity is a commonplace these days. Children cannot escape it. So why not encounter it in a true art form meant for the child. In a creative book where the nudity is a part of the whole, but only a part, where it is natural and seems right, not forced and vulgar like the centerfold in daddy's and mommie's magazines. Maybe a casual approach to sex and nudity occasionally in a children's book under the right conditions can some day make that centerfold less necessary.

And why not see life on the other side of the culture wall realistically, too. That suburban eighteen-year-old might have learned to resist the absurdities in life more if she had read *The Planet of Junior Brown* or *His Own Where*. Though such books may seem controversial to adults, they may be the essence of what life is like to the child or young person; they may be real enough to matter.

For any child of today whose daily existence is a ceaseless round of not necessarily stimulating activities and who is continually bombarded with too-distant-to-matter news and rock and roll lyrics and TV comedies and tragedies, all of which may tend to blend horror into a routine pattern, a book that carries a powerful, close-up, emotion-filled look at some aspect of life may be a jolt, a needed jolt. We need to be aware of life to live life. And not until we have really felt it touch us can we respond. Today's children and young people, as has always been true, will respond best to the thing they must admit is true and that touches them. If even part is false or remote, the whole can be cast aside. And a chance at true awareness is lost.

And that is the heart of the matter. A book done for our own time, especially for the children of our time, cannot speak to them, cannot get past the continual barrage of TV, newspapers, and rock and roll radio (have you ever really listened to the words of some of these songs?) without being honest, even if some people would prefer not to see it that way. And the impact that books that try to present life honestly will have on the young will not be the same as the impact they will have on an older generation, who are looking at events from a different past.

CHANGING MORES

Recently there have been protests about some of the words that have begun to appear in books for children and young adults. The words shock adults who see them. But for the most part they do not shock children and young adults. The free conversations of children in all parts of the country are filled with these words. And for them they have little meaning. Words, combinations of letters, have no inborn meanings. Connotations and denotations come from those who use them. Words we now would hesitate to say were once a part of common speech. And words we now say quite casually may one day be frowned upon. It is possible to say "Oh morning glory" or even "Oh coleslaw" with enough vehemence to make them sound truly hateful. At the same time it is possible for words that sounded ill on the ears of one generation to become gentle on the ears of the next.

And just as language changes, so lifestyles change. George Washington and Andrew Jackson had long hair. Ulysses S. Grant and Abraham Lincoln had beards. Teddy Roosevelt had a mustache. Franklin D. Roosevelt, Herbert Hoover, Dwight D. Eisenhower, and John F. Kennedy had short hair and no facial growth. Regardless of political affiliations, no one has ever judged the competence of these men in office by the amount of hair they allowed to grow on their heads. This is, of course, only a symbol for a larger truth. Dress is a symbol. Language is a symbol. And in many cases even the use or rejection of tradition is a symbol. The outside changes and the inside attitudes also change from generation to generation. What is accepted at one time is not in another. For centuries women wore their hair long. In the 1920s they cut their hair. Today young girls have long hair. Sexual mores change from culture to culture and generation to generation. Attitudes toward war, peace, and violence change and are still changing. The crowding of our world, the ecological problems that confront us, the greater awareness we have of other people and places, all make attitudes different. And the young are the focus of the change. They must change the most, for the world will alter more rapidly for them than for people of an older generation. Furthermore, today's young will soon seem old themselves, as their young cry out for still newer ideas. And to some extent the human species, like other species, will adapt or die.

This being the case it is a far greater crime to try to inflict the superficial mores of a generation past on a new generation than it is to break old shibboleths and let old taboos be laid to rest. Never fear, new ones will grow up. The young, once they begin seeking their own way, crowd together in fear of open spaces. They leave their parents, but cling to each other for support and create their own boundaries, different, yet sometimes even more restricting than the boundaries they have left.

To seem honest to them, books must fall inside these boundaries, not the boundaries created by others. Then how can we do our duty and pass on the weight of civilization to them? By digging deeper, by placing within the boundaries of their external super-ficial surface culture, the deep truths of life and of man's relation-ships to other men and to his universe. Though the surfaces change, the deeper truths do not change. This is why we can read books from other generations and enjoy them, recognizing both the surface differences and deep unchanging truths. We can do this, and young people and children can do this, when the boundaries of our time are clearly marked. But they will not accept the past when someone tries to palm it off on them as today.

It may be necessary sometimes to get ahead of today, to rush toward tomorrow if we are to make today's books not only real but useful. So the writers, editors, and buyers of books for the young need to keep alert, to sense what tomorrow's problems may be. Today we have sex, drugs, poverty, war, and intercultural con-flicts to contend with. And books do contend with them. Tomorrow we may see starvation, interplanetary exchanges in one form or another, subtle forms of mind control that must be exposed to avoid 1984, and goodness knows what more. The children who as adults will cope best with any problems are those who have an-ticipated in advance their own response to problem situations and found a way to handle them. An article I once read said that the child who daydreams well and yet functions effectively in social situations handles unexpected and new situations better than the child who does not daydream, because in the daydreams he has anticipated such events and dealt with them before. Reading can be like daydreaming, only perhaps more effective. The girl today who reads books about girls who become pregnant, girls who take drugs, girls who drop out of school, will live these situations in a way harmless to her, and yet because she has experienced them vicariously, she may be able to face the actual situations, or the forerunners of such situations, with greater poise and knowledge. It is better to read about the mistakes of a teenage bride, than to have to become such a bride just to see what it is like.

POSSIBLE BOOKS OF THE FUTURE

Not that books for children and young people should preach. Far from it. Rather they must offer valid information on all sides of an issue in nonfiction and valid experiences in fiction. Preaching is negative. Experience is positive and allows the individual to exercise his own intelligence. Decisions become his and hence are more likely to be firm and strong and made without destructive fears.

Books for the young are changing. For some adults they are changing too rapidly. For some not rapidly enough. If they are to survive, they must change in ways that make sense. They must change to meet the needs of the generation they are written for. And they may need to change in form as well as content. Microfilm and microfiche are in their infancy today. Someday a book may never be a book on paper at all. It may only come in film, as the need for space increases and available space grows smaller rather than larger. Small portable viewers may even make it possible to read these rolls and cards in all the familiar places, including in bed. Or microscopic books, perhaps two inches by three inches in size, easy to carry and store, will be read with special magnifying equipment, itself small and easy to carry. Paperbacks will certainly overtake hard bound books in popularity, as much for convenience as for cost. Who can anticipate all that may happen. No one. But all of us must be ready to accept change or see the book as a written record, a written story, die.

Content changes will reflect not only changing lifestyles and vocabularies, but changing ways of presenting material. In a freer world, for example, we might be able to allow a reader more freedom in determining the outcome of a book. It might be possible to write a book in which at a certain point a reader makes a choice between several alternative directions in the plot and as a result turns to one given page or another. Somewhat further on, the reader makes still another choice, and so on. In this way a reader can make a new book every time he reads it, by changing his choices. He can try out different patterns of action and different consequences. Or books could be, as one adult book I saw was, completely shuffleable. Each page contained a complete incident and was loose. The reader could put the pages in any order he chose, trying out different patterns to see what struck him as being most appropriate and real. A book could be written with no real end, letting the reader end it, or perhaps circling back to the beginning. Books on tape could be a few seconds of moving pictures, perhaps to establish the look of a locale. Music might somehow be built into a book. If these ideas seem extreme, they are. Yet we must expect change in this or some other direction. We cannot be content. To be content is to move back, because the world is moving on.

Is tomorrow a four-letter word? Yes, it may very well be. It may at least bring forth four-letter words from normally staid individuals who are too set in their ways to accept the quickened flow of culture and technology. Those who accept change or at least realize it is here to stay will not be thrown, however. Instead, they will fight to be a part of the action.

All of which does not mean that the future is necessarily going to be less moral, less concerned, less well structured, or even less comfortable than the past. To some people all change is, by its very nature, evil. But change in children's books, as anywhere, brings both good and evil. There will be new things that will be better than anything we have ever had before, perhaps, although sex and drugs and "bad words" and a lot of other things some people feel are "bad" will continue to crop up. The way ideas are treated will not always be even the same as now. As the cultural attitudes in our society change, books will change. Watch the newspapers and you will be able to match the current of the times with the current in books. And when others protest, suggest that they too watch the newspapers and the television and think twice about what they are saying.

Surface differences then, must and will happen, but beneath these we, all of us, can work to see that the books we give to children reflect truths, both current truths and those truths we feel have always been: respect for life and for all who share the earth with us; beauty, not sentimental beauty, but the beauty that finds its way into every worthy corner of the universe. We must not let honor die, nor human dignity, nor a sense of individual and collective worth. No matter what the surface, we must hope that every book will be alive in itself and will let some of the deeper values of living live in it. If these are lost to our civilization, then our hope for the future is indeed dim.

Adults write children's books, they edit them, and they buy them. But in the end children are free to accept or reject what they are given. How well we gear what we do to their particular surface world view, how much we respect them, and how much we give them to grow on — without preaching — may well determine the future of books and maybe the future of some other things we value as well.

A review of significant court decisions affecting students' free speech rights.

Freedom of Speech for Public School Students

PETER E. KANE
Professor of Speech
New York State University
College at Brockport

A discussion of freedom of speech for public school students begins most properly with a consideration of the extent and nature of the problem at hand. The only common and compulsory experience shared by the majority of Americans is public primary and secondary education. The Census Bureau estimates that school enrollment through grade 12 in 1970 was 51,476,000 pupils, and most pupils attend school half a day for the better part of 12 years.

All schools require a degree of regimentation and place some limits on freedom of activity. Even the most unstructured school begins and ends at specified times of the day, takes attendance, and deals with a given core of subject matter and skills. However, a student's constitutional rights are not suspended when he walks through the schoolhouse door. A student in school retains his rights, privileges, and responsibilities as a citizen of the United States even though those in authority in the schools, too often, try to deny those rights.

A recent explicit recognition that all children and, therefore, school children have constitutional rights is found in the case of *Re Gault*.[1] While the issue in this case was procedural rights, Justice Fortas in the majority opinion broadly stated, "Neither the Fourteenth Amendment nor the Bill of Rights is for adults alone." It is not unreasonable to conclude that this statement would cover attempts to deny school children their First Amendment rights. It is the purpose of this study first to review those free speech rights which have been clearly established and then to explore some of the areas in which the law is less clear.

ESTABLISHED FREE SPEECH RIGHTS

Flag Saluting. The first area in which students' free speech rights are clearly established is that of flag salutes. In 1940 and again in 1943 the Supreme Court dealt with cases arising from the expulsion of Seventh Day Adventists who refused to salute the flag. In 1940 the court affirmed the expulsion (*Minersville School District v. Gobitis*),[2] but after three years' consideration of Justice Stone's compelling dissent in that case, the court changed its mind. The decision written by Justice Jackson in *West Virginia Board of Education v. Barnette* is unequivocal.[3] "To sustain the compulsory flag salute we are required to say that a Bill of Rights which guards the individual's right to speak his own mind, left it open to public authorities to compel him to utter what is not in his mind." To this point was added a specific observation about the proper powers of public schools.

> The Fourteenth Amendment, as now applied to the States, protects the citizen against the State itself and all its creatures — Boards of Education not excepted. These have, of course, important, delicate, and highly discretionary functions, but none that

[1] 385 U.S. 1 (1967).
[2] 310 U.S. 586 (1940).
[3] 319 U.S. 624 (1943).

they may not perform within the limits of the Bill of Rights. That they are educating the young for citizenship is reason for scrupulous protection of Constitutional freedoms of the individual, if we are not to strangle the free mind at its source and teach youth to discount important principles of our government as mere platitudes.

Although this decision is twenty-seven years old, difficulties continue to arise regarding acceptable forms of non-participation in flag salutes and other patriotic exercises. In the case of *Sheldon v. Fannin* it was ruled in Federal District Court for Arizona that a student could not be excluded from school for refusing to stand during the singing of the National Anthem.[4] Non-participating students are asked to leave the room during the flag salute. However, being sent to stand in the hall can be viewed as a punishment. They are asked to stand although this action can be viewed as coerced partial participation in the ceremony. In 1969, both these points were affirmed in a pair of cases in Federal Court for the Eastern District of New York, and a ruling was issued which permitted students to remain seated at their desks during the flag salute.[5] The court added that based on the Tinker decision discussed below, to remain seated was a legitimate form of protest which could be suppressed only if the school could prove that it was subjected to substantial disruption as a result. On the basis of this limited case law, it appears that students may claim the right to remain seated in the classroom during patriotic exercises.

Wearing Symbols. The most recent court decisions affirming students' freedom of speech is that of *Tinker v. Des Moines Independent School District*.[6] The issue in this case was narrowly stated by Justice Black in his dissent:

Whether the First and Fourteenth Amendments permit officials of state-supported public schools to prohibit students from wearing symbols of political views within the school premises where the symbols are not disruptive of school discipline or decorum.

Seven of nine justices answered no. The facts of the case con-

---

[4]221 F. Supp. 766 (1963).
[5]*Frain v. Baron* (69-C-1250) and *Miller v. Schuker* (69-C-1347).
[6]395 U.S. 503 (1969).

cerned children who were suspended from school for wearing black armbands to protest the Vietnam war after the school district passed a regulation to prohibit such action. Through specific statements and reference to the case of *Burnside v. Byars*[7] the majority opinion written by Justice Fortas made it explicitly clear that buttons, armbands, and all similar political paraphernalia are recognized forms of speech entitled to First Amendment protection.

The key point in the Tinker decision, a point with broad implications, was that activity covered by the First Amendment must be substantially disruptive before it can be suppressed. The burden of proof that actions are disruptive rests with school officials, and mere fear of potential disruption is not sufficient.

> But, in our system, undifferentiated fear or apprehension of disturbance is not enough to overcome the right to freedom of expression. Any departure from absolute regimentation may cause trouble. Any variation from the majority's opinion may inspire fear. . . .
>
> In order for the state in the person of school officials to justify prohibition of a particular expression of opinion, it must be able to show that its action was caused by something more than a mere desire to avoid the discomfort and unpleasantness that always accompany an unpopular viewpoint.

The court's position on discipline and disruption is further clarified by Justice Black's dissent which was not supported by any other member of the court. Black's rejected argument was that school discipline is disrupted any time a student fails to obey a rule and that any action which distracts students' attention in any manner from their lessons is, in fact, disruptive.

In summary, the Supreme Court decision in the Tinker case did three things. First, it reaffirmed the constitutional right of public school students. In the words of Justice Fortas:

> First Amendment rights, applied in light of the special characteristics of the school environment, are available to teachers and students. It can hardly be argued that either students or teachers shed their constitutional rights to freedom of speech or expression

---

[7]367 F. 2d 744 (1966).

at the schoolhouse gate. This has been the unmistakable holding of this court for almost fifty years.

Second, the court reaffirmed the concept that there is symbolic and non-verbal behavior "closely akin to 'pure speech' which, we have repeatedly held, is entitled to comprehensive protection under the First Amendment." Third, the court clearly ruled that constitutionally protected behavior may be regulated only when the schools can demonstrate that the regulated behavior is, in fact, disruptive.

Hair Styles. The final area of clearly established First Amendment rights, surprisingly deals with hair style. For a variety of reasons, some of which probably have profound psychological origins, the great hair problem has received far more attention in recent years than it deserves. The course of recent legal history of the hair problem reflects the evolution in court thinking regarding the rights of juveniles.

Six years ago in the case of *Leonard v. the School Committee of Attleboro* the Supreme Court of Massachusetts upheld the disciplinary suspension of a long-haired student.[8] While the court recognized that hair styles may affect a student's private life, it ruled that the school had a right to regulate appearance which the school felt might be disruptive or distracting. The court felt that it was "reasonable" for the school to assume that "unusual" hair styles would be disruptive of school discipline and decorum. The question of whether the hair style was, in fact, disruptive was not considered.

The plaintiffs in hair cases brought in Federal courts have done somewhat better. However, as late as 1969 the results of a group of Federal District Court cases were mixed. In Boston, the court agreed that differences must be tolerated and ordered that a student's suspension be lifted and his record expunged.[9] In Indiana, the court ruled that while long hair is protected by the First Amendment, the hair in the specific case in question was in fact disruptive and, therefore, the proper subject of discipline.[10] In Chicago, the court ordered the admission of a student with shoulder length hair

[8]212 NE 2d 468 (1964).
[9]*Robert Richards, Jr., v. Roger Thurston*, 304 F. Supp. 499 (1969).
[10]*Crews vs. Cloncs*, N. 1p 69-C-405 (S.D. Ind., September 17, 1969).

and a mustache because the court viewed these styles as matters of personal freedom.[11] In Alabama, the court voided a school dress code because it "unreasonably" specified a single acceptable hair style.[12]

Apparently, the controlling decision in the area of long hair is that which has arisen from the case of Thomas Breen, a high school student in Williams Bay, Wisconsin. The Federal District Court ruled that Breen had been improperly suspended and observed, "It is time to broaden the constitutional community by including within its protection younger people whose claim to dignity matches that of their elders."[13] The school district with the support of the Wisconsin Superintendent of Public Instruction William C. Kahl appealed. In the case of *Breen v. Kahl* the Seventh Circuit Court of Appeals affirmed the District Court decision.[14] According to the opinion in that case,". . . the right to wear one's hair at any length or in any desired manner is an ingredient of personal freedom protected by the United States Constitution." The specific clause cited to establish this point was that of freedom of speech in the First Amendment. The court added:

> To uphold arbitrary school rules . . . for the sake of some nebulous concept of school discipline is contrary to the principle that we are a government of laws which are passed pursuant to the United States Constitution. . . .
>
> Although schools need to stand in place of a parent in regard to certain matters during the school hours, the power must be shared with parents, especially over intimately personal matters such as dress and grooming . . . [I]n the absence of any showing of disruption, the doctrine of "in loco parentis" has no applicability.

Wisconsin again appealed the negative decision, and on June 1, 1970 the Supreme Court issued an order letting the Circuit Court decision stand.[15]

In summary, students in the public schools apparently are as-

[11]*Miller vs. Gillis*, No. 60-C-1851 (N.D. Ill., September 25, 1969).
[12]*Griffin vs. Tatum*, 300 F. Supp. 1360 (1969).
[13]296 F. Supp. 702 (1968).
[14]419 F. 2d 1034 (1969).
[15]No. 1274, *Kahl v. Breen*.

sured the following rights under the freedom of speech clause of the First Amendment:

1. Students may not be required to participate in flag salute or other similar exercises.

2. Students may wear armbands, buttons, or other paraphernalia to express a point of view unless the school can demonstrate that such behavior is in fact disruptive.

3. Students may wear their hair as they see fit unless the school can demonstrate that such hair style, including beards, is in fact disruptive.

ASSUMED STUDENT RIGHTS

Beyond the rights supported by direct rulings, there are a number of First Amendment rights which can be reasonably assumed on the basis of court decisions in other areas. These rights include petitioning, leafletting, distribution of underground newspapers, freedom from censorship of regular school newspapers, freedom of dress, and a whole constellation of rights included under the heading of equal access to school services and facilities.

Distributing Published Materials. Circulating petitions, leafletting, and selling or distributing underground newspapers are clearly related activities. It is logical to assume that these activities are not subject to school control or discipline when performed outside of school. However, the only clear case in this area is a 1967 Federal District Court decision, *Hodes v. Neimowitz*, which lifted the suspension of a student who had distributed the *New York High School Free Press* across the street from his school.[16] Nevertheless, it is clear that schools do informally discipline students who support and/or disseminate unpopular ideas. This activity, viewed as evidence of "poor citizenship," is used to justify discretionary decisions such as denying membership in an honor society or exclusion from the school honor roll.

The right to petition, leaflet, or distribute newspapers within the school is less clear. Support for the assertion of such rights can

---

[16]Order entered without decision.

be found in a 1968 decision of the Second Circuit Court of Appeals in the case of *Wolin v. Port Authority*.[17] Robert Wolin brought suit when denied permission to distribute leaflets within the Port Authority Bus Terminal in Manhattan. Speaking for the unanimous court Judge Irving Kaufman first noted that public places were subject to the constraints imposed by the Constitution and then said:

> We cannot accept the argument that the mere presence of a roof alters the character of the place, or makes the terminal an inappropriate place for expression. The privacy and solitude of residents may require that apartment house hallways be insulated from the excitement of volatile exhortations, or the quiet dignity of judicial administration may dictate that courthouse passages be kept free from demonstrations. But that is a result based on wisdom and experience because the abrasions caused by any protected speech would too greatly interfere with other interests—and not simply because there is a covering on the building.

The point here is that leafletting and related activities are permissible inside public buildings and, therefore, should be permitted within the school if they do not in fact disrupt classes or otherwise "greatly interfere with other interests." There is, of course, no question of the students' legal right to be in the school building.

The leafletting issue has, however, been clouded by the recent refusal of the Supreme Court to review the case of seven East Tennessee State University students disciplined for distributing a pamphlet critical of that school's administration.[18] A scathing dissent to that ruling filed by Justice Marshall joined by Justices Brennan and Douglas insisted that the behavior being punished is clearly protected by the First Amendment. Although this case deals with a State University, the implications for the public schools of this ruling should not be ignored.

As the East Tennessee State case illustrates, one reason that school administrators and governing boards object to the distribu-

---

[17]392 F. 2d 83 (1968).
[18]No. 1011, *Norton v. The Discipline Committee of East Tennessee State University* (June 22, 1970).

tion of pamphlets and underground newspapers, even outside of the school, is that they have no control over the content which, at times, can be most unfavorable. This fact raises the question of the amount of control school officials may properly exercise over the content of the regular school newspaper. A reasonable position would seem to be that whether it is viewed as a channel for communication or an educational experience, the basic responsibility for the content of a school newspaper should rest with those who have been selected to write and edit it.

Most student papers have a faculty advisor who can and should offer guidance. This advisor should not function as a censor who passes on the acceptability of copy for the paper. Such a procedure promotes neither good communication nor sound education.

The court decision in the case of *Zucker v. Panitz* addresses itself to the question of the role of the school newspaper.[19] The specific facts of the case concerned a student's ad expressing opposition to the war in Vietnam which was approved for publication by the student editorial board and then suppressed by the school principal. In his ruling in favor of the students Federal District Court Judge Charles Metzner stated:

> This lawsuit arises at a time when many in the educational community oppose the tactics of the young in securing a political voice. It would be both incongruous and dangerous for this court to hold that students who wish to express their views on matters intimately related to them, through traditionally accepted non-disruptive modes of communication, may be precluded from doing so by that same adult community. . . .
>
> . . . , it is clear that the newspaper is more than a mere activity time and place sheet. The factual core of defendants' argument fails with a perusal of the newspapers submitted to the court. They illustrate that the newspaper is being used as a communication media regarding controversial topics and that the teaching of journalism includes dissemination of such ideas. Such a school paper is truly an educational device.

A frequently advanced reason for school control of the content of student newspapers is that of legal liability. The school main-

---

[19]299 F. Supp. 102 (1969).

tains that it must exercise control to protect itself from legal action by those whom the unregulated students might libel. To this argument there are three responses. First, in light of the current state of the law concerning libel the danger is extremely remote. Second, material which is actually suppressed is almost always not libelous but rather the expression of unpopular opinions or criticism of school administrators or trustees. Third, legal liability rests with the newspaper's editorial staff unless the school assumes that liability by exercising content control. Clearly the educationally sound way to handle a possibly libelous statement should the problem ever arise is through advice and consultation rather than suppression. When the students understand the nature of the problem, appropriate modifications will undoubtedly be made. Should they not be made, the legal consequences are clearly the students' responsibility.

Dress Styles. Not just hair styles and the wearing of armbands but all personal attire can be viewed as an element of personal expression and thus subject to First Amendment guarantees. From the decisions in the Tinker and Breen cases, it can be logically argued that students in the public schools have the right to personal expression by dressing themselves as they wish. However, many school systems still have enforced dress codes.

One approach to the problem of student dress is suggested by the 1925 Supreme Court decision in *Pierce v. Society of Sisters*.[20] The case concerned the attempt by the State of Oregon to compel attendance in public rather than private schools. In ruling against Oregon the court observed:

> . . . rights guaranteed by the Constitution may not be abridged by legislation which has no reasonable relation to some purpose within the competency of the State. The fundamental theory of liberty upon which all governments in this Union repose excludes any general power of the State to standardize its children.

If dress is a protected right as court decisions seem to indicate, then the question becomes one of determining what regulations have a "reasonable relation" to some educational purpose. One

---

[20] 268 U.S. 510 (1925).

thoughtful answer to that question is found in a 1966 ruling by James E. Allen, Jr., then Commissioner of Education for the State of New York.[21] Commissioner Allen said that while schools may properly establish dress codes, "such rules must clearly relate to the educative process and must be necessary to the protection thereof." Specifically, valid rules "may prohibit the wearing of any kind of clothing which causes a disturbance in the classroom, endangers the student wearing the same, or other students, or is so distractive as to interfere with the learning and teaching process." This answer makes the key point, again, one of disruption with the burden of proof again placed on the regulating agency.

Equal Access and Opportunities. The final area of free speech rights to be considered here is that covered by the legal concept of equality before the law. Simply stated, the idea is that those rights or privileges which are granted to one person or group should be granted on the same basis to all others. This concept has implications in matters of educational materials, school communications, school clubs and activities, and guest speakers. In regard to educational materials, the idea can be clearly illustrated by considering magazine subscriptions for libraries. If the school subscribes to *National Review*, it should also subscribe to *Ramparts, Progressive*, or some other journal expressing similar opinions. The educational materials made available to students should be representative of the broad range of American thought and not limited by someone's test of orthodoxy.

All groups and individuals should have equal access under equal conditions to school communication media and other facilities. If space on a bulletin board is granted to one group, it should be granted to all others. If the public address system is used to announce the outside of school meeting of a Boy Scout troop, the Young Socialist Alliance should be granted the same privilege. If the stamp club is a recognized school club allowed to meet in a classroom and have a picture in the yearbook, the draft resisters should be permitted to become a recognized school club by the same process, allowed to meet in a classroom, and have a picture

---

[21]*Dalrymple v. Board of Education of the City of Saratoga Springs* (No. 7594).

in the yearbook. The discretionary power to approve of one group but not of another or to grant privileges to one group or person not granted to another, almost inevitably leads to the tests of orthodoxy which are inimical to freedom of thought and expression. The previously noted practices of informal discipline would seem to be a violation of law in precisely this area.

The last topic for consideration is that of guest speakers. The concept of equality means here that every student or student group should be able to extend invitations to speakers on the same basis as all others. If regular administrative requirements, whatever they may be, are satisfied, a speaker should be allowed to speak. The absence of uniformity in requirements or discriminatory application of requirements would probably not be supported in the courts. If requests for speakers are routinely approved, the rejection of a request for a "controversial" speaker is unacceptable. If students have regularly had the right to select speakers for specific occasions, a veto may not properly be exercised when their choice happens to be "controversial." Just such a case was noted on the floor of the House of Representatives on June 18, 1970. Representative John Tunney of California called attention to the refusal of the Oceanside Long Island High School Board of Education to allow Representative Allard Lowenstein of New York to speak although he was the overwhelming choice of the Senior class as their commencement speaker. The board vetoed the students' choice because it considered Congressman Lowenstein to be a "controversial figure."[22]

In summary, although unequivocal court decisions have not been rendered, it is reasonable to assume that students in the public schools have the following free speech rights in addition to those clearly established rights enumerated in the previous section:

1. Students may not be punished for petitioning, leafletting, or distributing underground newspapers outside of school. These activities should be permitted inside the school as well if they are not demonstrably disruptive.

2. Control over the content of school newspapers can be safely vested in student editorial boards. It is both unnecessary and edu-

---

[22]U.S., *Congressional Record*, 91st Cong. 2d sess., H 5759.

cationally unsound to vest powers of review and censorship with the school authorities.

3. Students may dress as they see fit except in cases where the school can demonstrate that a particular dress is damaging, dangerous, or disruptive.

4. The educational materials made available to students by the schools should represent the breadth of American opinion and not some standard of orthodoxy.

5. All students and student groups should be treated alike in regard to the use of school facilities including the school's media of communication.

6. The procedures for extending invitations to guest speakers should be the same for all and applied in the same manner regardless of the specific speaker invited.

Any survey of the specific rights of freedom of speech of public school students must result in mixed feelings. On the one hand, we can all be proud of a system of government which has as high a trust in young people and as great a tolerance for diversity as has been suggested by this enumeration of rights. On the other hand, we all must clearly recognize the gulf which exists between our principles and our practices. It is no comfort that students must go to court to secure relief from the illegal oppression of school officials. Certainly the hypocrisy of teaching one thing in the civics class and doing the opposite outside of class is a major factor in the alienation of our young people and does "teach youth to discount important principles of our government as mere platitudes."

The first two sections of this article are by Thomas L. Tedford; the last two by Ruth McGaffey. They were all prepared for the Speech Communication Association as part of a continuing series to emphasize the importance of the free examination of ideas in a democratic society.

Freedom of Speech

THOMAS L. TEDFORD
Professor of Drama and Speech
University of North Carolina at Greensboro

RUTH McGAFFEY
Professor of Communications and
Chairman, Department of Communications
University of Wisconsin at Milwaukee

WHAT EVERY TEACHER SHOULD KNOW ABOUT THE SUPREME COURT OBSCENITY DECISIONS

The significant interpretations of the First Amendment by the United States Supreme Court have occurred during the twentieth century. In 1919, the Court enunciated the famous "clear-and-present danger" principle, and in numerous decisions between 1919 and 1957 developed a general doctrine of restricting freedom of speech only when the speech presented a *danger* to the community, the nation, or — in the case of defamation — to the good name of an individual.

In the 1957 "obscenity" decision of *Roth v. U.S.*, the Supreme Court departed abruptly from the "danger" restriction and allowed the censorship of sexual materials on the grounds of *worthlessness*, thus establishing a new category of prohibited speech. Roth, a seller of books, photographs, and magazines in the State of New York, was convicted of mailing "obscene" circulars and advertising. Justice Brennan, who wrote the majority opinion upholding the conviction of Roth, asserted that explicit sexual materials were not protected by the First Amendment if they *combined* the elements of prurience and worthlessness.

Every teacher should know that (1) the *Roth* case of 1957 was the Supreme Court's landmark case on the subject of "obscenity"; (2) that the Court did *not* hold that explicit sexual communications presented a danger to society; (3) rather, for the first time in American history, the Court attempted to formulate a doctrine of removing communications from Constitutional protection on the basis of the *worth* of that material.

Despite the unique grounds for censorship set forth in *Roth,* the Supreme Court did make an effort to insure the protection of ideas. Brennan stated that "all ideas having even the slightest redeeming social importance — unorthodox ideas, controversial ideas, even ideas hateful to the prevailing climate of opinion — have the full protection of the guaranties" of the First Amendment. Those who were dismayed by the censorship authorized by the "prurient-worthless" principle could appreciate the Court's strong commitment to the protection of ideas.

Decisions of Burger Court. From 1957 to 1973 the lower courts, both state and federal, attempted to apply the guidelines of *Roth.* The result was national confusion. The Supreme Court reviewed several decisions of the lower courts thus attempting to explain the meaning and proper application of its censorship standards. The confusion was compounded. Many prosecutors admitted that they did not know how to interpret Supreme Court opinions concerning "obscenity," and many judges in lower courts expressed uncertainty over the meaning of the guidelines.

In 1973 the Burger Court, led by the four appointees of President Nixon, announced in a five to four decision that the *Roth* test and subsequent "clarifications" were inoperable. Chief Justice

Burger spoke for the majority in five "obscenity" cases: *Miller v. California* (mailing unsolicited sexually explicit material), *Paris Adult Theatre I v. Slaton* (theatre showing sex films in which the sex acts were *simulated*), *U. S. v. Orito* (interstate transportation of sex films), *Kaplan v. California* (sale of unillustrated sex book in an adult bookstore), and *U. S. v. 12 200 Ft. Reels of Super 8mm Film* (attempt to bring sex films, slides and photographs from Mexico for private use of the defendant).[1] The Burger opinion so obviously undermines the First Amendment's protection of ideas and this nation's commitment to fair notice in matters of prosecution that those who are opposed to censorship can now debate the issues and persuade the public with preciseness concerning the principles at stake.

Burger asserts the following points in his opinion:
1. Only "serious" ideas are protected by the First Amendment.
2. Communications and art dealing with sex are guilty of "obscenity" until proven innocent.
3. No conclusive scientific proof exists to support the majority view on the censorship of "obscenity."

In the case of *Miller*, Burger removes the "utterly without redeeming social value" requirement which was an essential part of earlier decisions, and says that from now on communications and art which appeal to "prurient interest" or which are "patently offensive" may be censored if they lack serious literary, artistic, political, or scientific value. There is no mention of "educational" or "religious" value.

In the cases of *Paris Adult Theatre* and *Kaplan*, Burger asserts that no longer is expert testimony by the prosecution required to show that the material is "obscene"; rather, the material itself is adequate "proof" of obscenity." In short, sexual materials are now guilty until proved innocent!

Furthermore, Burger admits that the scientific evidence to support his views on censorship is inadequate in the Georgia case of *Paris Adult Theatre*. The Chief Justice states that "although there is no conclusive proof of a connection between antisocial be-

---

[1]*Law Week*, vol., 41, pp. 4923–66, 1973. Subsequent references from same source.

haviour and obscene material, the legislature of Georgia could quite reasonably determine that such a connection does or might exist." He argues that it is permissible to censor materials and to fine or imprison the distributors "on various unprovable assumptions. . . . Nothing in the Constitution prohibits a State from reaching . . . a conclusion and acting on it legislatively simply because there is no conclusive evidence or empirical data."

Burger makes two additional points in his opinion of 1973:
1. No longer will the question of "obscenity" be decided by national community standards; rather, the standards of the "forum community" are to apply. He neglects to define "forum community."
2. State laws must specifically define the sexual conduct which is to be classified "obscene."

Dissent to Burger Guidelines. Every teacher should grasp the significance of Justice Brennan's vigorous dissent to Burger's new censorship guidelines, for Brennan is the author of *Roth* and has been the voice of the Court in several pro-censorship decisions. When Brennan changes his mind and admits that *Roth* has failed, then there is cause for optimism by those who believe that the First Amendment protects the artist as well as journalists, preachers, and politicians. Brennan makes the following points:
1. The 1973 formula for censorship will fail, for it is too vague and it violates the fundamental principles of the First and Fourteenth Amendments.
2. The 1973 formula invites arbitrary and erratic enforcement of the law, places a "chilling effect" upon freedom of speech, and puts absurd stress upon the institutions of law enforcement and the courts.
3. The new formula allows the censorship of ideas which do have social value. "Before today," Brennan argues, "the protections of the First Amendment have never been thought limited to expressions of *serious* literary or political value."
4. The best solution is to allow each adult to act as his or her own censor, while providing protection for juveniles and unconsenting adults.

Burger does make one concession to intellectual freedom in his censorship opinion. He declares that the "states . . . may . . . drop all controls on commercialized obscenity, if that is what they prefer. . . ." Every teacher should know, therefore, that it is permissible for a state to have more "liberal" controls than those established by Burger. For instance, a state may allow consenting adults to purchase, read, or view what they wish, while providing protection for juveniles and unconsenting adults.

Points for Teachers. In brief, every teacher should know that the United States Supreme Court:

1. Has never held that "obscenity" presents a clear-and-present danger to society.

2. In its 1973 decisions made it easier to successfully prosecute the artist-communicator by asserting that only "serious" materials are protected by the Constitution, and that explicit sexual materials accused of being "obscene" are guilty until proven innocent.

3. Admits that no conclusive scientific proof exists to support censorship.

4. Says that it is legal for a state to have no censorship regulations, or no censorship for consenting adults; it is legal to provide procedural safeguards such as a mandatory adversary hearing followed by fair warning prior to any arrest; it is permissible to provide special protection to parents, teachers, librarians, and other such persons.

In addition, every teacher — and particularly teachers of literature, drama, art, and film — should note that the decision to censor the work of the artist-communicator was made by lawyer-judges, not by creative artists. Meanwhile, these same lawyer-judges have "declared unconstitutional" almost all restrictions upon their own speech and the speech of their professional colleagues in law and politics.

The censorship policies of the Burger Court demonstrate such artistic illiteracy and unsupported reasoning that they are certain to be amended or discarded in some future ruling. For the present there is hope that some state legislatures will be more considerate of the First Amendment than is the Burger Court. Until censorship is abolished in this country, the teacher who opposes censorship should fight back with information and persuasion, holding to the faith that soon the people of the United States will have the courage to set their artists free!

A DOZEN PAPERBACKS FOR TEACHER AND STUDENT

This brief bibliography, at once comprehensive and inexpensive, provides the teacher and the student with the key opinions, documents, and analyses of First Amendment issues in the United States — from censorship to sedition. When ordering be sure to specify the paperback edition, since some of the books are published in both hard and soft covers. A more complete bibliography can be secured from the Speech Communication Module, ERIC Clearinghouse on Reading and Communication Skills, Statler Hilton Hotel, New York City, 10001. Ask for *Freedom of Speech: A Selected Annotated Basic Bibliography*.

Bosmajian, Haig A., ed. *The Principles and Practice of Freedom of Speech*. Boston: Houghton Mifflin, 1971.
A valuable collection of basic documents concerning freedom of speech in the United States. Part I, "Antecedents and Determinants," includes Milton's *Areopagitica*, John Stuart Mill's *On the Liberty of Thought and Discussion*, and the Alien and Sedition Acts of 1778. Part II provides key selections from landmark court decisions. Part III presents seven contemporary essays on issues of freedom of speech, including key writings of Alexander Meiklejohn, Zechariah Chafee, and Herbert Marcuse. Senior high.

Chafee, Zechariah, Jr. *Free Speech in the United States*. New York: Atheneum, 1969.
Zechariah Chafee's First Amendment classic, originally published in 1941, is an interesting and scholarly study of free speech controversies in the United States from World War I until 1940. Chafee's interest is in the area of *political* speech,, including the prosecutions of World War I, sedition, and criminal syndicalism; only passing attention is given to other areas, such as defamation and "obscenity." This book is essential reading for students of free speech. Senior high.

Emerson, Thomas I. *The System of Freedom of Expression*. New York: Random House, 1971.
Thomas I. Emerson, Professor of Law at Yale, has written the most comprehensive subject-area analysis of contemporary First Amendment problems available in one volume. Although his purpose is to demonstrate how his expression-action theory of free speech can work in a variety of situations, he does review each type of First Amendment subject prior to the application of his theory. These reviews are com-

prehensive, clear, and carefully documented. Subject areas reviewed include external security, internal security, meetings and demonstrations, defamation, conspiracy, obscenity, privacy, the rights of government employees, academic freedom, and free speech in private "centers of power." Emerson also discusses the concept of the affirmative promotion of freedom of speech by the government. This book is a superior reference for all students of freedom of speech.

Gorden, William I. *Nine Men Plus: Supreme Court Opinions on Free Speech and Free Press.* Dubuque, Iowa: Wm. C. Brown, 1971. (An academic game simulation.)

William I. Gorden, a professor of speech communication at Kent State University, has a unique professional interest in academic games as an innovative way of teaching and learning. This volume is not so much a "book" in the traditional sense as an "academic game," which is intended to help the student enjoy learning a great deal about freedom of speech. The rules of the game include arguments and debates among the participants concerning how a case should be decided, voting on issues, and tabulating scores. Free speech topics about which the game is played include academic freedom, censorship, defamation, political dissent, privacy, and demonstrations. Teachers interested in academic games as a teaching method will find Gorden's publication worth examining. Senior high.

Haiman, Franklyn S. *The First Freedoms: Speech, Press, Assembly.* New York: The American Civil Liberties Union.

Haiman summarizes key principles of the First Amendment under the headings of The Public Forum, Schools and Colleges, State Security, and The Mass Media. The positions of the American Civil Liberties Union are included in the discussion. This inexpensive pamphlet is excellent for classroom use.

Haiman, Franklyn S. *Freedom of Speech: Issues and Cases.* New York: Random House, 1965.

Haiman has assembled summaries of the key First Amendment issues and cases of this century. He skillfully interweaves court decisions with selections from the writings of lawyers, philosophers, political scientists, artists, and clergymen to demonstrate conflicting views. Haiman classifies First Amendment issues and cases as follows: provocation to anger and the problem of preserving the peace; political heresy and the problem of national survival; and artistic expression and the problem of public morality. The court cases will need to be supplemented with a review of Supreme Court decisions since 1965. Senior high.

Levy, Leonard W., ed. *Freedom of the Press from Zenger to Jefferson.* Indianapolis: Bobbs-Merrill Company, 1966.
Leonard Levy's anthology includes numerous "classic" American statements on freedom of the press, beginning with Franklin's "An Apology for Printers" (1731) and ending with an 1823 document of Jefferson. The editor's lengthy introduction places the fifty-nine documents of this volume in historical perspective. The series is continued with Harold L. Nelson's *Freedom of the Press from Hamilton to the Warren Court.* Junior or senior high.

Meiklejohn, Alexander. *Political Freedom: The Constitutional Powers of the People.* New York: Oxford University Press, 1965. (Galaxy Book.)
Part One of this book contains the text of Meiklejohn's First Amendment study, *Free Speech and Its Relation to Self-Government*, originally published in 1948. The 1948 work includes the author's criticism of the clear-and-present danger test and his "private speech—public speech" proposal for judging First Amendment cases. Part Two presents a number of Meiklejohn's views on freedom of speech, including essays on academic freedom and on legislative investigations into the beliefs and associations of American citizens. No study of free speech is complete without attention to the views of Alexander Meiklejohn. Senior high.

Nelson, Harold L., ed. *Freedom of the Press from Hamilton to the Warren Court.* Indianapolis: Bobbs-Merrill Company, 1967.
Nelson's anthology of fifty-one documents, including essays and court opinions, is a companion volume to Levy's *Freedom of the Press from Zenger to Jefferson.* The editor's introduction places the documents in historical context, and is followed by a chronology of First Amendment developments from 1801 to 1964. The two-volume series is a valuable source for the student of free speech in American history. Junior or senior high.

O'Neil, Robert M. *Free Speech: Responsible Communication Under Law.* (2nd ed.) Indianapolis: Bobbs-Merrill Company, 1972.
Robert M. O'Neil, a professor of law, has written a concise analysis and explanation of the major subject areas related to free speech in the United States. His chapters include a discussion of the overall "concept" of free expression (including freedom of association, and privacy); limits on the right of free speech; the speaker's right to a forum; the regulation of time, place, and manner; legal protection of the speak-

er's work (copyright protection); and the speaker's legal liabilities (with an excellent summary of the law of defamation). The book is designed for the "layman," and is of special value to the teacher and student. Senior high.

The Report of the Commission on Obscenity and Pornography. Washington, D.C.: U.S. Government Printing Office, 1970. (Also available, with a special introduction by Clive Barnes, from Bantam Books.) In 1967 the Congress authorized a Presidential Commission to investigate the problems of "obscenity" and "pornography." This is the report of that Commission. Included in the recommendations of the majority are proposals to allow adults to make their own decision about explicit sexual materials, and to substitute sex education for censorship. The vehement dissent of the minority is also included in the *Report.* This volume should be required reading for any student of the censorship of sexual materials; it deserves a place in every secondary school library. Senior high.

The Supreme Court Obscenity Decisions. San Diego, California: Greenleaf Classics, 1973.
In June, 1973, the four Nixon appointees to the Supreme Court were joined by Justice White to deliver a majority opinion in favor of continued censorship of books, magazines, and films in the United States. This book reprints the complete texts of the five opinions, together with the dissents of Justices Brennan (who spoke for Stewart and Marshall) and Douglas. The "Miller" definition of "obscenity" is included, making this a valuable reference for English teachers. The introduction is by anti-censorship lawyer Stanley Fleishman. Also included are the briefs of the American Library Association and the Association of American Publishers urging a rehearing of the cases. Because the majority opinions here are currently "the law of the land," the contents merit study by teachers and students of all disciplines. Senior high.

FREEDOM OF SPEECH FOR THE IDEAS WE HATE

Perhaps every teacher of English is aware of the burning of copies of *Slaughterhouse Five* and *Deliverance* in Drake, North Dakota, and the disorder in West Virginia caused by textbook choice. The Wisconsin Education Association is concerned about incidents of censorship in Wisconsin schools, and I am sure that teachers all over the country share their concern. There is one type of censorship, however, which usually does not arouse the same depth or breadth of reaction: that is, the censorship of ideas that most of us, even confirmed civil libertarians, consider to be "bad" ideas. Such ideas have been censored regularly.

Last year, for example, the Harvard Law School Forum cancelled a speech by Professor William Schockley. Professor Schockley had become well known for his thesis that blacks are intellectually inferior to whites, and the officers of the Harvard Forum were afraid that black protestors would cause trouble. In Milwaukee, a municipal judge forbade the American Nazi Party to distribute hate literature within the vicinity of any public school. In Boston, a federal judge banned racial slurs on school property and ordered city officials to enforce stern measures against demonstrations near schools or school bus routes. In New Haven, Connecticut, the Southern New England Telephone Company cut off service to the National Socialist People's Party.

Two years ago, citing what he termed a "clear and present danger" to Atlanta, Mayor Sam Massell appealed to local news media to reject the political advertising of a candidate for the U.S. Senate who was an avowed white supremacist. Protests against the person were also lodged by the Anti-Defamation League, the NAACP and the Atlanta Community Relations Commission. The candidate, J. B. Stoner, said on his campaign broadcasts that "The main reason why niggers want integration is because the niggers want our white women. I am for law and order with the knowledge that you can't have law and order and niggers too. Vote White."[2] However, the Federal Communication Commission ruled that Mr. Stoner might continue his broadcasts. The FCC said, "If there is to be free speech, it must be free for speech that we abhor and hate as well as for speech that we find tolerable or congenial.[3] I agree with that statement and that shall be the thesis of this essay.

Support for Repression of "Bad" Ideas. To those familiar with the wording of the First Amendment, freedom of speech for the ideas we hate may not seem like a particularly controversial point

---

[2]*Milwaukee Journal*, August 8, 1972.
[3]Ibid.

of view. However, it is not necessarily the majority view in this country. As I have indicated elsewhere,

> Substantial groups of American citizens consider that there are some ideas too dangerous or too repulsive to be allowed expression. This was substantiated by the results of the year-long survey of about 90,000 persons made by the Education Commission of the States, a non-profit organization set up in 1964 with funds from the Carnegie Corporation. In a random sampling the subjects were asked if they would permit Americans to hear these statements on radio and television: "Russia is better than the United States," "Some races of people are better than others," "It is not necessary to believe in God." Sixty-eight percent of those aged 25 to 35 said they would refuse to permit the broadcast. So would 94 percent of boys and girls 13 years old and 78 percent of the 17 year olds.[4]

There appears to have been some improvement in that situation. The *Newsletter on Intellectual Freedom* reports some encouraging news.[5] It notes that in 1970, 57 percent of the persons polled by the Harris poll agreed that officials should be given the authority to censor films, television, radio, and theater for unpatriotic or revolutionary content; 52 percent agreed that newspapers that preach revolution should be banned from circulation; and 34 percent agreed that no one should be allowed to possess pornographic materials. In 1973, however, only 43 percent agreed that officials should be given the authority to censor; 40 percent agreed that newspapers which preach revolution should be banned; and 27 percent agreed that no one should be allowed to possess pornographic materials. However, while Americans may be slightly less inclined to censor repulsive ideas than they were a few years ago, there are still substantial numbers of citizens who find some viewpoints so repulsive and obnoxious that they want to suppress them entirely.

These would-be censors say that some ideas are worthless, that some content and language offends the sensibilities, that some ideas

---

[4]McGaffey, Ruth M. "A Critical Look at the Marketplace of Ideas," *Speech Teacher*, March 1972, p. 117.
[5]*Newsletter on Intellectual Freedom*, March, 1974, p. 47.

might cause violent reactions from opponents, and that other ideas may cause violent actions by supporters. These arguments may be substantially true. The question, however, is whether *any* or *all* of them justify the conclusion that "ideas we hate" should be repressed. I do not think they do.

All of these arguments are based on the idea that there is a hierarchy of content value, and the content at the "top" should be constitutionally protected while that at the "bottom" need not be. This theory has appeared many times in several forms. Some kinds of speech, such as obscenity, "fighting words," and libel, have usually been thought to have little value and thus have not been granted constitutional protection. The Supreme Court has consistently refused to grant protection to "commercial" speech. Philosopher Alexander Meiklejohn argued for years that while there should be no restriction on speech that is relevant to self-government, there could be restrictions on other speech. Others have thought that even within the category of "political speech" some topics are more important than others. During the 1940s, peaceful labor picketing was granted some constitutional protection largely because the topic was considered so important. The Court said:

> Freedom of discussion . . . must embrace all issues about which information is needed or appropriate to enable the members of society to cope with the exigencies of their period. . . . Free discussion concerning the conditions in industry and the causes of labor disputes appears to us indispensable to the effective and intelligent use of the processes of popular government to shape the destiny of modern industrial society.[6]

Why All Ideas Should Be Aired. It is hard to disagree with the idea that some speech is worth more than others. I would simply say, however, that that argument is irrelevant. There are at least two reasons why that is true.

First, the underlying purpose of the First Amendment is subverted if all ideas are not allowed expression. Oliver Wendell Holmes expressed the underlying philosophy of the marketplace of ideas in 1919 when he wrote,". . . when men have realized that

---

[6]*Thornhill v. Alabama*, 310 U.S. 88 (1940).

time has upset many fighting faiths, they may come to believe even more than they believe the very foundations of their own conduct that the ultimate good desired is better reached by free trade in ideas — that the best test of truth is the power of the thought to get itself accepted in the competition of the market."[7] Thus, if all ideas can not be expressed we are neither testing their worth in the marketplace nor considering all ideas in our search for truth and wisdom. It does not necessarily follow that the majority will hate only "bad" or "wrong" ideas. We take a risk in any suppression that something of value will be lost.

Secondly, if hateful ideas are to be repressed, someone must decide which ideas those are. Who should make the decision? Should it be the Attorney General, a Congressional committee, the Director of the FBI or CIA? The local vice squad or school board? By majority vote? Or perhaps the decision should be made by legislative bodies or the Supreme Court. We have tried all of those methods at one time or another, and the results have been sedition acts during world wars, the red scares of the 1920s and 1950s, and FBI and CIA counter-intelligence of the 1960s. To most people, the Supreme Court is the most suitable group to make such decisions. That body has tried to formulate tests to determine what speech should be protected and which can be repressed. For many years the most commonly used test was the "clear and present danger" doctrine. Then the court tried to use the "balancing test." That test tried to weigh the importance of the rights of the individual to speak against the possible harm to society that might occur from the speaking. The flaw in these as well as other tests, of course, is that the judgment is a subjective one. People disagree as to what constitutes a clear and present danger and people disagree in how they balance individual rights against societal interests. At one time the U.S. Supreme Court upheld the sentencing of several young Jews to twenty years in prison because they distributed a few Yiddish leaflets condemning the United States landing of troops in Russia following the Soviet Revolution. In times of war or threat of internal disorder, nothing becomes as important as suppressing ideas that frighten us.

---

[7]*Abrams v. United States*, 249 U.S. 47 (1919).

I think the writers of the First Amendment had a basic trust in the common judgment of the American people and a basic distrust in the judgment of any one person. Therefore, freedom of expression was put in a primary position in the Bill of Rights with the idea that a self-governing people must be able to discuss all ideas, regardless of how repulsive they might be. Anti-Jewish, anti-black or anti-Catholic statements may offend most decent Americans. Swastikas and SS uniforms as well as the white sheets of the KKK are not only offensive but frightening to the majority of our people. These ideas we hate must, however, be constitutionally protected if the marketplace of ideas is to survive for those ideas to survive for those ideas we love.

WHAT EVERY TEACHER SHOULD KNOW
ABOUT SYMBOLIC SPEECH

Everyone knows that "Congress shall make no law . . . abridging the freedom of speech." That's in the Constitution. But every teacher should know that the statement is not true. Congress has made many laws abridging freedom of speech: We have had laws prohibiting any speech that might cause disloyalty or insubordination; we have had laws forbidding advocacy of the overthrow of the government or saying anything which presents a "clear and present danger" of disorder. So "no law" does not mean no law. Does "speech" really mean speech? The United States courts have said "no." At least it does not include all speech. In one famous passage, the United States Supreme Court summed up its position:

> There are certain well-defined and narrowly limited classes of speech, the prevention and punishment of which have never been thought to raise any Constitutional problem. These include the lewd and obscene, the profane, the libelous, and the insulting or "fighting" words—those which by their very utterance inflict injury or tend to incite an immediate breach of the peace. It has been well observed that such utterances are no essential part of any exposition of ideas, and are of such slight social value as a step to truth that any benefit that may be derived from them is clearly outweighed by the social interest in order and morality.[8]

---

[8]*Chaplinsky v. New Hampshire*, 315 U.S. 568 (1942).

So speech does not mean all speech — but does it mean more than speech? Does it mean nonverbal expression as well? This is an issue that the courts have been wrestling with for forty years. Every teacher should know that speech *does* mean more than "pure speech." It includes some forms of what the courts have called "symbolic speech."

Cases Involving Nonverbal Expression. In 1931 the Supreme Court decided that the display of a red flag was a constitutionally protected expression.[9] In 1943 the Court ruled that the flag salute was a form of speech and that, furthermore, since the right to speak implied a right not to speak, the flag salute could not be required of public school students.[10] "Speech," thus, also means "*no* speech" or "silence." This right of silence was also made clearly applicable to public school teachers in 1972.[11]

In the 1930s the Court held that peaceful picketing was protected expression, and this protection was extended to demonstrations during the 1960s. Of these civil rights demonstrations Harry Kalven, Professor of Law at the University of Chicago, has written:

These are structured ceremonials of protest; they are not riots. The demonstrators were not, as the majority recited the record, trying to bring the government to a halt; rather they were expressing the concern of the young Negro about his situation. What was symbolized was a deep grievance, a break with society. . . . Whatever the power, the pressure, and anxiety generated by such large numbers, the demonstrations showed a tact, a grace, a patience, and a distinctive rhetoric of their own.[12]

The Court agreed that such peaceful demonstrations "reflect an exercise of these basic constitutional rights in their most pristine and classic form."[13] Subsequently, while some "time, place and manner" restrictions have been placed on parades and demonstrations, generally it has been agreed that such conduct is "speech" and warrants some protection.

Vietnam war protests followed the civil rights demonstrations.

[9]*Stromberg v. California*, 283 U.S. 359 (1931).
[10]*West Virginia State Board of Education v. Barnette*, 319 U.S. 624 (1943).
[11]*Russo v. Central School District*, 469 F. 2d. 623 (1972).
[12]Harry Kalven, "The Concept of the Public Forum: Cox v. Louisiana."
[13]*The Supreme Court Review* (1965), p. 7.

During these times the definition of speech for purposes of First Amendment protection was expanded in a manner directly applicable to high school students and teachers. In the landmark case of *Tinker v. Des Moines,* it was decided that the wearing of black armbands during school hours as a symbol of protest was protected expression.[14]

Mary Beth Tinker and several of her friends were suspended from school for wearing black armbands. Her parents applied to the United States District Court for an injunction to force the school to readmit the children. Neither the District Court nor the Circuit Court of Appeals was convinced by the Tinkers. However, the United States Supreme Court was convinced and reversed both lower courts. Justice Fortas wrote the opinion of the Court. He noted that the wearing of an armband was the type of symbolic act that is within the free speech clause of the First Amendment. He called it a "direct, primary First Amendment right akin to 'pure speech'."[15] He argued that students and teachers do not lose their rights when they enter a schoolhouse. Finally, he indicated that since there had been no resulting disturbance, this was not the kind of speech or action that "intrudes upon the work of the schools or the rights of other students."[16]

While Justice Fortas specifically stated that the ruling in this case did not involve dress code and hair regulations, it has been applied to them. There have been hundreds of cases challenging dress codes. Judges have not been able to decide whether this "lifestyle" issue really involves the right of expression at all. However, the majority of the decisions have used the *Tinker* rationale and have concluded that if there were no evidence of the particular dress or hair style causing disorder, the regulations were unjustified. In April 1974, however, a federal court upheld the right of a Chicago school board to terminate a teacher's employment because he wore a beard and sideburns.[17]

In the last 1960s two other forms of "symbolic speech" became widespread. One involved the desecration of the American

---

[14]*Edwards v. South Carolina,* 372 U.S. 229 (1963).
[15]*Tinker v. Des Moines School District,* 393 U.S. 503 (1969).
[16]393 U.S. 503, 504.
[17]393 U.S. 503, 505.

flag; the other concerned the destruction of draft cards. Both activities were expressly prohibited by state or federal law. While the courts were willing to admit that such actions were instances of symbolic expression, they hesitated to say that it was the kind of expression that should be constitutionally protected. In fact, while flag desecration was occurring in almost every section of the country, the Supreme Court avoided ruling on the issue. Not until 1974 when most of the activity had died down, did they declare a state flag misuse law unconstitutional. In this instance a young man placed an American flag upside down in the window of his apartment in Seattle, Washington. A peace symbol was attached to the flag. The man, Harold Spence, was convicted of violating the state law, but the U. S. Supreme Court reversed his conviction. The Court noted that Spence was obviously engaging in a form of communication, and that "the nature of the appellant's activity, combined with the factual context and environment in which it was undertaken, lead to the conclusion that he engaged in a form of protected expression."[18] Thus, in some circumstances, flag desecration may be protected speech. Nevertheless, if disorder is caused by such desecration or if the flag is a public one, the activity is probably still unprotected. The situation is different with regard to draft card burning. The courts had little difficulty in deciding that the interest of the federal government in the protection of the draft card was more important than the individual's right of expression. Draft card destruction, therefore, is not protected speech.

Pros and Cons of Protection of Symbolic Speech. Teachers should understand the arguments that are used to support the idea that nonverbal communication should receive the same protection as pure speech. Those who support this thesis argue that symbolic conduct may be the only method of communication which can provide an audience for those who can not afford access to the mass media. Burning a flag or conducting a demonstration will usually bring out the television cameras and news photographers. Furthermore, some say, because the Fathers of the Constitution did not know what kind of communication methods would be used in the 1970s, the First Amendment should protect the kind

---

[18]*Spence v. State of Washington*, 42 LW 5140 (June 25, 1974).

of communication that society actually uses. Finally, it is argued that symbolic speech is effective (not necessarily coercive), and that the Constitution is not intended to protect only innocuous expression.

Those opposed to such protection argue that since all action is expressive, it is impossible to decide which action should be protected. They also contend that symbolic speech tends to elicit an emotional response that is not conducive to the rational discussion that the First Amendment is intended to encourage. They also point out that some kinds of symbolic activity such as large demonstrations are inherently coercive, and that force should not be protected speech. These two sets of arguments have not been finally resolved.

Most acts of symbolic speech are acts of protest. When important issues divide the nation, those acts increase, and violent reactions to such acts also increase. When the nation calms down, protest calms down. This nation now appears to have entered a period of relative quiet; the number of symbolic speech cases reaching the courts has decreased. These courts, however, have not finished their task of defining speech. When the nation again becomes embroiled in conflicts about war, race or lifestyle, bizarre kinds of protest will probably increase. At that time the courts will once again be forced to face the issue and decide for teachers, students and all Americans just how much symbolic speech is protected by the First Amendment to the Constitution of the United States.

Attempts to censor literature, stemming from various motives, are a major threat to teachers of English. The Students' Right to Read *(NCTE, revised edition) is a helpful manual for teachers who must deal with such attempts. Professor Booth's discussion is a brilliant supplement to that publication.*

Censorship and the Values of Fiction

WAYNE C. BOOTH
Professor of English
University of Chicago

To the teacher, any attempt by outsiders to censor teaching materials is self-evidently wrong. To the censor, it is self-evident that a responsible society must supervise what is taught to its children. Little wonder, then, that attacks on "censorship," like defenses of "responsible supervision of materials," too often assume what they set out to prove: addressed to those who are already converted, they may be useful for enspiriting the troops, but far too often they do nothing to breach the enemy's line.

To convert any "enemy," we must show him not simply that respectability, or tradition, or the National Council of Teachers of English are against him but that he is wrong, wrong according to his own fundamental standards. To tell him that he is wrong according to *our* standards gets us nowhere, though it may be great fun; the problem is to find, somewhere among *his* standards, at least one that is violated by what he proposes to do.

In dealing with censors, as with other enemies, it may very well be that the enemy is in fact so far beyond reason that there is no possible point of contact. But if we assume, as I think we must, that at least some of the would-be censors are men of goodwill whose values, at certain points, coincide with ours, then we must work at the extremely difficult task of showing them that even according to their own values, the effort to censor is misguided.

The sources for such points of contact — and hence of real rather than merely self-comforting arguments — are many. Most censors want to preserve some form of society in which they can exercise their own freedom; we can argue, following Mill and many others, that the kind of society the censor *really* wants cannot be maintained if his kind of censorship prevails. Similarly, most censors respect and seek to further the "truth" as they see it, and some of them can be shaken by arguing, with Milton and others, that truth flourishes best when ideas can compete freely. Or again, many censors, irrational as they may seem to us, respect consistency and would like to think of themselves as reasonable; they can be shaken, sometimes, by showing the inevitable irrationalities and stupidities committed by any society that attempts to censor.

Every teacher in America today owes it to himself to have ready, either in his mind or in his files, a portfolio of these and other arguments against censorship, fleshed out, of course, with the details that alone can make them convincing. He can never know when the censors will move in his direction, nor can he know in advance which of his supply of arguments will be effective in a given crisis. But he can know that unless he has thought the issues through, he is likely, when the attack comes, to stand tongue-tied. Of course he may go under anyway, no matter how well-prepared his defense, if the censor will not listen to his reasons; one should have no illusions about the easy triumph of freedom or truth, in any market place, open or closed. But even if the censor wins, there should be some comfort in knowing that one has at least said what can be said for the free teacher, freely choosing his own materials.

SPECIFIC DEFENSES NECESSARY

Since many censorship drives begin with attacks on specific works, an important and often neglected section of one's "Freedom Portfolio" ought to deal with some such heading as "The Moral Quality of Individual Works." Though censorship cases are seldom fought without some appeal to general political and social arguments that apply to all cases, they would more often be won if, at the first threat of attack on any one work, the teacher had a battery of specific defenses ready for battle.

What is usually offered, in place of such specific arguments, is a standard collection of highly general claims, already known to the censor, about the moral value of literature. There is good reason why such claims do not convince. For one thing, some literature is *not* moral, and there is even much good — that is, clever — literature, which is quite obviously at odds with any moral values the censor can be expected to care about. For another, most literature, even of the most obviously moral kind, is potentially harmful to *somebody*, as Thomas Hardy pointed out in defense of *Tess of the D'Urbervilles*. The censors are thus always on safe ground, from their own point of view, so long as we talk about all literature, or even all "good" literature. Even the most ridiculous attacks — say those on *Robin Hood* — have this much validity: it is *conceivable* that such a work might alter a child's beliefs, and if we admit this, we must also admit that the alteration might be "for the worse," according to the censor's values. The child who reads *Robin Hood* might decide to rob from the rich and give to the poor, or he might even decide to support a progressive income tax. We do no service to our cause if we pretend, as some have done, that literature cannot have such effects because it does not deal with beliefs. Any literary work that we really read will play upon our basic beliefs, and even though fundamental changes of belief produced by novels may be rarer among mature readers than among novices, it would be foolish to pretend that they do not occur. If the change is "for the worse," from the censor's point of view, then the work has done harm, and it should be banned.

In contrast to our general claims, the censor usually has some specific danger in mind which is directly and literally related to something he has seen in the text. He has found profanity or obscenity or depravity, and we tell him that the book will, like all "good books," do the students good. In Austin, Texas, a pastor who was testifying in a hearing against *Andersonville* read aloud a long sequence of cuss words, excerpted from widely separated bits of the novel. The committee was quite properly horrified. The book they "read" was a bad book by any criterion, and certainly it would be a bad book to teach. But the horrifying fact about the episode is not that the committee members were offended by what they had heard but that none of them had enough gumption to read so much as a single page of the real book straight through. It would do no good to say to such committeemen, when the preacher was finished, that *Andersonville* is really a highly moral work; the "book" which they experienced was not. Similarly it does no good to say to the censor of *The Catcher in the Rye* that it is really "calling for a good world in which people can *connect* — a key word in twentieth-century writing." One can picture the reactions of the irate parent who has discovered the obscenities in *Catcher* as he reads the following defense of the morality of fiction-in-general:

> When the student learns to see great books, classic or contemporary, as metaphors for the whole of human experience, the study of literature contributes in a unique way to this understanding of these traditions. They help him to discover who he is and where he is going.
>
> An abstraction may have little emotional impact. But the dramatization of an abstraction, of concepts and values, offers us something we can grasp. We begin to feel and understand the abstraction.[1]

Now here is something for the parent really to worry about: if *Catcher* is on his mind, he will think that we teachers are treating its profanity and obscenity as standing for "the whole of human experience," suitable to help his child "to understand who he is

---

[1]*The Students' Right to Read.* Urbana: National Council of Teachers of English.

and where he is going"! It is surely no comfort to tell him that literature, by dramatizing the experience of profanity and obscenity, makes it have more emotional impact.

The obscene phrase that Holden tries to erase from the school walls toward the end of *Catcher* is concrete, literal, visible; our "defenses of poesie" tend to be abstract, metaphoric, intangible. We must somehow make them seem to the censor as real as the abuses he has found, but to do so will never be easy. To be concrete and specific about the moral values even of a short poem is terribly difficult, and the precise inferences through which a good reader constructs his reading of a complete novel are so complex that it is no wonder we draw back from the effort to describe them. Yet it is only by learning to follow such processes for himself — that is, by learning how to read — that the censor can discover what we really mean by the morality or immorality of a work. Unless those who wield educational power know at firsthand what we mean when we say that a literary work can be moral even though many of its elements are to them objectionable, the other defenses against censorship may finally fail.

I have a frequently recurring fantasy in which I am called before a censorship committee and asked to justify my teaching of such-and-such a book. As hero of my own dream, I see myself starting on page one of whatever book is attacked and reading aloud, with commentary and discussion, page by page, day by day, until the censors either lynch me or confess to a conversion.

A pipedream, clearly. And the one I use for substitute is not much less fantastic. An irate committeeman comes to me (I am a very young instructor in a highly vulnerable school district), and he threatens to have me fired for teaching *The Catcher in the Rye* (or *Huckleberry Finn*, or *Catch-22* — one can of course mold one's daydreams to suit current events). I look him boldly in the eye and I ask him one question: "Will you, before you fire me, do me one last favor? Will you read carefully a little statement I have made about the teaching of this book, and then reread the book?" And since it is fantasy, he says, "Well, I don't see why not. I want to be reasonable." And away he goes, bearing my neatly-typed manuscript and my marked copy of *Catcher*. Some

131

hours later he comes back, offers his humble apologies for what he calls his "foolish mistake," and returns my manuscript. Here it is:

WHAT TO DO WITH A LITERARY WORK
BEFORE DECIDING TO CENSOR IT

Let us begin by assuming that we ought to censor all books that we think are immoral. Learned men have offered many arguments against this assumption (you might want to take a look at Milton's *Areopagitica*, John Stuart Mill's *On Liberty*, or the NCTE pamphlet, *The Students' Right to Read*), but other learned and wise men, like Plato and Tolstoy, have accepted it, and we can do the same — at least for a time. What should determine whether a book is among those we want to censor?

The question will not arise, of course, unless you have found, as in *Catcher*, something objectionable. There you have found such things as teenagers speaking profanities, the phrase "Fuck you" — repeated! — and a schoolboy visit to a prostitute. It must seem to you that I am being merely perverse when I say that such a book is really highly moral, when "read properly." Yet I mean something quite real and concrete by this claim. Unfortunately, to see fully what I mean you would need to sit in my classroom every day, throughout the time we spend trying to learn how to read *Catcher* "properly." I know that you cannot spend the time that would be required for this experience, and the principal probably wouldn't allow it even if you could. But there are certain things you can do, on your own, to discover what a "proper reading" of this book might be.

The big job is to relate the seemingly offensive passages to the context provided by the whole work. To say this is not, as you might think, merely a trick to sidestep the true issues. We all relate literary parts to their contexts all the time, almost without thinking about it. If someone told us that a book talked openly about nakedness, we might, if we are worried by pornography, begin to worry. But we are not troubled to read "I was a stranger, and ye took me in: Naked, and ye clothed me: I was sick, and ye visited me." The context has transformed both the word "naked" and the concept of nakedness to obviously moral uses. Similarly, when we read about the woman "taken in adultery," caught "in the very act," we do not ask that the reading be changed to something less specific. Not only do we take for granted the piety of the Bible — something we do not and cannot do for *Catcher* — but the immediate context in John viii quite evidently requires a forceful statement of the nature of the sin that is being forgiven. If you doubt this, try substituting some lesser sin — say gossiping — for adultery in the passage, or some eupherism like "caught flirting with another woman's husband."

When we read the many other specific accounts of sexual abuses that the Bible contains — of seduction, incest, sodomy, rape, and what not — we do not put the Bible on the list of banned books, because we know that the context requires an honest treatment of man's vices, and that it at the same time changes the very effect of naming them. Though we might question the wisdom of teaching particular sections of the Bible to children of a particular age, we would never think of firing a teacher simply for "teaching the Bible." We would want at the very least to know what the teacher was doing with it. We know the context, in this case, and consequently we know there is at least one book with many bad things in it that is still a good book.

It is exactly this same claim that we teachers want to make about a book like *Catcher in the Rye* (though few of us would want to go as far as one theologian who has called it a piece of "modern scripture"). But since the claim is much harder to substantiate with a long work like a novel, I want to begin with a look at how the process of transformation works in a short simple poem. Any poem with possibly offensive elements would do, but I have chosen a highly secular one that is likely to offend in several ways: "ygUDuh," by E. E. Cummings.

> ygUDuh
>
>   ydoan
>   yunnuhstan
>
>   ydoan o
>   yunnuhstan dem
>   yguduh ged

<pre>
        yunnuhstan dem doidee
        yguduh ged riduh
        ydoan o nudn
LISN bud LISN

        dem
        gud
        am

        lidl yelluh bas
        tuds weer goin

     duhSIVILEYEzum
</pre>

This poem may very well seem unintelligible to you on first reading. I've seen a class of high school seniors flounder with it — until I asked one of them to read it aloud. But then they worked out something like the following "translation" (though there was usually some unresolved debate about whether it is spoken by one speaker or two):

<pre>
You've got to

        You don't
        Do you understand?

        You don't know
        Do you understand those
        You've got to get

        Do you understand? Those dirty
        You've got to get rid of
        You don't know anything
LISTEN, Bud, LISTEN

        Those
        God
        damn

        little yellow bas-
        tards, we're going

To CIVILIZE them.
</pre>

Now that the poem is out in the open, as it were (though limping badly), it obviously offers several possible kinds of offense. We can imagine, first of all, a National Association for the Advancement of Yellow Peoples rising in protest against the offending phrase *yellow bastards*, just as the NAACP of Brooklyn had *Huckleberry Finn* banned because it refers to Jim constantly as Nigger Jim. What right has a poet to use such language, degrading a whole people? Even though the poem was obviously written in wartime, when tempers ran high, that is no excuse for descending to such abuse.

"The context of the whole poem" provides an answer to this imaginary protest. Does Cummings, the poet, call the Japanese "yellow bastards"? Obviously not. There is a speaker, dramatized for our literary observation, a speaker whose tongue bewrayeth him, with every half-word that speweth out of his mouth. It is this speaker from whom the whole content of our paraphrase comes: he it is who would take those yellow bastards and civilize them. What Cummings says, of course, is provided only by inference from the way in which the statement is conveyed. The speaker provides, in the many signs of his brutish inarticulateness, evidence that Cummings is as greatly opposed to his foolish bigotry as the president of the NAAYP might be. And, of course, the poet expects us to take pleasure in the comic contrast between the speaker's lack of civilization and his bold program.

If the members of the NAAYP still feel dissatisfied with our effort to place the line in its dramatic context, claiming that they simply would prefer not to see such language in print, we can only ask, "Would you prefer that bigots who hate your group be portrayed more politely, hence more favorably, and hence more deceptively?" It is clear that as the poem stands, the more crudely the bigot is portrayed the stronger the indictment. Is it not likely that a student subjected to this poem in a literature course would come out of his experience *more* sensitive to the issue of bigotry, and *less* willing to accept the crudities of bigots than before?

Other readers, as we have learned in various censorship hearings, will object to the profanity. But again we see that the "poem" is no more profane than it is bigoted; it is the speaker who is profane. The purist may still say that he does not want profanity presented even as part of an indictment, but I have not noticed that censorship hearings have been marked by the censors reluctance to speak the words they object to.

STEPS FOR THE GOOD CENSOR

Though the steps we have taken so far with this poem by no means exhaust what the good teacher would want to bring out in discussing it, they show very well what the good censor will want to do before carrying out his job.

1. He will refuse to draw any conclusions whatever from any element of a work taken out of its context. This means that he will read the whole work.

2. He will not be satisfied with one reading. When a work is assigned and discussed in class, it receives several "readings," sometimes quite literally and always in the sense that first impressions are modified by sustained reflection. As a class progresses, a poem, play, or novel is traversed by the alert student again and again. What the censor should be interested in is what the student will get after such reflective rereading, not the errors he might fall into if he read the work without the teacher's encouragement to thoughtful rereading. But of course this means that the censor himself must go through the same process. Any censor who rejected "ygUDuh" on one reading would be a very foolish censor indeed.

3. The true values of a work — the real moral center which we may or may not want to rule out of our children's experience — cannot usually be identified with the expressed values of any one character. What we might call the *author's* values, the *norms* according to which he *places* his characters' values, are always more complex than those of any one of the characters he invents. To censor the Bible because Satan plays a prominent and sometimes even dominant and persuasive role would be absurd. It is equally absurd to censor any book for expressed values which are, for the proper reader, repudiated by the author's implied criticism.

If these three points apply to a short minor poem like "ygUDuh" they are even more applicable to the more complex reading tasks presented by long fiction.

The degree of difficulty varies, of course, depending on the reader and the work. It is easy for most readers to recognize, for example, that Mark Twain does not himself use the word "nigger" in *Huckleberry Finn*. "We blowed out a cylinder-head," says Huck. "Good gracious!" says Aunt Sally. "Anybody hurt?" "No'm. Killed a nigger." The whole point of this episode, coming as it does long after Huck has been forced by experience to recognize the nobility of "nigger Jim," is that even Huck cannot resist thinking as he has been taught to think. Huck here not only uses the word nigger, but reduces "niggers" to less than human standing.[2] But it is not hard — at least for a white man — to see that Mark Twain is far from making the same mistake; indeed, he would have no point in relating the episode except to show a lapse from his own values.

A Negro reader is given a more difficult task. To place the offensive word or concept into its transforming context requires a kind of dispassionate attentiveness that his own involvement with words like "nigger" may easily destroy. The word sets off responses which, though appropriate to most occasions when it is used, are totally inappropriate to the very special use that Mark Twain has made of it. It is likely that every reader sooner or later encounters books that he misreads in exactly this way. And it is highly unlikely that we will ever discover our own errors of this kind, because the very nature of our fault, with its strong emotional charge, keeps us from listening to those who might set us straight.

THE CATCHER AS EXAMPLE

With all of this as background, suppose we turn now to objections to *The Catcher in the Rye*. You said that you objected to the printing of the obscene phrase that Holden tries to erase. But in the light of your objections to the book, it is surely strange to

---

[2] A possible alternative reading would see Huck as himself master of the ironies here. Since he is author of his own anecdote, he may be thought of as choosing a moral language which he knows will be convincing to his auditor. Regardless of how we read the passage, Mark Twain is clearly guiltless, even from the most passionately pro-Negro viewpoint.

find that you and Holden have the same feelings about this phrase: you would both like to get rid of it.

> It drove me damn near crazy. I thought how Phoebe and all the other little kids would see it, and how they'd wonder what the hell it meant, and then finally some dirty kid would tell them — all cockeyed, naturally — what it meant, and how they'd all *think* about it and maybe even *worry* about it for a couple of days. I kept wanting to kill whoever'd written it.

Holden could hardly be more strongly opposed to the phrase; it is significant, surely that throughout the scene from which this passage is taken, the tone is entirely serious — there is none of the clowning that marks Holden's behavior in many other passages. But this immediate context cannot in itself be decisive; though it is unequivocal about Holden's serious repudiation of the phrase which *you* repudiate, the *author* after all does print the phrase and not some euphemism, and this surely suggests that he is not so seriously offended by the phrase, in itself, as you and Holden are.

Clearly we are driven to thinking about what kind of character the author has created for us, in his lost wild boy. What kind of person is it who, a moment later, concludes that his effort to wipe out the obscenities of the world is "hopeless, anyway," because they are unlimited.

You said this afternoon that you found him to be a terrible person. But supposing we begin from the other direction and ask ourselves why young readers find him, as they do (I have yet to find an exception), so entirely sympathetic. When I ask my adolescent students why they like Holden so much, they usually say, "Because he is so real" or "Because he is so honest." But it takes no very deep reading to find many additional virtues that win them to him, virtues that even you and I must admire. It is true that his honest, or rather his generally unsuccessful but valiant attempt at honesty, is striking. But a far stronger magnet for the reader's affections is his tremendous capacity for love, expressed in deeds that would do credit to a saint. The book opens, for example, with his visit, extremely distasteful to him, to the sick and aging history teacher. Holden knows that the old man loves him and needs him, just as he needs the love of the old man; it is out of real feeling that he subjects himself to the sights and smells of age and illness. The moral sensitivity revealed in this scene is maintained through the book. Again and again Holden reveals himself — often in direct contradiction of his own claims — to be far more sensitive than most of us to the feelings of others. He "feels sorry" for all the outsiders, and he hates the big shots who, like the Headmaster, allot their attentions according to social importance and try to shut out those who are fat, pimply, poor, or corny. He has genuine affection even for the Ackleys and Stradlaters ("I sort of *miss* everybody I told about"), and he is extraordinarily generous, not only with his possessions (almost everything he owns is on loan to some other boy) but with himself (he is the only boy who thinks of including the impossible Ackley in the trip to the movies). Though he often hurts others, he never does so intentionally ("I was sorry as hell I'd kidded her. Some people you shouldn't kid, even if they deserve it"). His heroes are those who are able to love unselfishly — Christ, Mr. Antolini, his sister — or those who, like James Castle, show moral courage. His enemies are those who deliberately inflict pain — for example, the boys who drive Castle to suicide.

A full catalog of his virtues and good works would be unfair to the book, because it would suggest a solemn kind of sermonizing very different from the special *Catcher* brand of affectionate comedy. But it is important to us in talking about possible censorship of the book to see its seeming immoralities in the context of Holden's deep morality.

The virtue most pertinent to the obscene phrase is of course Holden's struggle for purity. The soiled realities of the "phony" world that surrounds him in his school and in the city are constantly contrasted in his mind with the possible ideal world that has not been plastered with obscenities. His worrying about what Stradlater has done to Jane, his fight with Stradlater, his inability to carry through with the prostitute because he "feels sorry" for her, his lecture to himself about the crudities he watches through the hotel windows, his effort to explain to Luce that promiscuity destroys love — these are all, like his effort to erase the obscenity, part of his struggle to find "a place that's nice and peaceful," a world that is "nice and white." Though he himself soils, with his fevered imagination, the pure gesture of Antolini, revealing how helplessly embedded he is in another kind of world altogether, his ideal remains something like the world of the nuns, or the world of a Christ who will not condemn even Judas to eternal damnation. He is troubled, you will remember, when one of the nuns talks about *Romeo and Juliet,* because that play "gets pretty sexy in some parts, and she was a nun and all." Nuns ought to live in the pure, sexless, sinless, trouble-free world of his ideal, just as his sister ought to live in a world unsullied by nasty scrawlings on stairway walls.

All of this — the deep Christian charity and the search for an ideal purity — is symbolized in his own mind by the desire to be a catcher in the rye. He wants to save little children from falling, even though he himself, as he comes to realize, is a child who needs to be saved. The effort to erase the words is thus an ultimate, desperate manifestation of his central motive. Though it is a futile gesture, since the world will never in this respect or any other conform fully to Holden's ideal of purity, it is produced by the very qualities in his character which make it possible for him to accept his sister's love at the end, give up his mad scheme of going west, and allow himself to be saved by love. It is clear that he is, for his sister, what she has become for him: a kind of catcher in the rye. Though he cannot protect her from knowledge of the world, though he cannot, as he would like, put her under a glass museum case and save her from the ravages of the sordid, time-bound world, he can at least offer her the love that comes naturally to him. He does so and he is saved. Which is of course why he is ecstatically happy at the end.

Now none of this is buried very deep in the novel. I've not had to probe any mystical world of symbols or literary trickery to find it out; it is all evident in the actions and words of Holden himself, and it is grasped intuitively, I have found, by most teen-age readers. Their misreadings are caused, in fact, by carrying this line too far: they often overlook Holden's deficiencies. So strong is the persuasive power of his obvious virtues (obvious to them) that they overlook his limitations of understanding and his destructive weaknesses: they take him at his word. They tend to overlook the strong and unanswerable criticism offered by his sister ("You don't like *any*thing that's happening") and by Antolini, who tries to teach him how to grow up ("The mark of the immature man is that he wants to die nobly for a cause, while the mark of the mature man is that he wants to live humbly for one"). They also overlook the author's many subtle contrasts between what Holden says and what he does. In learning to read these and other built-in criticisms, students can learn to criticize their own immaturities. They learn that such a book has been read only when they have seen Holden's almost saint-like capacity for love and compassion in the light of his urge to destroy the world, and even himself, because it cannot live up to his dreams.

I am aware that what I have said does not "prove" that *Catcher* is harmless. I'm sure there are some young people who might be harmed by it, just as reading the Bible has been known to work great harm on young idealists given to fanaticism. I have not even "proved" that the book can be beneficial. Only your own reading can convince you of that; again I find myself wishing that you could reread the work with us, in class. But perhaps you will return to it now and try once more, moving from page 1 to page 277, thinking about Holden's moral life as you go.

I know I do not have to ask you (the dream continues) for your decision. As a man of honor, you can only have carried out our little experiment to the letter, and the book is now cleared of all suspicion. I should not be surprised if your experience has also made you wonder about other books you have suspected in the past.

You may have guessed by now that I have been inching my way all this while toward a repudiation of our original assumption. Is there really a place for *any* censorship other than the teacher's careful choice? The skill required to decide whether a work is suited for a particular teaching moment is so great that only the gifted teacher, with his knowledge of how his teaching aims relate to materials chosen for students at a given stage of development, can be trusted to exercise it.

Such a teacher can be trusted even when he chooses to teach works that reveal themselves, under the closest reading, to be immoral to the core. Let us suppose that you have performed the kind of reading I have described on a given work, say *Peyton Place* or one of Mickey Spillane's thrillers, and you find that it does not, as with *Catcher*, have any defense to offer for itself: it is immoral no matter how one looks at it. So you go to the teacher to insist that the book be removed from the reading list. You should not be surprised if the teacher replies: "Oh, yes, I quite agree with you. *Peyton Place* is inherently an immoral work; there are, in fact, far worse things in it than the few sexual offenses you object to. Read carelessly by high school students, it could do tremendous harm — like other books of the same kind. That's why I insist on spending some time, in my advanced sections, on this particular kind of shoddiness. I find that most of my students have read the juicier sections on their own, anyway. By placing those porno-graphic bits back into the shoddy context from which they have been torn, the student soon comes to treat Metalious' commercial sensationalism with the contempt it deserves."

So you see, sir (the drama has by now shifted, dream-like from manuscript to real-life drama, and I am hearty, confident, even slightly patronizing as I fling one arm across his shoulder), the only person who can conduct the fight for good literature is the person who has some chance of knowing what he is doing: the sensitive, experienced teacher. He it is who. . . .

*   *   *

Dreams of wish fulfillment always end with a rude awakening. My dream ends with the admission that even with the best of luck my argument about *Catcher* would do no more than shake a censor's confidence in his own judgment. Wide awake, I know that many censors will only scoff at any efforts we may make to reason about the issues of censorship. But as I write these final lines, I do not doubt for a moment that even an ineffectual defense of freedom is better than no defense at all.

By recognizing children's rights and developing procedures for ensuring that these rights are protected, schools can guarantee more democratic treatment for children. Counselors should be advocates of these procedures and rights.

Children's Rights and the School Counselor

WILLIAM H. VAN HOOSE
Professor of Counselor Education
University of Virginia

M any schools operate within a seventeenth century framework concerning the rights of children. This view gives adults almost total authority over children and denies them the natural rights accorded every other age group in society. It is argued that children do not know what is best for them, that they are too immature to make decisions, and that their best interests are served by benevolent adult domination. Children have few rights of their own; they are often denied fair treatment and are not afforded the right to participate in making decisions that directly affect them.

Educators give lip service to freedom, individual rights, and democracy, but in practice they often deny these rights to students. Schools espouse democratic ideas but at the same time engage in authoritarian practices that violate all principles of individual liberty. Such practices are antithetical to most of the principles of education in a democratic society. As I. Glaser has noted:

> What students learn—not from what they are taught but from the way the school is organized to treat them — is that authority is more important than freedom, order more precious than liberty, and discipline a higher value than individual expression. This is a lesson which is inappropriate to a free society — and certainly inappropriate to its schools.[1]

JUSTIFICATION FOR CHILDREN'S RIGHTS

Acting on Rawls' theory of justice, Worsford has described a philosophical framework for securing children's rights to fair treatment. The central theme in Worsford's argument is that all members of society must participate in deciding on those principles of fairness and justice which guarantee equal rights to all people. He states that when individuals make rational choices and when they come to an understanding of what constitutes "rights," only one set of principles of justice will emerge. He further says that:

> Individuals will choose two fundamental principles of justice. The first is that each person should have a personal liberty compatible with a like liberty for all others; no one should be any freer than anyone else in society to pursue his or her own ends. The second is that societal inequalities are to be arranged such that all individuals must share whatever advantages and disadvantages the inequalities bring.[2]

Within this conception, people have natural rights, including the right to be treated like everyone else. These rights are based on the nature of individuals, and to violate them is to violate the nature of the person.

In this theory, children are participants in the formation of the basic principles of justice and fairness. They have the capacity for

---

[1]Glasser, I. "Schools for Scandal: The Bill of Rights and Public Education," *Phi Delta Kappan*, 1969, pp. 51, 190–194.

[2]Worsford, V. L. "A Philosophical Justification for Children's Rights," *Harvard Educational Review*, 1974, pp. 142–57.

understanding and accepting these principles, and whether or not this capacity is fully developed, the child still receives the full protection of all principles of justice. Worsford, describing the Rawlsian view, points out that children, at least partially, can participate in deciding on principles and practices that lead to fair treatment. Children often do know what they want and are capable of weighing alternatives and making decisions. A major point in this concept is that children already have natural rights, but they must be recognized and protected.

Adults should provide direction, exert influence in helping children act responsibly, and assist them in decision making. In fact, children often seek help and willingly accept the authority of older persons, and this is necessary when special knowledge and experience is required to advise and guide one's actions. But adult expertise and intervention must be used to facilitate personal growth, not to inhibit or restrict an individual. Thus, the manner in which adult authority is exercised becomes the critical factor.

Maes' views on human freedom and counseling are pertinent to this subject. He has described two kinds of experiences commonly considered to be liberating.[3] The first of these is facility in action, which means "being natural," free from anxiety and tension. This freedom can also be described as a state of spontaneity, being oneself, feeling free to act without anxiety about external expectations and demands. This second definition includes an awareness of choices and the freedom to act on them. Trying out, experimenting, and making decisions are all necessary elements in the process of experiencing freedom.

The rights of children in school include opportunities for participation, involvement, and some independence of action. Rogers has stated that learning is facilitated when students are given the right to explore and to make choices and when they are in a climate that assures personal freedom and security.[4] When such principles are understood and accepted, certain actions must be taken to implement them.

---

[3]Maes, W. "Human Freedom and the Counselor," *Personnel and Guidance Journal*, 1968, pp. 777–81.
[4]Rogers, C. *On Becoming a Person*. Boston: Houghton-Mifflin, 1961.

DUE PROCESS

Children in school are entitled to due process of law if they get into difficulty with rules or school authorities. Due process implies a fair procedure: the right to defend oneself and to confront one's accuser, the right to a fair and impartial hearing, and the right to appeal. In schools, due process should include the right of a child to be heard and the assurance that school authorities will give impartial treatment.

Since due process means a fair process and since no educator wishes to be unfair, it seems unlikely that any teacher or administrator would object to providing the necessary procedures for due process for children.[5] This is often not the case however. As M. D. and J. A. Lewis state, "All across the country students are regularly denied due process; and the presumption of innocence is almost unheard of when young people are accused of violating school rules."[6]

It is not only schools that deny due process of law to children. From early times both common and statute law have imposed disabilities on persons under age. Under common law, for example, parents could (and did) claim the earnings of their children. Children have few legal rights unless exercised through a parent or guardian. In most states a minor cannot sue except when the litigation is conducted by a parent or guardian in his or her behalf. It is also generally true that a person under fourteen — sixteen in some states — accused of a crime is not treated as a criminal but as a delinquent. On the other hand it seems paradoxical that in some states a fourteen year old accused of a crime may be tried as an adult but otherwise denied adult status.

Although some laws create disabilities for children, others provide privileges and special protection for them. Several recent statutes and court decisions illustrate a growing concern for the rights of children and youth. Two supreme court decisions during the 1960s (Dixon and Alabama State Board of Education, 1961 and

---

[5]Dunlop, R. "School Law For Educators" in Peters, et al., eds., *The Practice of Guidance.* Denver, Col.: Love, 1972, pp. 508–29.
[6]Lewis, M. D., & Lewis, J. A. "The Counselor and Civil Liberties," *Personnel and Guidance Journal*, 1970, pp. 9–13.

in the Matter of Gault, 1967) deal directly with due process in schools. The court has made it clear that students have a right to due process of law and that schools must recognize some basic rights of pupils.

PERSONAL RIGHTS

> There was an old woman who lived in a shoe.
> She had so many children she didn't know what to do;
> She gave them some broth without any bread
> Then whipped them all soundly and put them to bed.

This nursery rhyme reflects some eighteenth century views on how to deal with children. We like to think that such views are uncommon today and that our level of sophistication has led us to more appropriate methods of dealing with children. However, there are several exceptions.

Each year in the United States 50,000 to 60,000 children are wilfully beaten, starved, and mistreated — or "battered" — by adults, usually their parents. About one-fourth of these children die as a result of such maltreatment.[7] These statistics refer to physical abuse — cases in which evidence of mistreatment is tangible. We have not even begun to deal with psychological abuse, which is often equally damaging.

In education, we have made some progress from the time when "readin', ritin', and 'rithmetic was taught by the rule of the hickory stick." Nevertheless, some schools still inflict corporal punishment, and courts tend to uphold the school's authority to use the paddle. Supposedly, punishment must be moderate, reasonable, and administered without malice. It is sometimes recommended that a neutral party administer the whipping, with a witness present — as protection for the adult, not the child. The contradictions here are obvious. Children have personal rights, and these include the right to freedom from physical assault. Adults may seek redress when physically assaulted. Therefore, under the principles of equal treatment described above, children should have the same right.

---

[7]Leavitt, J. *The Battered Child—Selected Readings.* Morristown, N.J.: General Learning Press, 1974.

Educators are obligated to maintain some control of the school, and reasonable rules are necessary. They may often have to resort to physical force to control fights, to restrain violent pupils, or to protect other children, but I believe that such situations are quite different from a planned assault on the physical person of a child. Such practices are clear violations of human dignity, human rights, and human liberty.

We do not know the extent of the psychological abuse that follows physical punishment. We do know, however, that children who are whipped also suffer psychologically. Some children develop an unusual degree of hostility toward the person who punished them and toward the school as well. This hostility, which may be released on other children, poses a greater problem not only for the child but for the school as well.

I do not think that educators are sadists or that schools are ruled by physical force. Instead, I argue that physical punishment in schools is wrong, that it has the potential for creating more problems than it solves, and that physical punishment violates all the human rights known to civilized man. The present level of expertise and sophistication in our society suggests that we can find better ways to deal with children in school.

RIGHT TO PRIVACY

The doctrine of the right of privacy is fairly recent, yet its roots go back to the principles of English common law. The early philosophers also recognized that humans not only had personal rights but they also were entitled to a degree of privacy which should not be invaded.

Ethical codes that apply to the work of counselors recognize to some extent the right to privacy. Generally these codes or standards suggest that counselors should not release confidential information to unauthorized persons and that confidential information obtained from records or from counseling should not be discussed with those who are not involved.

The rights of privacy of students are frequently violated in two different ways — first by revealing information students believed to be confidential and through misuse and/or release of information from student records. Each of these instances presents some professional dilemmas for the counselor and illustrates how the counselor often gets caught in the middle.

Both counselor training and professional counselor reference groups place a major emphasis on the confidential nature of counseling. Many authorities believe that effective counseling cannot take place without sure guarantees against disclosure of counselee secrets. At the same time, the effectiveness of counseling in elementary schools largely depends on counselors' relationships with teachers. Teachers expect, and perhaps even have the right to, information about their students. This raises the question of whether counselors can withhold information about students without damaging their working relationships with other personnel.

A second dilemma is created by the fact that counselors are liable if the information that is revealed is misused or results in "unwarranted publicity"; and it may not matter whether the information revealed is correct or incorrect. Counselees have a right to be protected from wrongful intrusion into their private lives which would cause shame, mental suffering, or humiliation.[8]

The use of cumulative records presents a third dilemma for counselors. Today, schools are recording and dispensing more personal information about students. Cumulative records, which once consisted mainly of grades, attendance data, and test scores, now contain anecdotes, personality profiles, medical information, and family evaluation. The counselor is a primary user of records and in some schools may be the custodian of some or all of the types of information mentioned above. Thus, several questions arise with respect to the counselor and student records. Can or should counselors deny other school personnel access to pupil records? If they cannot or do not, then how do they protect privacy rights of counselees? How do counselors handle confidential information provided by other professionals such as psychologists or psychiatrists?

The Family Rights and Privacy Act of 1974 provides for paren-

---

[8]Butler, H., Moran, K., & Vanderpool, F. *Legal Aspects of Student Records*, National Organization on Legal Problems of Education. Topeka, Kan.: 1972.

tal access to their children's school records. In its present form this act is ambiguous and leaves many questions unanswered. However, the right of parents to inspect, challenge, and limit the use of a child's records is quite clear. This legislation has several positive implications in that it may limit access to student records by unauthorized personnel and agencies, and it may lead to more judicious preparation and maintenance of school records. In any case, the intent of the Family Rights and Privacy Act is to preserve the rights of privacy, and this is a step in the right direction.

A dilemma arises for counselors, not because of the intent of the law but because of the problems involved in developing procedures for implementing it. Counselors should be careful not to get caught in the middle by assuming total responsibility for access and release of pupil records. The records in question are school records not just counseling records, and their proper use is a responsibility of the administration as well as the counselor.

IMPLICATIONS

In our society there is a growing concern for individual rights. Counselors have traditionally committed themselves to the concepts of human dignity, freedom, and the democratic process. The Lewises' analysis of the counselors' position on civil liberties is perhaps one of the best available.

> If we as counselors are to believe the rhetoric of our profession, there are certain things which, almost by definition, we favor unequivocally: the right of the individual to work toward the fulfillment of his own potential, to obtain self-understanding, and to make decisions based upon an examination of alternatives. . . . If we counselors really believe all that we say we do, then it must be assumed that we are against the denial of any human being's rights and liberties, regardless of his age.[9]

Elementary school counselors are not hired as social reformers nor for teaching children to break rules. They are, however, concerned about individual development, and when this development

---

[9]Ibid., p. 11.

is thwarted by institutional or societal practices, the counselor has a clear responsibility to try to change such policies. In fact, the very nature of counseling places the counselor in a position to bring about positive change in significant others and in the institution itself. When a counselor's professional behavior exemplifies a commitment to the rights of children, other school personnel may reexamine their own views on personal rights, due process, and privacy.

In conclusion, there are two important things to consider. First, in the future, counselors and other educators will be required to be more alert and responsive to the rights and freedoms of those they counsel. Second, increasingly more counselors will be held accountable for the judgments and decisions they make about counselees.

In matters of children's rights, counselors may find some help in codes of ethics of professional associations and in the professional literature, including statements on the role and function of counselors. However, such information often deals in generalities about what a counselor should do and provides little help on how to do it. Thus, answers to questions raised here probably will not be found in the literature, in professional association statements, or in laws dealing with human rights. Nevertheless, some partial answers may be found as we examine our own values and our own beliefs about justice, human rights, and children.

FREEDOM TO CHOOSE

How can enthusiasm for learning best be engendered? What is the significance of the phenomenal growth of "free school" alternatives within the past few years? This is an impassioned call for a thoughtful look at alternatives to conventional schools and schooling.

Assessing the Alternatives

CHARLES H. RATHBONE
Chairman, Elementary Master of Arts
in Teaching Program, Oberlin College

Take a card — any card!" cries the mustachioed prestidigitator, and when later he produces the precise card we selected, we laugh in surprise at his legerdemain. I recall receiving a special deck as a birthday gift when I was nine or ten. Though never especially adroit at cards, with that deck I too could perform all sorts of tricks — for one simple reason: each of the fifty-two cards was a three of clubs! Those on whom I played my tricks stood no chance whatever — no chance, because they were permitted no real choice.

Unfortunately, that's precisely how the deck has long been stacked in American education: you paid your money and you got the three of clubs — and too bad for you if your suit wasn't clubs.

Luckily, times are changing: in the world of schools and schooling, a whole host of alternatives have sprung up; the educational landscape is now abloom with a colorful variety of very different classrooms. Accounting for this phenomenal proliferation requires caution, for the origin of each is unique. Some undoubtedly provide self-serving ego trips for their directors; others represent slick exercises in acronymic grantsmanship; still others offer cut-rate political excursions. But more often than not these newly evolved educational ventures owe their origin to the conviction of a single individual that his particular dream deserved substantiation, that his theory was owed an honest test. Most, too, came into being because of someone's despairing dissatisfaction with the status quo.

Considering the full range of these present-day alternatives, I find they fall into two rather broad categories. On the one hand are those concerned with tightening up what they perceive to be an inherently flabby school organization: disarmingly straightforward about their objectives, comfortable with modern technology, business-like in their analysis of the activities of teaching and learning, theirs are the schools for which systems analysis, behavioral objectives, cost-efficiency computation, modular scheduling, computer-assisted instruction, and the like seem eminently appropriate. Their objectives seem clear, their assumptions patent.

The second general category of alternatives includes the free schools, informal and experimental colleges, drop-out centers, radical non-schools, educational communes, and the like. They go by such names as Knowplace, Rough Rock, Bensalem, Trout Fishing in America Inc., Walden Center, SDS Education Collective, Noscuela, Play Mountain Place, Summerhill West, Storefront Learning Center, Whole Earth Truck Store, Skitikuk, Timberhill, World of Inquiry, Stone Soup, and Pegasus. Among them one finds educational objectives less often and less explicitly stated, philosophical and pedagogical assumptions less precisely specified, and formal and systematic evaluation procedures neglected in overall program planning.

Yet precisely because they bring unparalleled vitality, imagination, conviction, and plain good will to the educational scene, they must now be challenged to explain themselves, to make available for public scrutiny their ideals and assumptions — as well as their daily practices. For only then can they be fairly and usefully assessed by those responsible for teaching in the public schools.

UNDERNEATH THE RHETORIC

Though no absolute consensus exists among these *free* or *open* or *informal* settings, they share certain areas of special concern, areas that bear closer examination.

Classroom Boundaries. While once we assumed that on one desk and in one chair each child would draw, compose, do sums, and conduct experiments, a less formal, more functional organization of classroom space is now in vogue. Moreover, from Lillian Weber's "open corridor" in Harlem's P.S. 123 to Parkway's "School Without Walls" in Philadelphia, the physical boundaries of the classroom are being pushed back. As new schools challenge the assumption that all meaningful learning takes place in a single officially designated "educational" space, they are sending their students out into the neighborhood to test and taste reality — just as they are inviting various community resources back into the classroom. Either way, the walls dividing school and life come tumbling down.

Curriculum. Because proponents of the new open schools view knowledge as inherently indivisible, organic, and idiosyncratically formed, they adamantly oppose prepackaged, sequentially organized curriculum units. Similarly, because they consider the prime organizer of curriculum to be the child himself, they have abandoned traditional goals of "coverage," while encouraging the child to introduce his own concerns into the classroom. Prepared curriculum is no longer considered an *end*, but rather a *starting place* for learning.

Direct Experience. Whether by way of work-study programs in high school or introducing manipulative materials in kindergarten, the new alternatives are accentuating the value of experiential learning. Coupled with an emphasis on *process* over *product* (which allies them with Maslow's "Third Force" people in psychology) and a concomitant *time-now* orientation (". . . the best preparation for being a happy and useful man or woman is to

157

live fully as a child," asserts the *Plowden Report*), this learning-by-doing answers for many the current cry for relevance.

"Teacher" and "Teaching". The new schools acknowledge that children learn not only from "official" teachers, but through interaction with the environment, from peers, from the very structure of school. They acknowledge, too, the myriad unintended learnings that occur in school — meaningful but unplanned lessons over which the teacher has minimal control. The teacher's job, as they see it, is to *assist*, not to *direct* children, and this obligates him to two masters, not one: he agrees both to serve society's surrogate, the school, and to honor each child's private agenda, no matter what that may entail. Obviously, much of this must be accomplished on a one-to-one basis; large group activities have all but disappeared.

Student Rights. The rights issue has progressed beyond censorship and dress code: the new schools have realized that just a little compulsion goes a long way in complicating personal relationships between students and teachers; they have discovered that learning, like marriage, is best when freely entered into. They have learned, too, that without freedom (to attend class, to choose one's work) there can be little individual dignity, pride, integrity, nor can freedom be "given" by one person to another.

As Roy Illsley, headmaster of Battling Brook County Primary School, Leicestershire, once told me: "The basis for learning should be that the child wants to know, not that somebody else knows, or that somebody says he ought to know." Each child's curriculum must therefore reflect his needs, his interest, his assertion of personal right to direct his own learning. Thus the message to each child is clear: you have certain inalienable rights; people are the products of their own decisions; in this setting you are respected as one whose choices count.

Affective Conditions. Love and apprehension, joy and discord are endemic to the open classroom: teachers and students therefore have a responsibility, first to acknowledge and then to cope with the release of strong emotions. Teachers especially must be sensitive to the fear and humiliation children may experience while learning; their task is not so much to cushion stress as to help children understand it. Teachers also have a special obligation, it is held, to know themselves in some depth — since insensitivity to their own needs often permits gross misuse of praise and punishment in classrooms. Finally, proponents of these new alternatives are aware that all groups of thirty-six children are not identical: every social group, if allowed to develop naturally, evolves its own unique lifestyle, which is to be fostered and respected, not put down or neglected.

Sources of Authority. The arbitrary authority of age and degrees and expertise is out; to learn "that there's no one over you" is now an acknowledged goal. School is seen as a place for finding out who *you* are, not for learning to accept others' standards. For the teacher, this means presenting himself as an essentially neutral resource, not as a cajoling, demanding, ego-involved participant in the child's learning process. For the student, this means crafting his own yardstick, not measuring himself by someone else's.

CHOOSING TO CHANGE

The attractiveness of such alternatives is compelling. Their ideals, however audacious, are undeniably noble. Yet we can all too easily don the outward trappings of someone else's innovations without understanding or accepting the substantive, philosophical positions on which they implicitly rest. Fortunately, sources of information about these new kinds of classrooms are plentiful: Toronto, Santa Barbara, and New York have hosted recent experiential "festivals"; several of the so-called romantic critics have gone practical (Kohl's monthly contribution to *Teacher*, Holt's *What Do I Do Monday?*, Kozol's Storefront Learning Centers in Boston); newsletters and mini-periodicals abound (*New Schools Exchange Newsletter, The TDS* [Teachers for a Democratic Society], *Red Pencil, MANAS*); Postman, Silberman, and others are on the lecture or *Today Show* circuit. Besides, most alternative schools welcome visitors. Indeed, there is little excuse these days for not being well informed of what's going on and where.

But being informed is not enough; we must probe deeply to discover the real significance of these alternatives. If choosing to change demands responsible assessment of the possible effects of a change on children, it also means taking a careful look at oneself. For intellectual consideration of educational philosophy is one thing; being open to feelings of confusion, elation, disappointment, and vulnerability is quite another. Alternatives come and alternatives go, but until the teacher is ready to risk himself — to put his own beliefs on the line — no significant classroom change is possible. Choosing to change means more than taking on the "system." It means taking on full responsibility for one's own professional actions. And that is about the most difficult, most mature action a teacher can ever demand responsibility for.

Change, of course, needn't take place in a vacuum. In fact, broad-based support systems are essential. One principal I know used to keep in his outer office an "I Want Box," into which teachers poured all sorts of requests — for materials, for machines to be repaired, for field trips, or for conferences on problem pupils. That's one kind of support. Other schools have discovered ingenious ways of involving parents in the operation of the school: besides providing cheap labor, this practice keeps vital communication lines open and provides basic political support in time of strife. Perhaps the most comprehensive support system exists within certain Local Education Authorities in England, where full-scale advisories have been established to assist practicing teachers. The advisers are in no way concerned with evaluative functions — they aren't even allowed to enter a classroom unless invited by the teacher. Their sole function is to help teachers to grow.

To begin is never easy. Having assessed the alternatives and having looked squarely at one's own motives, having evaluated the odds and sized up the opposition, having decided the cause is just, one needs but the courage to act. At the end of the final chapter of *What Do I Do Monday?* John Holt puts it bluntly:

> Every day's headlines show more clearly that the old ways, the "tried and true" ways, are simply and quite spectacularly not working. No point in arguing about who's to blame. The time has come to do something very different. The way to begin is—to begin.*

---

*New York: E. P. Dutton, 1970.

*A thoughtful analysis of recent
efforts to challenge the monolithic
nature of the public schools. "Over
time, we could emerge with a redefined
system of public education that is
diverse, self-renewing, and responsive
to a pluralistic society."*

The What, Why, and Where of the Alternatives Movement

MARIO D. FANTINI
Dean of Education and Professor
New York State University College
at New Paltz

There is an alternative schools movement beginning in this country that could very well become the major thrust of reform in the decades ahead. This trend toward educational diversity has grown out of several decades of frustration: We tried to make a monolithic public school system work for everybody. We were preoccupied with improving a single model of education. We updated courses of study, such as new math and new physics; we introduced new technology and new devices, such as programed learning, team teaching, and non-gradedness; and for those who were the most obvious casualties of the schools, we mounted compensatory programs of remediation. In short, we spent our fiscal and human resources attempting to improve a uniform nineteenth century institution. The result is, at best, an improved outdated institution.

Our compensatory, add-on efforts at reform are now slowly being assessed as general failures. President Nixon rendered the verdict on compensatory education in his 1970 Education Message. Disappointment in the results of these innovations is best depicted in the 1972 Ford Foundation Report entitled *A Foundation Goes to School*, which reviewed a decade of investments in school improvement efforts that utilized many of these innovations, with less than satisfactory results.

The problem of providing a pluralistic, technologically advanced society with universal quality education continues to be a problem requiring a basic reform of our educational institutions. Because quality education has an important survival value in today's world, the absence of it becomes increasingly a matter of personal urgency. Quality education has become a value to most American households. However, it is difficult, if not impossible, for a monolithic system of public education to respond to the different conceptions of quality education held by a pluralistic society, and consequently these differences result in increased confrontations.

BEGINNINGS AND BACKGROUND

We can trace the roots of the current alternatives thrust in large measure to the civil rights movement of the 1960s. As the quest for desegregation gained momentum, parent, teacher, and community boycotts of public schools led to the establishment of temporary freedom schools in storefronts and church basements. Teachers, community residents, parents, and college volunteers collaborated to continue the education of black children in the "freedom schools."

An excerpt from a memorandum to Mississippi freedom school teachers participating in a summer project during the mid-1960s illustrates the departure from the standard program of the public schools:

> The purpose of the freedom schools is to provide an educational experience for students which will make it possible for them to challenge the myths of our society, to perceive more clearly its realities, and to find alternatives and, ultimately, new directions for action.

162

For many blacks and whites alike, the freedom schools provided a glimpse of alternative programs tailored to their perceived needs, which included sympathetic adults working with children, curriculum specifically geared to the self-determination concerns of black people, and involvement in the immediate political life of the community.

To pursue these educational concerns, those involved departed from established procedures by assuming a flexible stance that advocated expanding the boundaries of schooling to include the community and its resources, establishing smaller educational units to humanize the experience for those involved, and relating educational experience to the life of the community. These ingredients remain prevalent in the current alternative schools movement.

Another social trend that continues to contribute to alternative education is the so-called counterculture movement. Viewing public schools as repressive and authoritarian institutions reflecting the deteriorating values of the dominant society, members of the counterculture have attempted to sponsor alternative institutions that are free to develop new learning environments that are personally liberating and geared to individual and group life styles.

Participants in this search were quick to embrace the new educational philosophies of A. S. Neill, Ivan Illich, and a host of the so-called romantic education writers, such as Paul Goodman, John Holt, Herbert Kohl, Everett Reimer, and George Dennison. Underlying this philosophy is the central concern with individual freedom. A. S. Neill states his philosophy clearly: "My view is that a child is innately wise and realistic. If left to himself without adult suggestion of any kind, he will develop as far as he is capable of developing."[1]

To Illich and Reimer, schools, especially public (but also, perhaps, free schools) get in the way of real education. To them, the best idea, one that maximizes both freedom and individual development, is one that gives each person the right and the means for orchestrating his own distinctive plan.

---

[1]Quoted in Graubard, Allen. *Free the Children: Radical Reform and the Free School Movement.* New York: Pantheon Books, 1972. p. 11.

Another movement stimulating alternative education grows in part out of the British experience (including the World War II years) supporting the progressive principles of education articulated by John Dewey. This is the currently popular view of education variously called "British infant," "integrated day," "open," or "informal" education. While not as radical as the alternatives embraced by those in the counterculture category, the open classroom has become increasingly prevalent within the public system of education. Such books as *Crisis in the Classroom,* by Charles E. Silberman, helped popularize this philosophy with the general public. Moreover, teachers, school administrators, and professors have embraced it, rekindling a new interest in John Dewey and the progressive education movement of the earlier part of this century. While the open classroom advocates believe in giving the learner more freedom, they limit this freedom when it comes to determining the common content areas for which the school is responsible, such as the three R's, sciences, languages, and so forth. Open classrooms have become alternatives in which the learner is free to explore these academic areas in a more natural, personal, and experiential way. Teachers are more likely to be resources to the learner in these settings. In other words, there are still schools and classrooms, only now the structure is more informal.

These major movements helped highlight other alternatives that had either been around for years or were in recent operation due to growing consumer dissatisfaction. For instance, Montessori education became an important alternative. In New York City, Harlem Prep and the Street Academy became prominent specimens of schools that took public school casualties and made them success- ful college bound students. In Philadelphia, a school without walls triggered a nationwide awareness of the concept of the city as a classroom.

One other project, the voucher plan, has significantly influenced alternative education and deserves comment here. Growing out of free market economics, this idea was formulated by Milton Friedman at the University of Chicago and Christopher Jencks at Harvard University. Several Office of Economic Opportunity experiments in voucher education are currently in progress — for example, in Rochester and New Rochelle, New York, and Alum Rock, California.

In brief, the voucher plan calls for recasting education into a free market system in which each family is given a voucher worth a certain sum of money (usually enough to cover basic tuition) for each school-age child. This voucher is redeemable in any private or public school the family may choose after shopping around. Vouchers increase the purchasing power of the consumer and provide him with the right of choice.

Predictably, the voucher plan has elicited stormy, critical resistance from professional educators — especially those within the public schools, including the two major teacher organizations (NEA and AFT), who view the plan as a serious threat to public schools. However, the threat of having a voucher that would stimulate alternative schools *outside* the framework of public education has encouraged a movement for alternatives *within* the public schools themselves. Ironically, as an external threat, vouchers have helped to generate an internal reform effort, thus fulfilling in part their original purpose.

If we put these developments together, the alternative schools movement appears to fall somewhat as follows.

EXTERNAL FREE SCHOOL ALTERNATIVES — TOWARD RADICAL REFORM

Free schools have sprung up from coast to coast in the past five years. Estimates show that over 400 such schools exist. The life span for free schools is about two years, and their average enrollment is estimated at thirty-three students. The turnover rate of both students and teachers is high. Yet these schools have at times captured a spontaneous quality that any educator would applaud. Allen Graubard, in his book *Free the Children*, provides numerous examples of this quality. To cite one illustration, financial problems prompted a free school to use the public park as its educational setting. The facilities of the park — grassy grounds, trees, picnic tables, fireplaces, electric outlets, sinks, and sports fields — were fully utilized. Graubard quotes one of the leaders in this school as remarking:

The great virtue of the park has turned out to be its openness, which has greatly improved communications among and between the teachers and students. Everyone can see everyone else; we know where the students are and what they are doing and they know where we are and what we are doing. This has eliminated the need we felt last year for schedules. Furthermore, the teachers, instead of being sequestered to [their] rooms, with [their] groups of students, are now all together in the equivalent of one big room with all the students. The result is that we tend to work more closely together, to plan together, and coordinate our efforts much more than we ever did before. We don't, moreover, have to pay the price usually paid by large groups of people together in a big room — noise.[2]

The free school movement includes two wings. The free schools embracing an A. S. Neill philosophy that "freedom works" are primarily white middle class. The other wing of the free school movement emphasizes the school as a political environment in which to prepare the next generation for the active transformation of society. Obviously, those who consider the present fiber of society oppressive and unjust want to use free schools as the vehicle for societal renewal. In certain quarters, free schools reflect this political orientation. Some nonwhite schools as well as counter-cultural white schools have developed such formats. Descriptions of these schools can be found in the writings of activists such as Herbert Kohl, Jonathan Kozol, and Larry Cole, who themselves have developed free schools.

Free schools are not free in the financial sense; tuition is charged in most of them. Rather they are free from the ponderous bureaucracy of the massive public schools. They gain their momentum from the dedication of staff and parents. Teachers, for example, often work round the clock for subsistence wages. The important point is that there is a flexibility about these schools that represents a refreshing departure from the uniformity of public schools. Yet despite their aspirations of love, independence, self-direction, tolerance, and social responsiveness, their real impact, like that of the voucher plan, has not been to achieve radical reform out-

---

[2]Ibid., p. 81.

side the system of public schools, but rather to stimulate a more progressive, albeit moderate, reform effort *within* the public school system.

ALTERNATIVES WITHIN PUBLIC SCHOOLS — TOWARD PROGRESSIVE REFORM

Eighty-five percent of the nation's children attend public schools, and the bulk of our support for school improvement has been with this public education sector. Yet, while polls reveal that from 60 to 70 percent of those who use public schools express satisfaction with them, a critical mass of over 30 percent do not.

At a time when quality education is critical to the survival needs of the individual, the inability of our public schools to deliver quality education to significant numbers of users has resulted in frustration and retaliation. Many of those who are dissatisfied with the services of public schools and cannot afford private schools are now placing pressure on the public schools to change; those who are satisfied are trying to keep them as they are. This tug-of-war is beginning to affect everybody, sometimes disturbing the climate for those students who are profiting from standard school programs.

Caught in this cross fire are the professional educators, some of whom want to change the system, while others want to keep it the same. The result of these developments is an arena of power politics. Teachers, parents, and students are organizing into groups in order to achieve their own objectives. Desperate attempts to achieve quality are proposed; vouchers, performance contracting, and decentralization are fiercely opposed or supported. But each proposal is embattled by the politics of contemporary public education.

All the while, the costs of education rise as the results decline. A public that needs quality education demands accountability. The professionals — caught in the middle, trying to play by the norms of a system that was forged in the last century — resist this public review, become defensive, and look to their professional organizations for protection.

It is at this point that alternatives enter the picture. Catching on to the possibilities of developing other ways of educating a pluralistic student body, many teachers, parents, and students have begun to plan and implement alternative public schools. Teachers and administrators are swarming to workshops on open education. Hundreds of open classrooms have sprung up across the nation. (For instance, half the public schools in the state of North Dakota are considered to have open education.) Dozens of cities have begun their own versions of a school without walls.

These new alternatives differ sharply from the options traditionally available in public schools, such as vocational and special education, schools for dropouts and unwed mothers — tracks that carried with them a psychological classification that was negative when compared to those in the academic track. Moreover, these options were based more on chance than choice.

Before the alternatives movement, the child was assigned to a teacher whose teaching style may or may not have been congruent with the child's learning style. Some students responded, others did not, but neither teacher nor child had any choice in the matter.

Alternatives provide new opportunities for a match in teaching and learning styles. Choice lets students select programs that best fit them. Parents, who have played key roles as teachers at home, are in a good position to help select the alternative that best suits their child's distinctive pattern for learning. Similarly teachers can select the alternative that best supports their temperament and approach.

On a national basis, public school alternatives fall into several categories:

Classroom Alternatives. Some alternatives are found at the classroom level of neighborhood schools. For instance a first-grade teacher who favors open education may be the only one of three or four teachers who does. Hence she offers an option to any first-grade parents who wish an open classroom. The same principle applies at any grade level and with any legitimate educational pattern. A teacher may offer, for example, a Montessori, behavior modification, or a multiculture alternative classroom.

Alternative classrooms have certain advantages. They start slowly. Parents and students are introduced to options gradually and within the confines of their own neighborhood school. No one is forced to participate, and even if no overwhelming dissatisfaction with the school exists, alternative classrooms provide a choice to those parents or teachers who are dissatisfied.

Schools Within Schools. Another manifestation of alternative education is the idea of schools within schools, or mini-schools within a formerly single school. Any neighborhood elementary, junior or middle, or high school can become two or more smaller schools, each school emphasizing a distinctive pattern of education. Each subschool is made available to students, parents, and teachers by choice. There are many such schools, both urban and suburban, in various stages of development. Examples are:

☐ Haaren High School in New York City has a mini-school arrangement. This boys school is organized into a complex of fourteen mini-schools within a single building. Each mini-school has its own coordinator (who is responsible to the principal), 5 teachers, 1 street worker, and from 125 to 150 students.

☐ Walt Whitman High School in Montgomery County, Maryland, a middle class suburb, was one of the first to consider schools within schools similar to that of Haaren.

☐ After comprehensive planning, the high school in Quincy, Illinois, is now developing subschool alternatives. With extensive faculty, student, and community participation, a range of alternatives were sketched. The Education By Choice planning team proceeded to propose seven options, in terms of learning environments, as follows: 1) primarily teacher directed; 2) direction from both teacher and student, but for the most part teacher directed; 3) students and teachers together plan the experiences for the participants; 4) primary focus on considering the various areas of learning in relation to the arts; 5) primary focus on career orientation and preparation; 6) learning environment for special education students; and 7) learning environment for dropout prone students.[3]

☐ Jefferson Elementary, a K-3 school in Berkeley, California, offers three distinct options: traditional, individualized, and multicultural.

---

[3]"Education By Chioce." Application for Operational Grant under Elementary and Secondary Education Act, Public Law 89–10, Title III. Submitted by Quincy Public Schools, Quincy, Illinois, January 1973. pp. 31–32.

Schools within established schools have certain advantages: (1) they are convenient for parents, students, and teachers; (2) they provide opportunities for staff and community to participate in the development of alternatives; and (3) by using the facilities of an established school, they can make fuller use of existing resources such as physical education, music, and art facilities and counselors.

Their disadvantages are the problems that arise when any established social system is disturbed. There may be serious resistance by those who perceive alternatives as a threat to existing arrangements.

Separate Alternative Schools. A popular mode for alternative education is the development of a new public school in a facility separate from existing schools. The Village School in Great Neck, New York, is housed in a church basement. An abandoned missile base in Long Beach, New York, houses the Nike School. The Brown School in Louisville, Kentucky, uses a downtown office building for its location. Such descriptions are repeated across the country:

☐ The St. Paul Open School is actually a three-story former factory building now brightly decorated. This alternative school does not mandate attendance. Each student pursues his own tailored plan. The major learning areas — humanities, math, science, and industrial arts — make up the organization. Teachers serve as learning facilitators. The classrooms have an informal, family-type flavor to them (armchairs, sofas, tables, lamps, and so forth).

☐ The Murray Road Alternative School in Newton, Massachusetts, is located in a former elementary school and has about 115 college bound high school students and 8 teachers who participate in an informal educational community. With only British and American history required, there is great freedom to pursue individual interests and concerns.

Separate alternative schools have advantages. For one thing, they can start from scratch. Away from traditional constraints, they are free to mold new concepts of teaching and learning with sympathetic participants. However, disadvantages may arise if a separate alternative school becomes the only experiment in optional education, thus leaving out other parents, teachers, and students.

Systems of Alternative Schools. Several school systems have attempted to transform significant portions of their districts into alternative school patterns. For example, the Berkeley Unified School District in California has generated over twenty distinct alternative schools. Such alternatives fall into four broad patterns:

☐ *Multiculture schools.* These schools include children carefully selected on the basis of diversity of race, socioeconomic status, age, and sex. During part of the school day the students meet and work together. At other times they meet in their own ethnic, social, or educational groups, learning their own culture, language customs, history and heritage, or other special curriculum; later, these aspects are shared with the wider group.

☐ *Community schools.* The organization, curriculum, and teaching approach of these schools comes from outside the classroom — from the community. There may well be total parent involvement, with both the school day and week being extended into shared family life. There will be use of courts, markets, museums, parks, theaters, and other educational resources in the community.

☐ *Structured skills training schools.* These schools are graded and emphasize the learning of basic skills — reading, writing, and math. Learning takes place primarily in the classroom and is directed by either one teacher or a team of teachers working together.

☐ *Schools without walls.* The focus of these schools is the child and his development. The staff deals with the child rather than the subject. The schools are ungraded, and typically their style and arrangements are structured. Their goals are to have the students grow in self-understanding and self-esteem, learn how to cope with social and intellectual frustration, and master the basic and social skills through their own interests.

The School District of Philadelphia has a director of alternative programs who is coordinating the development of more than fifty alternative learning environments. These are modeled after open classrooms, schools without walls, and mini-schools, and include schools for students with special problems (such as gifted learners, academic failures, and disruptive and pregnant students).

The Minneapolis Public Schools have initiated a Southeast Alternatives Program serving all students in that area of the city. Elementary students can attend any of the following four types of schools:

1. A contemporary school, Tuttle, which offers curriculum innovations but maintains a teacher directed, structured curriculum and grade level school organization.
2. A continuous progress school, a part of Pratt and Motley Schools, in which each child advances at his own pace without regard to grade level and in which instruction is by teams and based on a carefully sequenced curriculum in basic skills.
3. An open school, Marcy, which combines flexible curriculum, scheduling, and age grouping in the style of the British infant schools. Children take a great deal of initiative for their own education, with the emphasis on pursuing their own interests.
4. A free school, the Minneapolis Free School, which extends through the twelfth grade. Students, parents, volunteers, and faculty develop the courses, and much off-campus experience is included. The initial enrollment of 70 students was expanded to 150 during 1972–73, and, according to school officials, a more structured, content oriented program was developed.[4]

The Alum Rock schools in California are participating in a voucher experiment. Parents in this pilot project receive vouchers worth about $680 for children in elementary school and about $970 for those in the seventh and eighth grades. Six schools and about 4,000 students are involved. Each of the schools offers at least two alternative programs. If the evaluation of the first year proves positive, the demonstration will expand during subsequent years.

POLITICS OF THE ALTERNATIVE MOVEMENT

It should be clear by now that, educationally speaking, alternatives run the entire gamut from student directed to teacher directed. On the one end, there are alternatives that accord the learner considerable freedom to determine how he will learn, what he will learn, when, where, and with whom. On the other end, these elements are predetermined by the school itself. In between, there is a vast range of possibilities. With such a perspective, we

---

[4]National School Public Relations Association. *Alternative Schools.* Washington, D.C.: the Association, 1973. p. 23.

can see the overall pattern into which are fitted free schools, open classrooms, ungraded schools, schools without walls, prep schools, and so forth.

A few words on the politics of the alternative schools movement are always appropriate. We have learned that any change involves politics. Alternatives as a change effort is significantly different from many other reform plans in that it is based on choice and is, therefore, voluntary. It is chosen by teachers, parents, and students by attraction; it is not superimposed. The "something for everybody" flavor of alternatives reduces the inevitable political conflict that results when people have no choice in the reform proposal being implemented.

No real reform can be achieved without the support of the front line agents — teachers, parents, and students. Alternatives are grassroots oriented and cater to these three basic publics. The role of the school administrator is to provide an enabling structure. This means giving basic information on alternatives to interested parties and arranging and facilitating meetings among teachers, parents, and students.

Alternatives often run into resistance when they make exaggerated claims following a negative diagnosis of the standard process in the public schools. Such behavior by advocates of alternative schools only solicits resistance. First, the "blasting" of what exists makes those associated with standard education feel inferior, a mood hardly conducive to cooperation. Second, projecting high expectations of the proposed alternatives serves both to increase the resentment of those in the standard process and plants the seeds of frustration for those participating in the alternative itself. No one alternative can do it all.

It would be a far better approach for those in the alternatives movement to indicate that the standard process is an alternative that works for many, but not for everyone. There are teachers and students who would profit from an entirely different educational approach. Whatever the proposed alternative, it is, at best, another legitimate way of offering a choice. Since each alternative is aimed at the same common educational objectives, the idea is to develop different means to common ends. Evaluation, of course, should be built into all alternatives, including consumer satisfaction.

In very practical terms, preventing political resistance may mean something as simple as avoiding a particular label for the alternative, such as "humanistic," "open," or "individualized," which implies that other alternatives, including the standard, are "inhuman," "closed," or "unindividualized" — a verdict certain to cause defensiveness.

Most important, a proposed alternative should not carry a price tag that makes it more expensive than what already exists. Strong attempts to keep the per student expenditure the same will enhance its attractiveness. Furthermore, wherever possible, alternatives should help use existing resources differently and more effectively. Some alternatives actually cut certain costs. The School Without Walls in Philadelphia, for example, does not need a school building and can save on construction costs. The St. Paul Open School reports that because it utilizes many volunteers and student self-direction, the per pupil cost is actually less than the average for the city.

By far the greatest danger facing alternatives is that the movement will be viewed as a fad. Education has had its share of them: team teaching, programmed instruction, humanizing the schools, and so on. Ironically, these movements were all intended to be services, but unfortunately we have fallen into the box of thinking up a theme for each year, as though by discussing it we had taken care of the matter. It would be tragic for the alternatives movement to fall victim to such faddism. Certainly educators like John Bremer and organizations like the National Consortium on Options in Public Education at Indiana University are emphasizing the virtues of alternatives in educational reform.

Our experience to date with the infant alternative public school movement has taught us certain ground rules that need to be applied if we are to minimize problems and to guide the legitimization process:

1. Alternatives are not superimposed, but are a matter of choice for all participants — teachers, parents, and students.
2. Alternatives are viewed as another way of providing education alongside the existing pattern, which continues to be legitimate. They are different from special programs for dropouts, unwed mothers, and so forth.

3. They do not practice exclusivity.
4. They do not make exaggerated claims of accomplishments that may be deceptive in the long run.
5. They are aimed at a broad, common set of unlimited educational objectives. Alternative public schools are responsible to the public for comprehensive cognitive and affective goals that cannot be compromised; these include basic skills, learning-to-learn skills, talent development, socialization of basic societal roles (citizen, consumer, worker), and self-concept development.
6. They do not cost more money than existing per student expenditures.

Significant numbers of individual teachers, parents, and students could be attracted to alternative education if given the opportunity. But teachers belong to strong professional organizations that must also be supportive if alternatives are to have a chance of working. Thus far, the NEA has generally favored alternatives and has featured the theme in its meetings. The AFT has remained somewhat neutral. However, as alternatives within the public schools grow, and as more teachers become involved actively, the attitude of both major teacher associations is bound to be affected. Their leadership will certainly be welcomed during the years ahead.

On the other hand, if teacher organizations turn against the alternatives movement, then conflicts among teachers, parents, and students are sure to follow. Such collision can hardly serve the best interests of children, the public, or the profession.

During the remainder of this decade, we should see more growth in alternative education. What can result is a gradual expansion of the framework of public education to include many former alternative private schools. Over time, we could emerge with a redefined system of public education that is diverse, self-renewing, and responsive to a pluralistic society.

An exciting vision of a re-formed,
person-oriented school that will be a
"helping system" for enabling
adolescents to gain control
of their own lives.

The Helping System: Fostering Autonomy in Adolescents

MOSHE SMILANSKY
Professor of Educational Sciences
University of Tel Aviv

DONALD P. SANDERS
Professor of Education
and Associate Director
Center for Human Resource Research
Ohio State University

The process called modernization is endemic in societies around the world. Based on the methods of science, technological innovation, and on their consequences in human institutions, attitudes, and fates, modernization imposes enormous challenges to human personalities and institutions. It may not be an exaggeration to assert that the processes of modernization carry with them the potentiality of the destruction of civilization through erosion of the bases for human security, personality development, and simple self-esteem and satisfaction.

The authors wish to acknowledge with gratitude the contributions made to this article by their research associate and colleague Deborah Dye Coleman.

EFFECTS OF MODERNIZATION

Modernization, spreading and deepening in its impact at an accelerating rate, confronts people with an increasingly wide and complex set of choices — occasions on which individual decisions are required in order to deal with opportunities or problems. At the same time, modernization processes are removing or weakening the traditional institutional arrangements for supporting and developing effective self-concepts, conceptual tools, and frames of reference, which earlier provided bases for understanding and guides for personal decision-making.

As modernization flourishes it affects increasingly diverse segments of the society and additional institutions. For example, technological discoveries in the area of contraception increasingly are available to larger proportions of the populations of modernizing societies and are influencing the institution of the family and the institutions of schooling. These ramifying pressures raise for the institutions of society no less than for the individual human members of it, an obligation to change, to adapt, to adjust to new problems, to new opportunities, and to new potentialities. The basic point about modernization can be made in a sentence: modernization imposes on all institutions of society a requirement for reform or adaptation. In many places in the world this requirement is pressing very heavily on the institutions of education.

Having briefly considered the impact of the process called modernization, let us now consider the question: Who are the culturally disadvantaged? The concept "culturally disadvantaged" can be used to describe social groups (ethnic, religious, social class, regional, etc.) that, as modernization proceeds, are found in a position of low status, power, and influence relative to the dominant groups at that stage and pattern of modernization in a given society.

Even though there may be general agreement on the definition of the concept "culturally disadvantaged" as given above, there are wide differences of opinion among lay and professional persons alike as to the identification of groups as culturally disadvantaged and the specific factors or circumstances that contribute to their being so. Many feel that the designation of a group as being culturally disadvantaged is but an expression of prejudice by the representatives of the dominant cultural group. They prefer to use the concept "culturally different." Some claim that it is the influence of differential social class opportunities that causes persons to become culturally disadvantaged, and would rather refer to them as "socially disadvantaged." Others, who view economic factors to be of primary importance, see the culturally disadvantaged as simply "the poor," those who have little or no money.

Our assumption is that these generalizations are only partial explanations of the causes and behavioral manifestations of what we describe as being culturally disadvantaged. We prefer, instead, to utilize a single concept as a generalized basis for explaining both the causes and the behavioral manifestations. This concept refers to the *configuration* of sociocultural forces dominated by *cultural pattern.*

Each group, whether it be of ethnic, social class, economic, or geographic origin, possesses its own unique cultural patterns as well as its own social interests, which contradict and clash with the expectations of the cultural patterns and interests of the dominant group and the institutions that serve as its agents. As a result, the group is unable to obtain certain sociocultural privileges and opportunities and consequently becomes culturally disadvantaged. Any sociocultural group that remains in a certain sociometric position for a long period of time acquires certain attitudes, norms of value orientation, and behavior patterns of its own which are transmitted to the next generation through the socialization process of family interaction and childrearing and which are exhibited in schooling in the form of abilities, skills, knowledges, and motivations.

When we label a group culturally disadvantaged, we are not making a value judgment regarding that group's culture. For example, when we say that children of immigrants to Israel from Kurdistan, Yemen, or Tripolitania are culturally disadvantaged, we are not condemning the value orientation or behavior patterns of the traditional, agrarian, Moslem societies. On the contrary, we are aware of many positive features of life in that environment, and we might even agree with someone who says he prefers these traditional, rural, patriarchal, religious patterns of life. But once

178

these immigrant children were brought from developing countries to Israel, a modern country, they were forced to compete in schools in which the expectations and patterns of interaction were those required in an urban, industrialized, secular, democratic, and predominantly middle-class society dominated by Western European patterns of interaction; patterns that are more advanced in the modernization process. In this situation, relative to students of Western European background, they became culturally disadvantaged.

Parallel examples exist in other countries and cultures. In the United States, children of black, Puerto Rican, American Indian, and Mexican-American parentage develop cultural values and attitudes which are different from those of the predominant white culture. Numerous immigrant children suffered the same fate when other ethnic groups first came to America. In the same way many children of farmers, whether in Russia, Germany, the United States, or any other country, become culturally disadvantaged when the modernization process in their country becomes more compatible with the value orientation and patterns of behavior of the middle-class urban dweller. The rural, traditional culture of farm children simply does not prepare them to cope successfully in achieving their own goals or to adjust to the expectations of modernizing social institutions. A similar fate has befallen children from lower class families of dockworkers, miners, or rail operators in cities such as Hamburg or Amsterdam. Having been reared and socialized according to expectations in the closed system of the family, neighborhood, and community school, they are unprepared to function in the open system with the mobility and wide-ranging interactions that come with the process of modernization.

In short, it is not the quality of a given culture that determines whether a group becomes disadvantaged but, rather, it is the relative ability of the group to function according to the cultural norms influenced by the modernization process as established by the dominant group and accepted by the group under consideration.

Modernization places oppressively heavy obligations on human personalities, particularly those of persons from culturally disadvantaged groups. The individual must accept personal responsibility in unprecedented form for active, self-directive participation in a rapidly changing and increasingly complex social environment. Formal organizations take over provision of services and support to the individual in an impersonalized and often bureaucratic form. These services and support in an earlier age were provided by family and friends who knew and cared about the welfare of the human person as a whole being. As the support structures assisting the individual become differentiated and formally organized as public services, they may become less effective because they must serve many "cases" on a functional basis rather than a few persons on a holistic basis. Responsibility for protecting personality and defending individual integrity devolves upon the individual alone or upon the individual with support from a weakened extended family. Only the prepared, well-equipped, secure, self-directive, autonomous person capable of looking out for his own self-development and able to cooperate with others able to support him can flourish under these conditions. In our view, therefore, the goal of educational services to be provided in modernizing societies should be to cultivate the capacity of each of its members to be in charge of his own learning and developmental processes.

SELF-DEVELOPMENT AND COPING

We view self-development and coping capacities as skills which can be, and naturally are, learned by all men. In fact, the development of these skills is fundamental to the process of modernization and to the evolution of civilization, which, as Dunn argues, can be seen as a process of social learning.[1] Globally speaking, we see self-development as including three main categories of capacities:
1. The capacity to be aware or to sense;
2. The capacity to understand and comprehend;
3. The capacity to engage the environment (to transact with it, to decide or choose with regard to it, to act in it).
When we speak about cultivating these capacities in another per-

---

[1]Edgar S. Dunn, Jr. *Economic and Social Development — A Process of Social Learning.* Baltimore: The Johns Hopkins Press, 1971.

son, we refer to "person development." When we speak of his being in charge of his own development, we use the term "self-development." It is our fundamental assumption that most persons can learn to engage in self-development and that there is a threshold level of learning of this capacity which, if reached, provides a basis for essentially infinite further refinement and cultivation. We assert that it is the obligation of schools to enable all the young to reach at least that threshold of self-development.

We view man holistically and recognize that learning and behavior involve both "knowing that" and "knowing how." While for some purposes it may be useful to distinguish between cognitive learning and affective learning, for our purposes such a distinction is distortive. In our view *all learning must be affectively based and cognitively oriented.* Motivation precedes knowing; conscious, explicit knowing is the aim of learning.

Our assertion is that if a person is highly aware (if he has a well-refined capacity to perceive stimuli originating both internally and externally), advanced in understanding (if he has refined images and the capacity to use them to reflect on, to fit or to recognize a lack of fit between his knowings and the responses of his environment), and if he is skilled in engaging his environment (if he has refined capacities to transact with persons, with tangible and intangible phenomena in his environment), then he is well-equipped to live successfully in modernizing societies.

To be more specific, we conceive that the process of modernization requires that all persons who would live effectively in modernizing societies have certain capacities:
1.   Openness to experience and adaptability — an orientation toward change with the ability to project opportunity in it rather than to be fearful of it;
2.   Self-identity — a conscious awareness of himself, knowing who he is in relation to others; explicit knowing of the differentiated self and positive self-esteem is a necessary base for secure, autonomous, and self-directive behavior;
3.   Literacy and numeracy — the capacity to be aware and to engage in modern society requires these basic skills;
4.   Ability to relate to others — involves capacities such as listen-

ing, empathizing, presenting the self, helping others, and the like, in order to build supportive interpersonal relationships in a mobile society with many relationships of a temporary nature;

5. Ability to define and solve problems — the capacity to delineate and focus problems, set criteria, identify alternative courses of action, and to predict the consequences of choices is vital in flexible, dynamic social circumstances;

6. Ability to make a differential or specialized contribution to the community through taking specific roles and being able to do so effectively in cooperation with other specialists is essential in complex modern economies and communities;

7. Ability to learn readily and to be willing or ready to do so — an essential characteristic if a person is to remain capable of engaging effectively over a lifetime in a changing society;

8. Ability to use cognitive processes and content (images in the Boulding sense[2]), which are relevant and effective in understanding and coping with the problems and opportunities faced. Undoubtedly the content required varies substantially with the present and desired future social circumstances of individuals as well as with their individual learning patterns. It is vital, however, for each individual to be aware of and able to comprehend the salient dimensions of his social environment and how to relate himself to it.

The concept of *coping* is central to our concerns and closely related to self-development. We conceive coping to be active behavior of an individual in dealing with problems and opportunities in his environment. It involves:

1. Self-awareness — knowledge of who he is;

2. Values — knowledge of his own priority structure;

3. Repertoire of behaviors — knowledge of possible optional behaviors;

4. Capacity to predict — ability to estimate consequences;

5. Self-discipline — ability to choose, pursue, and follow through on a self-chosen course of action;

---

[2]Kenneth Boulding. *The Image — Knowledge in Life and Society*. Ann Arbor: University of Michigan Press, 1961, paperback.

6.   Capacity for social interaction — ability to transact effectively with other persons.

The Significance of Self-Development and Coping. Basically, there are two principal reasons for our concern for cultivating the self-development and coping capacities of individuals, one based on our values and one based on our interpretation of social dynamics.

We view the good society as a democracy in which each individual has the opportunity and the capacity to participate as a free and equal, though unique, person. A free person in a democracy is one who, knowing who he is, chooses and acts to overcome his problems and to utilize his potentialities for purposes and goals of his own choice in collaboration with other free persons. Every person's ability to cope is based on his view of himself: awareness of who he is, his origins, his experiences, his aptitudes, opportunities, values, and goals. Self-directive participation in a democratic society is our ideal and our value base.

We interpret social change as a process of dynamic modernization, as was described earlier. Given that interpretation, we recognize that modernization is irreversible, persistent, and that its principal consequence for the individual person is to make a wider range of options or choices available to a progressively larger proportion of the population. Therefore, more persons require skill in making choices as modernization progresses. The choices or options with which we are concerned may be called strategic choices, those of major magnitude in terms of their consequences and the degree to which they influence the configuration of possible options in the future.

Industrialization and progressive differentiation in society produce the following kinds of strategic options for larger proportions of the population:

1.   More opportunities for education, continuing education, and specialized programs of education;
2.   More occupational specialties, many requiring progressively greater levels of knowledge and skill;
3.   More functional relations with a larger set of people who are purveyors of services, products, and obligations.

Technological development opens to individuals more options such as a wider range of potential mates, friends, living patterns, housing and entertainment possibilities, and a wider range of choices in family planning and childrearing. Secularization and expanded communications make possible a much wider range of choices with regard to possible ideologies, values, attitudes, and ideas.

When an individual in a democracy is confronted by a wider range of strategic options, he needs to be aware of their existence, to be able to take advantage of them, and to be able to choose from among them wisely in terms of his own value structure, needs, and criteria; otherwise, he is relatively disadvantaged in comparison with those who are able to utilize those possibilities. As we indicated earlier, the disadvantaged may be conceived as those who, relatively speaking, have less power and are less well-equipped to live in modernizing society in its present stage and pattern and as it changes into the future.

For these reasons, therefore, we believe that democratic societies have an obligation to enable their members, particularly the young and especially the disadvantaged, to learn to be fully participating in freedom and responsibility. This is the basic aim of schooling as we see it: *to support the young in learning how to be in charge of their own lives and to cope with the conditions of modernizing society.*

Being in charge of one's own self-development and coping capacity can also contribute, we expect, to a reduction in the incidence of human failure, which seems to increase along with modernization. We would expect that the disadvantaged, by being more fully able to pursue their self-fulfillment, would be less subject to:

1. The failure syndrome now associated with schooling;
2. Mental illness;
3. Isolation and anomie often caused by an inability to choose associates well and to accept their assistance;
4. Fatalism, acceptance of fate and a feeling of powerlessness;
5. Anti-social behavior.

Reduction of the frequency of occurrence of these negative states in disadvantaged persons could be seen as the goal of social policy with regard to schooling as viewed from a rehabilitative perspective. Our fundamental and preferred perspective, however, is one of the prevention of negative effects and the positive cultivation of human potentiality.

A Preventive Strategy. How does one learn to be in charge of one's own life under modernizing social conditions? That is a central question in modernizing democratic societies, and one for which answers must be sought vigorously. The weakened extended family, the mobile nuclear family, and other institutions in their traditional forms cannot accomplish the task. Schools in their customary form do not, although schools are social institutions deliberately created to share responsibility for socialization of the young in cooperation with other socializing institutions such as the family, the church, the community, and the peer group. When these other institutions change in response to the pressures of modernization, schools too must change if effective socialization is to occur. Schools which once were appropriate to the task may no longer be so. Schools designed to transmit a relatively stable culture, to socialize the young differentially according to their social status, to select the able or talented for higher status positions (and to select *out* those deemed unable or untalented) are not adequate in secular, democratic, industrialized, and urbanized modern society. They are not adequate to the task either from the point of view of the society as a whole or from the point of view of individuals who must learn how to live a satisfying life in that society. For these reasons, we believe, schools must be reformed.

But we also believe that the conventional responses of schools to the demands of modernization are inadequate. Generally, they have simply added new programs, usually of a compensatory nature, intended to provide additional support to the disadvantaged to enable them to succeed in school as traditionally defined and operated. Spending more money, adding more programs, making quantitative but not qualitative adaptations has been the generally adopted solution. There are serious limits to this type of adaptation: resources of money, personnel, and facilities are limited, and so are the capacities of the young to endure repetitive, "irrelevant," ineffective, "unreal," and interminable schooling. The solutions generally have been based on some notion of "deficit" in the target population and have been intended to provide rehabilitative effects to overcome the deficits (in reading, in employment skills, and so on) of that population.

While under some conditions rehabilitative programs no doubt will continue to be required, we suggest in addition, and potentially in place of many such programs, that a preventive strategy should be pursued. Such a strategy would seek to work with persons at as early an age as is feasible; it would invest in their learning as heavily as necessary to facilitate their learning to be in charge of their own lives. Such a strategy of public policy could be expected, we believe, to reduce but not eliminate the need for publicly supported programs of rehabilitative and maintenance types. It could be expected in the long run, however, both to conserve public resources and to increase the numbers of citizens with the capacity to arrange fulfilling lives for themselves.

The Target Population — Adolescents. We believe that such a strategy should be pursued by creating social institutions which focus on cultivating the self-development and coping capacities of adolescents. The stage of human life called adolescence is potentially the richest age for fostering self-development and coping capacities for several principal reasons.

First, adolescence is the period in life when the young person confronts directly the problem of differentiating his personal identity and begins to make the strategic decisions and choices which will determine ultimately who he is and how he will live his life.

Secondly, available evidence in human development indicates three basic characteristics of adolescence that suggest that this may be the optimum state for a person to confront himself in his environment cognitively but on an affective base. This is the stage of formal operations at which fundamental cognitive processes transform. The adolescent is able to deal with hypothetical reasoning and to confront issues "as if" they had been experienced. It also is the stage at which a person has capacity for a higher stage of moral judgment — a period of feeling and searching for the true, the good, the ideal. Further, it is the stage at which there is a need for identification with and support from the peer group. An adolescent needs peer group interactions for intellectual, emotional, and social development.

Further, in contrast to the many psychologists who consider that adolescence marks a period when it is too late to bring about major personality and social changes, and to those parents, teachers, and psychologists who view adolescence negatively as a period of problems and difficulties, we suggest that it offers the potentially most promising and rewarding stage for initiating social development through change in the individual.

There are eight psychological and sociological characteristics of adolescence which, if perceived and used by schools in organization, curriculum, and expectations as positive forces, can serve powerfully to enable adolescents to be creative, active, self-directive participants in building social systems in which they live:

1. *Marginality.* Adolescence is a marginal position. The adolescent, already not a child, is not accepted as an adult in society. He is in a position of changing orientation, of changing roles, and status. He is open to new propositions and, therefore, the school can orient him toward continued socialization of desired values and behaviors.

2. *Potential Awareness.* The adolescent has matured enough to be able to become aware of the relations between his environment and himself (the configurations of his parents' sociocultural setting, his early experiences, expectations of the present and future, and the like). He can be made responsible for his future and encouraged to confront his "as if," predicted reality. He can be an active partner in a cognitive and affective reorientation-resocialization-development process. By coping creatively with the present reality of his life, he can experience growth.

3. *Differentiation.* Adolescence is an age of accelerated differentiations according to age, sex, abilities, knowledge, aptitudes, motivations, and so on, which are influenced by both hereditary and environmental factors. These differences can be perceived and realized as positive potentialities if they are approached positively, being legitimized and fostered rather than denied through static evaluation of the individual against a fixed, stereotypic standard.

4. *Cognitive Maturity.* Adolescence is an age of movement toward "formal operations" in cognitive development. Those helped to reach this potentiality find new worlds opened to them; they can abstract relationships, comprehend unexperienced po-

tentialities and transcend apparently fixed boundaries. They can cognitively master the place of man and social institutions within systems of differential dimensions of time and space. Therefore, for them direct experience is not the only possible reality.

5. *Searching for Self-Identity.* Adolescence is an age of affection — feeling, social searching, and commitment. Because of the adolescent's marginal and changing position created by his widening horizons, his search for an answer to the many questions opened in the movement through childhood toward the adult world, and the loneliness encountered in facing those who do not understand him, and secondly, because of his present needs and aspirations, he is ready to accept whatever promises to be different, better, or ideal. A school that can help him to identify the potentialities in his environment and assist in learning to take advantage of them, that has an affective approach, even in cognitive confrontation, will be building a student who is active, feeling, and committed, instead of passive and alienated.

6. *Peer Influence.* Within a school, peer groups can be utilized as reference groups toward new and diverse value orientations. By systematically and flexibly composing groups for different purposes, assigning them appropriate responsibilities, and facilitating their emergence and maturation as contributing forces in the system, the stereotypic, mass-oriented single reference group may be replaced by a variety of divergent, emerging models.

7. *Family Influence.* Since the adolescent is living with his family of origin, he has need for their support in his present crisis situation and in his need for self-identity formation. Further, on the basis of his new orientation he can support his family. This reciprocal support can be fostered through a good system of home and school relations.

8. *Crisis.* Adolescence should be an age of tension or crisis. To actualize the potentiality of adolescence, we should see it as an age of potential tension and crisis; we should value, foster, and capitalize on crisis. The extent to which the adolescent will be able to confront reality, develop new insights, and define personal commitments will depend on his initiation into crisis under the supportive guidance of the school.

Finally we recognize that the adolescent population represents the next generation of adults. They are, or soon will be, entering as adult members of the community, the polity, and the economy. As parents, they will be rearing the next generation and will do so on the basis of what they know and aspire to for themselves and for their children. If they are alienated, poverty stricken, or fatalistically subject to the whims of forces beyond their ken, it is likely that their children, too, will be enmeshed in the cycle of poverty and disadvantagement. On this basis alone, it seems to us, a preventive strategy directed at disadvantaged adolescents is desirable. To do otherwise is to jeopardize the positive fulfillment of two generations.

The Reform of Schooling for Adolescents. How might school reform be undertaken as a preventive strategy for enabling the members of a modernizing society to cope and to pursue self-development? Basically, we believe, by treating school as an experimental proposition and by systematic, persistent, and deliberate efforts to answer this fundamental question: What might the schools be like which will foster learning by adolescents to cope with the problems and opportunities of modernizing societies?

We do not know in detail how this question can be answered. It is our assumption that no single type of school will be appropriate for all adolescents, but that all adolescents should have access to an appropriate school, given their individual needs and the sociocultural configuration of their community. The task is to create and to test alternative models of potentially appropriate schools.

In various countries, substantial experimentation has been going forward with innovative, but usually compensatory or rehabilitative, partial programs directed at improving content- and skill-oriented abilities of a specific population. While these programs may be successful in terms of their limited objectives, they have little or no effect on the overall development of the majority of students. The reason for such failure, we assume, is that incremental program development inside a schooling context which is little changed is too weak to produce the needed results. Changing the mathematics curriculum or the science curriculum or the guidance process in a social organization unchanged in other respects cannot produce more than marginal positive effects. Our assumption is that metamorphic development is needed which can change the climate and the interpersonal relationships within a school; changes which will produce forces that can be brought to bear in the learning process which are powerful enough to have fundamental effects on students' capacity to be in charge of their own lives. For this reason the *focus must be on the whole school,* not on a single part of it.

We assume that it is now time to concentrate attention on creating schools which can begin to deal with the holistic nature of the learning and schooling processes, and which can begin to search for answers to the fundamental questions stated above. What might such schools be like?

TOWARD THE DEVELOPMENT OF A HELPING SYSTEM

We suggest that the required school should be seen as an active, self-directive, developing social organization responsible for helping adolescents to be in charge of their own lives. Transforming the concept of school toward the concept of a "helping system" is what is required, in our view. A helping system is an alternative conception of schooling, but it is broader than that concept, and it is more powerful in its potentiality than schools normally are.

What Is a Helping System? A helping system takes as its central focus a specified group of adolescent clients with their particular needs, potentialities, backgrounds, problems, and opportunities. Its members see themselves as part of an organization with particular patterns of interaction and certain tangible and intangible resources of know-how, materials, equipment, buildings, and so forth. These persons see themselves cooperatively sharing the task of facilitating the learning of those client adolescents.

All of these statements might be made about a school, but most schools do not understand those statements as a helping system must. A helping system is a flexible, responsible, client-centered organization. A school conventionally is a rigid, nonresponsible, school-centered organization of teachers, administrators, and counsellors which accepts client adolescents, requires them to undertake specified common experiences in particular ways, and approves those who fit while rejecting those who do not. This is a subtle point, very difficult to express, but essential to understanding the meaning of a helping system.

A helping system, as contrasted with the conventional school, differs largely in the way it approaches the task of fostering adolescents. Its orientation is not so much the teaching of the young as it is the facilitation of their learning processes. Learning experiences, especially those intended to foster self-development and coping capacities, must be individualized and personalized in order to maximize their value. Reasons for this are that learning is an individual matter based on the cognitive style, experiential background and affective base of each person. To be effective, any learning experience must be fitted to the individual's perspective. This means that flexibility in the design, sequence, duration, and media of learning must be available. The fixed schedule and organization of learning experiences in most schools is contradictory to this requirement.

A helping system's mode of operation must be responsible, not permissive. It must treat the individual student as responsible for his own learning if it is to achieve its goal of students learning to be in charge of their own learning process and to be self-directive. Behavior of all staff members must reinforce this responsibility, and they must be responsible for their own learning in turn. Further, since the system is sponsored by society as a public institution, it must be responsible in fulfilling its charge to socialize the young toward the necessary perspectives and capacities required for active participation in democratic society. In another dimension, the system must be responsible for its professional members as well, providing them with the support necessary to enable them to perform their roles effectively and in a personally satisfying way. Schools, by and large, avoid responsibility; this phenomenon underlies current cries for "accountability." No individual is seen as responsible for any specific learning in most schools. Too often, school people tend to attribute deficiencies in students to the students themselves or to their family background, not to the school and to its professional staff.

A helping system takes as its focus the developing, growing student and seeks to arrange ways to facilitate that growth and to support him while he confronts it. A conventional school takes the subject matter as given, and requires the student to accept it or to get out. The helping system adjusts subject matter and instruction to the individual's growth pattern and guarantees success to each student. With this general perspective in mind, let us now turn to some detailed proposals intended to elaborate this concept of the school as a helping system.

Organizational Patterns. The population to be served should include a wide range of diversity of background, interests, ability, and ethnic origin, so it can reflect as fully as possible the heterogeneity of the community in which the adolescent will live. Since the school is a social system, systematic grouping and building peer units is a vehicle for facilitating student coping ability, intellectual growth, social adjustment, and emotional maturity. At the same time, the sequential process of creation of a new school may limit the diversity of persons immediately available for composing groups representative of the full range of age, interest, ability, and social groups. Grouping should be planned flexibly, taking into account four main criteria:

1. The needs of individuals for security and autonomy in cooperative learning;

2. The needs of individuals for association over time with peer groups that may serve as reference and support groups;

3. The needs of individuals for participation in groups selected for their value for interaction and modeling;

4. The needs of individuals for participation in a flexible, open-ended system that can accept changes in individuals' aptitudes and interests as well as changes in value orientation and attitudes, thereby supporting a person toward achieving a new self-chosen goal.

A second issue is to determine what administrative arrangements are necessary in a system that stimulates creative exploration by students and professionals working in a particular place, while simultaneously guaranteeing to students, parents, and society mastery of basic academic skills and preparation of adolescents for responsible citizenship. Building such a responsible relationship between the school and its sponsoring public agency (the local school district, for example) would require clear definitions of responsibility, granting to the school the right for autonomous development and experimentation, allocation of authority to the responsible school leaders, and the provision of adequate financial support.

Beyond the need for a responsible relationship between the helping system and the external context in which it must survive and toward which it is responsible, another issue is the building of similarly responsible relationships among those persons who comprise the internal environment of the school, the students, and the staff. Specifically, several basic types of role assignments in addition to other teaching, counselling, or administering roles should be expected of all personnel. These are designed to facilitate the capacity of adults for assuming responsibility toward adolescents as persons as well as toward adolescents as students.

To ensure that teachers and administrators, as cooperative partners in a social system with adolescents, will be involved at the center of crisis, confrontation, learning, and celebration by adolescents who grow and learn together, each member of the school staff should be assigned to work part-time as a personal tutor with a small group of adolescents. In this way these adults can get to know a few students very well. Secondly, all administrators will teach as part of their responsibilities. In this role administrators can understand adolescent problems as they relate to learning in school and, therefore, better perform administrative duties. Finally, since both of these requirements help provide a relatively high ratio of adults per student, each adult in the school can serve multiple roles as tutor, role model, facilitator of personal development, and friend. In the helping system, teachers and administrators, as well as other adults in the school, are people who volunteer to serve as facilitators of, and supportive agents for, the development of adolescents in a democratic social system. They also are partners with students and community members in defining problems and experimenting with alternative modes of coping with these problems. To provide additional opportunities for adolescents to interact with adults of different backgrounds, ages, professions, and interests, the concept of school personnel needs to be enlarged to include members of the community who wish and are capable of participating in teaching and counselling roles.

The goal is to build teams of people with different abilities and interests who can cooperate to achieve a mutually desired end: facilitation of the self-development and coping capacities of all students who attend that particular school. Therefore, community members and professional educators must be sought who are ready to share a common value orientation, and who can enrich each other by offering different perceptions for dealing with similarly defined problems. In the same way that teams must be built so that teachers extend the abilities of each other, teams of students and teachers must be planned so that teachers are perceived as supportive to adolescents. Complementary teams of teachers, men and women, young and old, experienced and inexperienced, should work together according to their ability to serve as models, reference groups, and facilitators of the growth of the adolescent. Teachers are needed who can directly interact with students, who can work with parents, and who will be active in community affairs. Teachers and administrators, as members of a learning community, must play many roles: as models for adolescents, sources of information, partners in learning, and as persons who care what happens to each other.

A Responsible, Not a Permissive School. The school seen as a helping system is responsible to adolescents, to parents, and to the community. The helping system serves responsibly in supporting, intervening, teaching, and counselling roles to help adolescents to understand their present personalities, attitudes, and knowings which are products of the past and which establish the starting point for building their potential futures. Further, it is responsible for helping adolescents develop the skills and knowledge they need to take positive steps toward accomplishing personal goals.

Reciprocally, the helping system assumes that adolescents are responsible, growing persons and should be treated accordingly. School organization, social climate, patterns of learning, peer association, student-teacher relations, and diagnosis and evaluation can be used to facilitate students' learning to be responsible. Interpersonal relationships and teaching strategies should be aimed toward demonstrating that adolescents are responsible for their own development according to their increasing awareness and capacity for coping with their present and future life situation.

Adolescents also need to share in responsibility for facilitating the self-development of their peers and for the maintenance and development of the school and community.

Another part of the school's responsibility is to recognize that the home is the primary unit of socialization for youth and the basic unit for the support and security of the adolescent. For this reason, the school must interact in cooperation with, and in support of, the home to support collaboratively the adolescent's growth. This cooperation between home and school is both necessary and possible because each has a different role, different cultural pattern, and different interactive framework; they share, however, responsibility for the socialization of the same person.

In reflecting on the impact of modernization on the institutions of the school and the family it seems possible to pose several basic propositions that may be of use in defining possible new relations between these two agencies. We suggest that these may be particularly important when the school serves a heterogeneous population and when students come from culturally disadvantaged backgrounds.

1.   It is important to recognize that the home and the school are different, though parallel, institutions for the socialization of the young person. School is not a continuation of the home. Home and the school differ in their roles, status, and mode of operation, in what they demand of the child, and in the form of their rewards for the child.

2.   The adolescent must be helped to understand the different role patterns and expectations of the home and of the school. He must and can learn to play different roles (of the son or daughter in the home and of the student in the school) and benefit from the complementary and supportive contributions of each kind of experience.

3.   The home must be helped to understand the role of the school, its organization, cultural patterns, and expectations. It must learn to assist the school in helping young persons to progress by supporting the child in his effort toward developing autonomy and a positive self-identity. In this way, the home can help to build the capability of the child to cope with the potentialities and expecta-

tions of modernizing society as they are represented by the school, peers, and the community. Taken together, the home and the school can develop anticipatory socialization processes toward future alternatives for each young person with regard to identity, family building, and participation in community development.

4. The school must learn to understand the cultural patterns of the home, its socioeconomic conditions, and potentialities for supporting the child. The school must learn to interact with the home in ways that will maximize the potentiality of each to provide students with experience and the basic security needed for gradually developing autonomy and increasing personal responsibility.

School-Community Interaction. In addition to working with the home in support of adolescent development, the school should systematically build reciprocal relationships with other agencies of the community which can serve as additional resources for instruction, role modeling, and expanding awareness of adolescents. We suggest that there are four avenues of interaction between the helping system and the community at large which should be explored.

1. In virtually all towns and cities of any size there are many institutions which can serve as laboratories for learning. Institutions of higher education, public libraries, museums, governmental departments, public service agencies, health service centers, commercial and industrial firms, stores, and voluntary agencies are but a few of the rich resources that are part of the community. Whether a student wishes to study health care, art, technology, public sanitation, welfare, education, or something else, the most relevant source of information and experience possible exists in the operational model. Beyond these institutional settings lies an unlimited number of potential learning opportunities which can be utilized without any formal arrangement by the school. Prepared with the necessary skills in cognitive development, adolescents can use the world of the community as a focal point for self-directed inquiry and confrontation.

2. A wide range of people should be associated with school personnel in teaching special courses or in tutoring. Either because of professional or personal qualifications (hobbies, special abilities, or

personality traits), many people in the community can serve as positive models and friends of adolescents. The supportive staff could well include some professionals who are paid for their services, as well as those who volunteer. Parents should be a part of this group of supportive staff members of the helping system.
3. Students need to participate in work-related or vocational experiences. We suggest that the school should require some minimum amount of experience in this realm. For example, for two or four weeks each year, students might be expected, as a part of their schooling experience, to participate in personally selected areas of the world of work. Schools around the world have had a substantial amount of experience in generating work-related experience for students which can be drawn upon in the design of this dimension of the helping system's program. In addition, however, it will be necessary to develop new designs for articulating work experience with the cognitively oriented portions of the curriculum in the school.
4. Students should be expected to give service to their community. Service experiences can be generated in such forms as tutorial work with younger children or adult illiterates, assisting in preschool and elementary education, voluntary work in fire stations, hospitals, or medical care centers, work in community action programs, environmental protection programs, and so forth. Again, we suggest there should be a mandatory requirement that certain amounts of school time be allocated for adolescents to engage in making responsible contributions toward the improvement of their community. All students, especially the gifted ones, should be encouraged to develop a high degree of involvement in service to the community.

Cooperation in Learning as a Cultural Pattern. The basis for the social climate of the school should be that of a community or a culture of cooperation which can serve as a model of patterns of interaction in community participation and learning for adolescents. While the terms "cooperation" and "democracy" are frequently used in traditional schools and are concepts which carry positive connotations, today's schools do not socialize youth to be able to cooperate. Through their standard procedures of grouping, grading, selection, promotion, and so forth, schools emphasize competition. This orientation toward competition denies a belief in the capacity and in the responsibility of the student to direct his own learning. Every hour, in the form of grades or nods of approval, teachers communicate to students whether they are good or are bad. This treatment teaches the "good student" to maintain his security at the expense of others, while for the "poor student" it undermines whatever security he may have started with. In undermining personal security one cripples autonomous growth, distorts self-image, stifles initiative, and denies the opportunity for creative exploration.

Not only is self-development based on competition costly to the student who fails, but in modernizing society it may be costly to all individuals. Specifically, there are three reasons why we believe that it is necessary as well as possible to foster a culture of co-operation.

1.   Because of the legal and political decisions taken to promote social integration through school desegregation, educators are responsible for ensuring that all students have the security of co-operation, the potentiality of success, and the possibility of participation in the mainstream of school activities. For this reason, the school must foster cooperation and mutual rseponsibility of all persons, no matter what their background, interests, or abilities may be. It is the responsibility of the school to recognize student differences and their potential strengths, and then to work with students toward the maximization of the potential of each of them.

2.   The complex problems of post-modern society require co-operative efforts of professionals from many disciplines who are able to integrate knowledge and skills from diverse specializations and put them to work cooperatively. Problems in modernizing societies do not come neatly packaged in academic disciplinary packages or in forms that are relevant to specific occupational roles. Rather, problems exist as wholes and must be attacked in many cases by cooperative but differentiated teams of specialists. If, as students, specialists are socialized to maintain security through competition, as adults they cannot know how to work together cooperatively.

3.   The modern nuclear family demands that its members be able to operate in complementary and mutually supportive role

relations.[3] In the traditional families of the past, members did not expect or need to cooperate in decision-making. Decisions were established by tradition or made by the traditionally defined hierarchy. Each member of the family performed his traditionally prescribed role. Today, however, the cultural assumptions of democratization and secularization suggest new forms of cooperation and new differentiations in role taking among family members and require, therefore, that adolescent boys and girls be helped to learn how to cooperate with each other in the roles of husband and wife and mother and father.

In short, the helping system should assume a role in socializing adolescents to gain satisfaction from working creatively in cooperation with others so that they will become adults successful in solving future social problems in which they are personal participants.

Postive Self-Image — A Focus for the Development of Adolescents. Basic to a student's willingness to participate in any programs designed to foster his self-identity is his expectation of success; consequently, the school must be able to assure him of success. To realistically provide this assurance, however, the school must have assurance from the student that he is ready to cooperate in efforts toward individually-stated and group-stated goals, and that he will be persistent in his efforts to confront the necessary tasks. This reciprocality of responsibility is essential to guarantee success for each student.

Success is guaranteed through mutually accepted and shared responsibility by the student and the teacher, and through student-student dyads of responsible helping relationships. In a one-to-one relationship, the student must be accepted as a person who is responsible for being open to experience and for becoming aware of and confronting his life situations, commonly called problems. Through the process of "dynamic diagnosis," teachers assume responsibility for making decisions concerning desired experiences, intervention points and techniques, and guidance so they can support the adolescent in assuming ever-increasing, but never overwhelming, levels of personal responsibility.

---

[3]For an elaboration of this point see Deborah Dye Coleman, *Family Building for Adolescents: A Model of Developmental Learning Tasks.* Ph.D. diss., The Ohio State University, 1973.

Cogentive Orientation — Affective Base. The focus on self-identity must be supported by systematic development of curriculum and teaching methods toward reorientation and transformation in cognitive capacity. Such a development can be achievable only in a context which is affectively favorable.

In the discussion of the complexity of problems created by the configuration of forces which form the modernization process, major emphasis was given to man's need to develop capability for autonomous and intelligent confrontation with problems, including the abilities of questioning basic assumptions, critical reading, continuous learning, awareness of self and situation, and social intercourse in a fragmented, changing, mostly unfamiliar, potentially hostile, and hardpressing environment.

To resocialize an adolescent against an early childhood and elementary education which has stressed obedience, conformity, and passivity, the teaching pattern in all school disciplines should be planned to restore the basic potential capacities of adolescents to develop such capabilities. Cognitive orientation and affective behavior are nonseparable elements in the mentally healthy composition defined as personality. Therefore, changes in conceptualization and cognitive orientation must be associated with changes in patterns of feeling, in perception, and in the interpretation of behavior exhibited in the roles men take and in their interaction.

Motivating adolescents to go through the crisis of reorientation and resocialization requires a social climate that is based on the affective interaction of people who care what happens to one another. Seen as a helping system, the school requires the exhibition and exercise of that care.

Threshold Achievement in Basic Skills. The emphasis placed on fostering cooperation, in developing a positive self-image, and in building an affective base stresses areas that schools have not systematically emphasized in the past. In contrast, achievement in basic skills represents the core of traditional schooling. Yet every year a large proportion of students reach secondary school with limited achievement in basic skills such as reading and computation.

The failure of a student to reach a mastery level in basic skill areas such as reading and mathematics means that this student will always have reduced options for gaining satisfying employment, continuing his education, or participating in various forms of social interaction. Therefore, the helping system has responsibility for ensuring that all students, except those with permanent learning disabilities such as mental retardation, do reach mastery in basic skill areas.

Individualization, Personalization, and Socialization. Because wide ranges of personal differences in capabilities, backgrounds, knowledge, and motivation exist, the school must attempt to provide a diversity of instructional systems designed to meet the needs of students with different entry characteristics, learning styles, and interests. Further, the basic philosophy of the helping system requires honoring the right of an individual to study the same subject as his peers according to his learning style, as well as to study different subjects according to his present level of curiosity and motivation. Yet learning is also a social experience, a process of social intercourse in association, affiliation, confrontation, and friendship. In building grouping patterns, curriculum development, and evaluation, therefore, the helping system must consider the three complementary process needs: individualization, personalization, and peer socialization.

Broaden the Base of Instruction. In addition to concentrating on achievement in basic skill areas, it is important to broaden the base of instruction to include physical education, music, and graphic and performing arts. The unique contribution of experience in athletics and in the arts is that they allow more opportunities for direct and vicarious experience, expand the options for recognition possible, and meet the need for students to learn to be able to use leisure time suitably.

Therefore, in the helping system it should be compulsory for each student to be active in at least one area of sports and one area of the arts. There must be a choice from a variety of athletic and arts programs. Resources for providing these additional courses could be acquired through community recreational programs, agencies, museums, and other civic, cultural, and recreational services.

Learning to Teach — Teaching to Learn. In any content area a dyadic teaching-learning relationship has many advantages. First, different studies of tutorial approaches demonstrate that the tutors learn, progress, and improve their self-image through their work assignment, even though their students may not demonstrate positive results. Further, our observations show that he who is given the responsibility to teach a "man," and who receives the appropriate support, develops motivation to achieve in this assignment, and puts forth great effort to understand what he is expected to teach. He also demonstrates improvement in his skills of perception, listening, empathy, perseverance, and communication. He clarifies problems for himself and tackles processes that he never before bothered to understand. Finally, he perceives himself as one who is capable of performing an important role.

Secondly, economic considerations in maintaining a helping system make it financially advantageous to ask adolescents to share in providing resources for making learning opportunities available. By asking each adolescent to serve as a tutor at least four hours per week, either for his classmates or in elementary schools and preschools in the region, tutors can be provided for many students.

Thirdly, tutorial experience is an important element in developing the sensitivity of persons to each other and in preparing adolescents for family building and childrearing. Through this approach, the adolescent can be helped to ask himself what the other human being feels, how he learns, what and how he, with his own abilities, can help the other overcome obstacles in learning.

Finally, supporting disadvantaged adolescents in performing the tutor role is a cognitively-oriented, indirect form of support that does not damage their self-image as members of the peer group and which allows them to experience being people who can "take" from others and "give" in return.

Dynamic Diagnosis, a Foundation for a Helping System. There is no way to progress toward the goal that the new school will be a cooperative social system — person-oriented, process-oriented, and change-oriented — without investment in the development of a new evaluation pattern to replace the present competitive, impersonal, summative, and static grading and "matriculation" pattern. The diagnostic pattern must serve the school as a cortex for institutional learning: a means through which its members acquire sound, useful information on which to base their individual actions and, therefore in the aggregate, to base the actions of the school as a social system.

Diagnosis in the helping system should be based on the following assumptions:

1. It will be a comprehensive, diversified, longitudinal process shared cooperatively by all those concerned — students, teachers and tutors, administrators, and parents.

2. Since the school is a central institution for socialization toward democracy and a social lifestyle for both family and community management, all participants in the school will share responsibility for establishing criteria, and developing and practicing diagnostic and evaluation designs.

3. Since it is to be a person-oriented institution, there will be a system of diagnosis that will be supportive of persons in perceiving, reflecting, and decision-making when relating to themselves, their fellow men, the environment, and the interaction process.

For the student, a base line evaluation should be aimed at understanding his history of growth and development, his socio-cultural home environment, and his entrance characteristics — in motivation, value orientation, ability, skills, and feelings. Also, there must be a formative evaluation — his pattern of confrontation (the achievements, mistakes, and needs for support in coping) with expectations and acquisition of knowledge, attitudes, and capacity to confront issues and to progress. And, at each stage, there needs to be a summative evaluation that serves to identify what has been mastered: where are the gaps; what are the needs for further consideration; and what appropriate support is required in guidance, tutoring, or a change of orientation.

The teacher needs knowledge about himself (in addition to that part of knowledge and feelings that he will acquire from diagnosis of the student and the socialization process). The teacher, like the student, needs dynamic diagnosis supportive to changing his attitudes and behavior — self-perception, self-understanding, and differentiation between his needs and the needs of significant others (students, parents, administrators, consultants, and so forth). He needs diagnosis of his progress in changing his attitudes and behavior toward the aspired goals of maturity — greater adequacy and assumption of responsibility for self and others in the social interaction process.

Administrators and consultants need a similar type of self-diagnostic process, but they also need to have additional knowledge available for performing their roles. Such knowledge should be the necessary information for intelligent decision-making and improved policy orientation in daily operation.

For the parents there should be diagnosis of the growth and development of their child in all areas relevant to understanding and supporting him as a person — in home, school, peer, and community situations.

To develop a diagnostic process relevant to students, teachers, administrators, and parents, there must be a diagnosis of the environment affecting the school and its members — home culture and socio-economic conditions, feelings of parents and others in the community, resources in the community that may support school programs, needs in the community that the school may confront, etc. And in addition to a dynamic diagnosis of people, the diagnosis must include the process of development of curriculum and materials for teaching.

Schools for adolescents — operating as helping systems — clearly would be different in important ways from secondary schools as we now know them. Yet such schools need not (indeed could not) be created *de novo*. Most of the features of such schools as we have described them exist in various places in many countries. Nowhere, however, to our knowledge, are they all brought together into an effective and powerful whole. We believe that they can be brought into being if school leaders seriously choose to do so. And we believe that the decade of the seventies will be the period when educators must and will choose to reform adolescent schooling.

*Here is an actual case-study of what
happened when a principal undertook
the task of "humanizing and democratizing
his school through the collaborative
learning inherent in sharing the
decision-making process of the
school with his students."*

Are Students
Involved
In Deciding
Crucial Issues?

JAMES E. CALKINS
Assistant Superintendent, Staples High School
Westport, Connecticut

I n order that men may be prepared for self-government, their apprenticeship must commence in childhood. The great moral attribute of self-government
cannot be born and matured in one day; and if school
children are not trained to it, we only prepare ourselves
for disappointment if we expect it from grown men.
— *Horace Mann*

Who cares about student decision making anyway? How many
public secondary school administrators care about creating an
apprenticeship for self-government by involving students in the
school's decision-making process?

Before answering, be sure that the topic of this article is clearly
understood. It refers first to the young people who innocently enter

school expecting a democratic experience but who generally receive a lesson in dictatorship instead. "Involved" refers to meaningful participation. "The school's decision-making process" pertains to the school's crucial issues, not the typical student council's "sandbox" governmental decisions.

RESPONSIBILITY OF THE PRINCIPAL

Before you decide that this article is not for you because your school already involves students in decision making, ask yourself whether students in your school have a voice in such things as curriculum, scheduling, marking, testing and examining, and teacher evaluation.

What kind of voice do your students have in the real issues of your school? Who holds the power? Do students have, through representation in some democratic structure, an equal voice in making the most significant decisions in your school? In short, do they have a fair share of the action? Unless positive answers can be given to these and similar questions, the students are not really involved in the decision-making process of the school. What exists otherwise is phony, and the students know it. If you are honest, you know it too.

If the students are unaware, for some reason, the responsibility of the principal is clear. He should provide the leadership for raising the students' level of consciousness to enable them to realize the need for becoming involved. Only when the principal is ready to take this step — action designed to share power willingly without pressure — will it be possible for the students to become truly involved.

SHOULD STUDENTS BE INVOLVED?

Students in a public secondary school should be involved in the school's decision-making process only if the administrators are willing to take prudent but definite risks. A necessary risk involves a willingness to have faith, trust, and confidence in young people to the point of allowing them to share mistakes with administrators and staff in crucial areas of the school.

Only if the administration believes that students can learn to be responsible and to make meaningful decisions can it share its power. Confidence must exist that students can contribute significantly to the decision-making process. Both administration and staff must *want* to involve their students in what is essentially a collaborative learning experience in democracy.

Likewise, students must want to become involved. Not all students want to carry that burden of responsibility, and the greater the number of students falling into that category, the greater is the need for student involvement. When the real opportunity to share actively in school decisions is explained to them, most students will be eager to participate.

Students obviously cannot be expected to participate beyond the level of their knowledge and expertise. However, they can become informed, and it is possible for them to make sound judgments based on facts and information. Herein lies the challenge of collaborative learning. Students who are participating in decisions about curriculum, for example, can learn from teachers and administrators collaboratively what they need to know to render judgments. Certainly what is to be taught to students ought to be justifiable to them.

If the school is to be humane and democratic, students should be involved in the decision-making process. If that is not the intent, it really makes little difference what is done. Unless the students are given their fair share of power, neither humanization nor democratization is possible. What exists otherwise is benevolent despotism at the worst, or condescending paternalism at best.

If the freedom of each individual is paramount in the philosophy and the management of the school, individualization and socialization in a democracy would appear feasible. Without participation in self-determination, freedom is not possible. "Any situation in which some men prevent others in the process of inquiry is one of violence. The means used are not important; to alienate men from their own decision making is to change them into objects."[1] This warning is applicable to the public school.

---

[1] P. Freire. *Paulo Friere Cultural Action for Freedom.* Harvard Educational Review and Center for the Study of Development and Social Change, 1970, No. 1, p. 73.

Finally, students should be involved in the decision-making process of the school to counteract the effect of the current behavior of many public officials. Students need to know that our system of democratic government can work on a national level as well as in their own school. Again, however, the students must be involved in real decisions involving crucial areas of the school.

STUDIES ON INVOLVING STUDENTS

If administrators are interested in learning about involving students in the school decision-making process, a variety of sources can be consulted. The research of Lekander, Fahey, Schmerler, and Calkins[2] provides comprehensive coverage of the topics of shared decision making and/or shared governance in the management of the public schools.*

Lekander dealt primarily with the extent to which one hundred Southern California high schools were achieving the goals of citizenship enumerated in their student council constitutions. He, not surprisingly, concluded that these schools were achieving these goals.

Fahey based his study on a survey of samples of shared power and shared decision making in the public high schools in the United States conducted by the Commission of Training Programs-Implementation of Shared Power of the Association of Supervision

---

[2]J. E. Calkins, "A Praxis for Developing a Model of Shared Governance in the Secondary School," unpublished doctoral dissertation, The University of North Carolina at Greensboro, 1974.

J. J. Fahey, "Shared Power in Decision-Making in Schools: Conceptualization and Implementation," unpublished doctoral dissertation, The University of Michigan, 1971.

L. M. Lekander, "Student Participation in Secondary School Government: An Analysis of Purposes, Values, Practices," unpublished doctoral dissertation, University of Southern California, 1967.

G. R. Schmerler, "Student Participation in High School Governance: A Framework," unpublished doctoral dissertation, Columbia University, 1972.

*EDITOR'S NOTE: A more recent study of the governance structures of six alternative schools is that undertaken by the Educational Change Team of the Research Project on Educational Innovation at the University of Michigan: *Student Power: Practice and Promise* by Glorianne Wittes et al (New York: Citation Press, 1975).

and Curriculum Development (ASCD). He identified and described seven schools that demonstrated promising procedures for shared power in decision making. The high school identified as having the most promising procedure for shared power in decision making in his study was Staples High School in Westport, Conn.

Schmerler conducted an extensive literature search that led to the identification of five models of school governance based primarily on the relationship of students to the decision-making process. The five model designations were collaborative, parallel, adversary, independent, and individual choice. These categories were based on the extent of student involvement in shared decision making.

Calkins provided a rationale for both a model and a concept of democratic organization in the public secondary school, devised a theoretical model for the concept, described in great detail an operational model related to that theoretical model, and showed a potential innovator how to replicate the operational model. The operational model is the Staples Governing Board of Staples High School in Westport, Conn., cited by Fahey above.

BURDEN OF PROOF RESTS ON PRINCIPAL

In order to be involved successfully in the process of decision making, students must become convinced of the intent of the administration to share real power with them. The students must believe that the administration will not cop out at the first sign of public criticism. Only by repeatedly demonstrating commitment to sharing their power can administrators convince students that they mean what they say. They will have to publicly bleed in behalf of the students.

Students everywhere have a long history of demonstrated hypocrisy reminding them to be skeptical. The burden of proof rests squarely on the shoulders of the principal. His words will be measured against his deeds by all the students as he attempts to change the stereotype of his image and administration in general. Humanization of the school as a prerequisite to involving students in the decision-making process begins with the principal.

At Staples High School a four-year period of humanization preceded efforts to develop and implement a vehicle of shared power. Each of the actions listed below contributed to student acceptance of the commitment of the principal on controversial issues in the school and the community. While these items are not in chronological order, they do emphasize a developmental sequence of events that provided impetus to the initial discussions about finding a means of sharing power in the school's decision-making process. Some of these actions were:

☐ Elimination of tracking in all subjects

☐ Elimination of all bells

☐ Elimination of homerooms and systematic attendance taking on a daily basis

☐ Provision of a system of shared responsibility between the home and school for attendance and progress

☐ Elimination of mandatory study halls

☐ Creation of option areas for serious and quiet study, talk-study tutorials, smoking, and blowing off steam

☐ Opening up the cafeteria as a coffee and doughnut shop for breakfast and provision for pretzel stands, soda machines and snack machines

☐ Elimination of detentions and detention halls

☐ Provision for a suspension review board of students and faculty as an initial step in eliminating suspension

☐ Provision of complete freedom of campus and buildings as long as classes and rights of others were not interfered with

☐ Initiation of an open-ended schedule for all students that permitted them to come when their first class began and leave when the last class was over

☐ Provision for faculty professional self-evaluation through a program of professional development and appraisal based on a management-by-objectives concept

☐ Elimination of dress codes for students, faculty, and administration

☐ Elimination of prerequisites for participation in extracurricular activities or athletics

☐ Elimination of the traditional class governments and the student government

☐ Modification of ranking of students to deciles as a step toward the eventual elimination of class rankings

☐ Subdivision of courses into a variety of elective units which students could select to build a year's work

☐ Expansion of opportunities in individualized programs, which included self-evaluation for students who have completed all requirements for graduation ahead of time, independent study, independent work projects, and cooperative programs with colleges in the area

☐ Provision for an uncensored school newspaper

☐ Provision of students' access to their own records

These actions were not always well received among the faculty or within the community. However, two very obvious conditions were developing that kept the criticism and pressure in check. In the first place, Staples High School was flourishing under the aegis of this new leadership and the atmosphere of mutual faith, trust, and confidence. It also involved love and genuine concern.

MAKING FREEDOM WORK

Students were happy. Their activism was channeled into constructive activities because the administration was trusted to help them to do anything within reason that was educationally defensible. In this connection a visitor at one time remarked to the principal, "This is the only school I've heard of where the kids will come and ask the principal for permission to riot." There never was a riot, but all the collaboratively planned activities kept students headed in a positive and constructive direction.

The second condition that kept parent and faculty criticism in check was that teachers really did not want to change what was happening to them. The principal hit upon a very understandable human equation in dealing with his staff. Teachers will not complain or criticize loudly if they are receiving concomitant benefits from the actions taken with students, even if they are fearful of those actions or do not believe in them.

As the restrictions were lifted from students, the teachers were relieved from imposing those restrictions. If students did not have

211

to go to study hall, teachers would not have to supervise them. If students were allowed the freedom of the halls and access to the lavatories without passes, the teachers would not have to be there or check passes. As the lot of teachers improved and they became increasingly aware that they were being permitted to be more professional because they were being treated that way, criticism abated, and the teachers sought ways to make the new approach work.

Each new change was the outgrowth of dialogue and collaborative effort involving students, faculty, and administration. In retrospect it is possible to see clearly how the efforts to humanize the school provided the foundation upon which to build the democratic structure for involving students in the decision-making process of the school. Humanization was the forerunner of democratization.

If the principal has the courage to democratize the decision-making process in his school, he must be willing to accept a series of interrelated challenges which include:

☐ Undergoing a personal and professional self-evaluation
☐ Assessing conditions in the school and community favorable to change
☐ Reviewing the professional literature relative to involving students in the decision-making process
☐ Visiting and/or communicating with places which are experimenting with involving students in the decision-making process
☐ Taking prudent risks to effect change
☐ Taking a definite and visible stand on the issue of involving students in the decision-making process
☐ Making a commitment to sharing real power
☐ Demonstrating faith, trust, and confidence in young people
☐ Establishing a humane school as a prerequisite to democratization
☐ Reducing the vulnerability and dependency of students
☐ Raising the levels of consciousness of students to the point where they recognize and understand the need to become involved in the decision-making process of the school
☐ Assisting in the development of a vehicle for shared power in decision making

☐ Establishing the constitution for the vehicle for change as policy for the school system

☐ Working for public acceptance of the concept and the practice of sharing power with students in the decision-making process

☐ Recognizing that the new concept and practice require collaborative learning among students, teachers, and administrators

The above list does not represent priorities. It is suggestive of the actions and positions that a principal must take to promote the concept of involving students in the process of decision making in the school. Although the list may sound like rhetoric, every item presents a real challenge to the principal. This list represents practical commitments that cannot be viewed lightly. Each item, or a similar action or position, must be accepted by the principal as a real challenge if involving students in the decision-making process is to succeed.

If the research of Fahey can be believed, there have been few public high schools in this country willing to share real power with students. One exception has been Staples High School where shared governance equals shared power in a unique form of collaborative administration involving students, faculty, and administrators called the Staples Governing Board (SGB). The SGB is not a student council. It is not an advisory group. It is a school governing agency that actually shares the power with the administration of a public high school of 1,900 students covering grades 10 to 12. It is an agency that gives students and faculty a real piece of the action.

HOW THE SGB SHARES POWER

The SGB truly provides representative participation in the *meaningful* decision-making processes of the school. It does not concern itself as most student councils and faculty senates do with the collateral functions of the school. The SGB can and does make collaborative decisions about curriculum development, schedule construction, non-classroom teacher assignments, graduation requirements, evaluation of teachers and programs, to name a few of the areas of its involvement. It serves as a step in the administrative line organization of the school. Its meaningful involvement is guaranteed by a set of bylaws that have been empowered by the policy of the Westport Board of Education.

The SGB consists of twenty members (ten students and ten adults). The ten students are four seniors, three juniors, and three sophomores. Seven teachers and three administrators make up the ten adults. Students, teachers, and administrators are elected annually by their respective peer groups in open elections. Candidates must seek election through primaries beginning with petitions to their constituencies. There are no restrictions on who may run for office as long as they can meet the requirements of the petitioning process for access to the primaries. The complete election process is supervised by the Staples Governing Board.

The SGB is the unicameral legislative branch of the governance of Staples High School. The principal and his office constitute the administrative branch. In effect the SGB can pass laws and direct the governance of the school in any area normally authorized to the principal, subject to the limitations that may be imposed by state law, local town ordinances, or board of education policy. It passes laws that govern the school when they are ratified by the principal.

The principal has two kinds of veto power that he may exercise. He may deliver an absolute veto, which kills a bill. This action, rarely taken, comes about when in the principal's judgment a bill contradicts a law or board of education policy. This action can be appealed to the superintendent and to the board of education. A suspensive veto may be used if the principal wishes the bill to be reconsidered and revised by the SGB. In this instance the SGB may accept the veto and let the bill die; they may override this veto with a two-thirds vote; they may choose to rewrite the bill and resubmit it at a later date. Through the use of the absolute and suspensive vetoes, the balance of power is maintained under this concept of shared governance.

As the concept has evolved and operated, the SGB has served as the alter ego of the principal. When Staples High School buried the remnants of its student government, the principal of the school provided the leadership for the exploration and the evolution of the Staples Governing Board. The principal stimulated cooperative and collaborative efforts among students, faculty, and administrators to initiate a year-long process of study that culminated in the present bylaws of the SGB. He led the struggle to obtain the ratification of the bylaws and the acceptance of the concept on campus and in the community. The whole process provided a significant lesson in participatory democracy for the entire community as well as the faculty and students.

It is apparent in establishing and nurturing the concept of shared governance at Staples High School that the principal has the most significant role to play. His leadership must convey a genuine and honest belief in the concept of shared governance and participatory democracy. His actions and words must from the outset attest to his conviction that shared power as a basis for shared governance can exist in an atmosphere of mutual faith, trust, and confidence among students, teachers, and administrators.

WHAT THE SGB HAS ACCOMPLISHED

The best source of evidence that supports or refutes the faith expressed in the SGB is to be found in the variety of legislative actions taken by it. A brief review of only a few of the hundreds of actions taken by the SGB and approved by the principal includes the following:

□ Teacher and Course Evaluation Bill — This requires anonymous student evaluation of course and teacher by a standard questionnaire at the end of each semester. Only the teachers get the results.

□ Examination Option Bill — This permits a variety of options during exam week, including not having an exam and varying the effect of the exam on a grade. The options are arrived at cooperatively by student and teacher.

□ Pass/No Record Bill — This allows a student to select this option in lieu of a grade. Pass will be recorded, but failure will not.

□ Amendments to Charter Forms Bill—This amends a bill granting charters for activities at Staples to establish that only activities recognized by the SGB will exist on campus.

□ Recommendations on Conserving Energy — This spells out a variety of actions to be taken, all of which were implemented.

☐ Professional Non-Classroom Responsibility Bill — This establishes a procedure for assigning teachers non-classroom responsibilities.

These bills are samples of the variety and importance of hundreds of responsible actions taken by the SGB since its inception. Two salient points should be made about these actions. At no time has there ever been a student-versus-adult vote by the SGB members; and of the fewer than a dozen vetoes by the principal, none has been overridden or appealed by the SGB. The faith and love that founded the SGB will nurture its existence.

SOME OF THE FUNCTIONAL DILEMMAS OF THE SGB

The Valhalla of education has not been discovered in the form of the SGB. There are many problems inherent in its operation. Time and energy demands on the SGB members are great, and these are only partly compensated by course credits for students and in-service credits for teachers and administrators. Legislated policy is not always readily distinguished from administrative action. There is the continuing dilemma of keeping separate those decisions which can be legitimately made in-house and those which must be passed along as recommendations to the superintendent and the board of education.

Providing equal representation to the various social elements of the Staples community poses a very real and persisting dilemma. There is always the danger of creating an additional excessive bureaucracy in the school. Coping with a waning constituent interest and public misapprehension places a demanding communications burden on the SGB. Finally, there is the potential outcropping of the suppressed adversary relationships among faculty, students, and administration to be faced.

While the dilemmas are formidable, they are not insurmountable. Each year the SGB grows stronger and more viable. The present position of the SGB is still a transitional one. However, each passing year of accumulated actions by the SGB provides a basis for the resolution of these dilemmas. As the SGB becomes increasingly the vehicle for effecting change at Staples High School, these dilemmas will be resolved.

WHAT IS THE FUTURE?

The SGB is an idea whose time not only has come, but philosophically it is also supported by national and state legislation recognizing the earlier maturation of students. It is not only logical but also it is necessary to provide realistic and meaningful involvement in sharing governance if we expect students to assume the responsibility of citizenship at age eighteen. The future of the concept of the SGB is clear. It will continue and it will grow. It has become the administrative way of life at Staples High School.

In a very real sense the future of the SGB is closely allied to the future of the principalship in this school. Board of education policy has created a unique role relationship between the SGB and the principal. This policy represents a critical commitment to mutual faith, trust, and confidence among traditional adversaries in the public secondary school. It is a promise akin to that of the government of our democracy.

The greatest tragedy of recent student activism on high school campuses is to be found in the relatively few subsequent attempts by administrators to direct this tremendous motivational force into constructive and significant channels for change. While many educators and critics of the educational scene recognized the need to humanize and democratize the public secondary school, few of them offered or tried to implement any significant or meaningful changes in the way that students were treated or decisions were made in their schools.

The full measure of this tragedy may still lie before us as more and more high school youngsters become disenchanted with the decision-making process at the highest levels of our government. This disenchantment only reinforces the helplessness many students feel under the existing governance of their schools. Public high school organizational structures and management practices reflect an unfortunately prevalent characteristic of educational thought — hardening of the attitudes.

No high school principal can find a greater challenge to his leadership skills than to share willingly his power with students. No greater satisfaction awaits the principal than that of succeeding in humanizing and democratizing his school through the collaborative learning inherent in sharing the decision-making process of the school with students. The principal who willingly heads in this direction will have his energy and imagination challenged and tested, but he will be a happier person and have a happier school for the experience.

A piercing analysis of "the child who won't" with concrete suggestions for ways to build environments for self-actualization.

The Antiachiever: Rebel Without a Future

STANLEY R. SHERMAN
Director of Inservice Training Programs

DAVID ZUCKERMAN
Co-director

ALAN B. SOSTEK
Clinical Director

Center for Alternative Education
University Center, Inc., Boston

The most frustrating challenge of the guidance counselor has always been motivation of underachieving children — those with high aptitude scores (upper quartile) but marks below the average for their grade. In recent years, school administrators and teachers have developed new curricula, new structures, and new methods in attempts to reduce the scope of the problem. Yet today, three-quarters of the brightest third of America's students still do not manage to fulfill their potential even to the point of finishing college. Moreover, the most serious form of underachievement — the neurotic refusal to achieve — appears to have become more prevalent.

The antiachiever is the child who won't. He won't accept adult values, adult goals, adult forms of competition, adult dress habits, or adult social codes. It is not a new phenomenon for normal young people in the adolescent reaction phase to rebel against adult roles and goals by temporarily poor performance and even disruptive classroom behavior. But once they have discovered and established more mature roles, most youths from middle-class homes have returned to previously established success patterns. The antiachiever's behavior, in contrast, has long-standing neurotic roots, often stretching back to childhood, and seldom changes to a responsible adult mode without therapeutic intervention. In truth, it is more accurate to say that he can't accept the adult world instead of that he won't.

THE DILEMMA OF THE ANTIACHIEVER

The child who rejects achievement as a goal is heading toward a lifetime of frustration. This society has a high regard for academic credentials and little or no respect for those who fail to achieve. Its rewards — responsibility, recognition of accomplishment, prestige, status, and money — go to the achiever. The anti-social and extra-social goals of the antiachieving adolescent, who seeks gratification from his peers rather than becoming involved in the "games" adults play, are considered aberrations. Thus his foothold in traditional socioeconomic institutions is today at best marginal. Now unlikely to finish high school or to attend college and graduate if entered, the antiachiever faces probable failure as an employee and as a parent. Even the temporary and low level jobs now open to him in the "straight" world will "dry up" as he ages unless at some point in his career he has demonstrated the ability to hold down a job for a year or two with some degree of success. Moreover, the inevitable replacement of today's youth culture by a new wave and simultaneous absorption of its maturer members into the mainstream — after their introduction of significant cultural adaptations — will drastically reduce his peer group audience and thus the potential for rewards from this source.

The development of a rebel youth "counterculture" over the past 10 years may appear to provide alternative constructive channels for the antiachiever, but this is a mirage. The youth culture provides him with no really satisfactory avenues and, in fact, only serves to reinforce his self-destructive behavior. True, many young people have gained important new insights from the movement: learning processes and roles more creative than those currently accepted by U.S. society are indeed possible. But they are still only possibilities which require hard work and development of new disciplines before they can become realities. The antiachiever, unable to formulate concrete personal goals, lacks the motivation necessary to acquire the required skills and to implement new ideas. After years of negative conditioning, he is so present-oriented that he is unable to think with any validity in future terms. Indeed he may only dimly perceive the values of the counterculture's more positive aspects. Typically the antiachiever simply seizes on its more negative life styles, so highly publicized by entertainers and the media as desirable alternatives to "straight" life, to justify his unrealistic goals and self-destructive behavior patterns. He primarily uses counterculture verbiage to cloud his underlying problems in a miasma of nebulous generalities.

The counterculture has already produced a number of new career opportunities, but they too go to the motivated achiever — however disguised with long locks and authentically frayed jeans. The media specialist who promotes youth paraphernalia and entertainment must write well enough to prepare enticing copy; the pottery maker must judge her profit margin and potential market accurately enough to recover costs and living expenses. The underground hawker must compete with the 10 other drop-outs striving to sell newspapers in Harvard Square to recoup the cash he has paid out to his middle-class publisher; the commune farmer must persevere knowledgeably and skillfully to harvest crops. The completely altruistic poet must have self-discipline to produce enough work to gain an audience; and even the pusher must be sufficiently "together" to meet his commitments and stay out of jail.

Stymied by false "cultural" barriers, many parents, counselors, and teachers are unable to "reach" and communicate with the dissident antiachiever. And, even where positive relationships are established, most find it difficult to help him discriminate between the new "culture's" real values and its negative aspects because of their own ignorance or feelings of impotence. (Some adults refuse to admit the existence of this very real though fragmentary subculture movement while others tend to accept it as a mysterious semi-institutionalized, monolithic alien culture, totally divorced from, and thus not open to question by, the "straight" adult world.) Yet the antiachiever needs their help. Unless he settles for dependency — whether a welfare-supported subsistence lifestyle, carefully masked reliance on family funds, or institutionalization in a hospital or prison — the social drop-out has no option but to acquire at least some of the skills and attitudes of working members of the "system" for survival. The antiachiever is headed toward a lifetime of dependency or frustration: in both "societies" he must be able to participate in some tangible way to attain respect.

Already burdened with a wide range of other adolescent and children's problems, educators need to be able to distinguish between antiachievers and students with other serious academic handicaps to facilitate immediate referral to appropriate remedial programs. They also need to gain insights into the conditions which appear to contribute to escalation of this phenomenon in order to design preventive solutions. Thus in the following section, we shall first explore the traits exhibited by antiachievers to determine how their behavior and motivation differ from those of achieving students. Then we shall consider the impact of various family child-rearing patterns and give particular attention to the impact of the school environment on children. Finally, we shall describe some approaches which have proved successful in preventing or remedying the antiachievement syndrome.

TRAITS OF THE ANTIACHIEVER

Antiachievement obviously does not simply involve a poor academic record. Antiachievers can be found in progressive non-graded schools which assign no marks for classwork. And a brilliant few are able to sustain high marks throughout high school (though still performing substantially below their aptitude levels). What then distinguishes the antiachiever from the normally rebellious adolescent?

His classroom teacher may describe the antiachiever as lazy, immature, or neurotic. When asked, this student will say that his poor grades are the result of boring subject matter, inability to concentrate, teachers who don't like him, teachers he doesn't like, or plain bad luck. His generally defensive attitude, obvious lack of school-directed energy, and distaste for adult-proposed solutions indicate little desire to achieve. Almost all underachievers display a perfectly normal range of life energy except in school and certain work situations. But simply put, the antiachiever invests great energy in drives and actions that assure his continued nonachievement. His predominant psychological state, which both causes and is caused by this behavior, is a feeling of helplessness, a conviction that effective action is really impossible. He is afraid that if he tries he will fail, and the prophecy is self-fulfilling. The cyclical relationship of belief and behavior is obvious: each acts to reinforce the other and thus to maintain and prolong the individual's failure to achieve. Moreover, external sanctions like threats and bribery aren't effective in stimulating a change in his performance. Thus the choice of behavior pattern does not appear to be within his conscious control.

Since all behavior is motivated, the question is what distinguishes antiachievers' goals and methods of accomplishing them. There appear to be three distinct types of antiachievement goals: continued dependence, extraordinary status, and sheer failure avoidance.

Continued Dependence. Studies have shown that many antiachievers choose to fail academically as a means of maintaining immature, dependent relationships with their families and avoiding the risks of independent action — as well as the consequent responsibility. But the attempt to avoid crossing the adolescent threshold to adulthood is entirely unconscious. Like his normal peers, the antiachiever will complain about parental and school restrictions and insist on his need for greater independence. However, his behavior is regressive, with an infantile reaction to stress and a general resistance to accepting personal responsibility. He retreats and complains in the face of demands; he procrastinates when opportunities for successful achievement arise. Then when failure inevitably occurs, he blames forces outside himself or beyond his control.

Extraordinary Status. A particularly crippling motivation is the need to be extraordinary, which is linked to a low sense of self-worth fostered by adverse reaction to the school environment. Caught in a pattern of failure, this antiachiever finds little risks — such daily "tests" as taking part in class discussion or even doing homework — of threatening importance. Previous failures indicate little chance of success so he finds the best and safest approach to be attempting as little academic work as possible. Typically such children battle failure feelings by selecting extraordinary status as their goal. (For example, in answer to the question, "What do you hope to become?", such antiachievers answer "somebody important," "famous," or even "omnipotent.") Thus this type of antiachiever tends to dismiss the school's normal academic and behavioral demands as unreasonable and/or worthless. They are unrelated to his goals and should not apply to him; even if he does the work, it will lead to only "ordinary" success, which is simply not enough; attention to such petty details offers no rewards and will distract him from his glorious search; and so forth.

In seeking achievement gratification in school, this antiachiever thus concentrates on gaining peer group rather than adult esteem. As a classroom rebel, a role considered respectable even for achievers, he can win recognition simply by giving vent to his feelings or playing power games which are "stacked" so the teacher can only lose. From the antiachiever's point of view, his "smart," unproductive, disruptive antiauthoritarian actions are highly productive and quite successful. His need to be extraordinary is satisfied by becoming the "funniest," the "wildest," the "most disruptive" kid, a status which most of his peers talk about with relish.

Failure Avoidance. The third type of antiachiever does not try for any form of success, but seeks to avoid failures or at least displace the blame for those which he cannot avoid. He never commits himself to an honest attempt since this would involve risk; whereas, venturing nothing, he cannot be blamed for what has not even been attempted. He procrastinates to defer confronting failure. He shirks personal responsibility to avoid blame — thus if something goes wrong, it remains the failure of the anonymous "they." His lack of initiative is appalling. As a further protective cloak, this antiachiever denigrates school success: how can he be said to fail at a worthless activity? How can she "fail" to win a prize if she isn't involved in the contest?

However, over the longer term, this antiachiever does not gain feelings of success. Try as he might to avoid the responsibility for his school failure, he still knows that only he lives his life and that he, at root, is responsible and is failing. This knowledge, while not sufficient to cause him to abandon his mode of action, does extort its toll; the avoider is usually miserable, prone to frequent depressions, and extremely self-deprecating. He feels lacking in self-worth, less adequate than his peers, weak, bad. Typically he is quite angry about his trap, but cannot express his hostility except in limited areas, most particularly through self-derogatory comments. His passive-aggressive behavior saps his energy and draws his attention away from adopting and developing more successful life strategies.

CONDITIONS WHICH FOSTER UNDERACHIEVEMENT

But descriptions of behavior don't tell why some children become antiachievers and why they are increasing in number. To find out why more and more underachievers have chosen to walk through the swamps of failure, we must look first at their home lives and second at their school environment.

The Family. Some researchers have gone so far as to say that almost all the causes of underachievement are found in the home rather than the school. However, their research is based on very limited data; causal relationships linking family characteristics and poor performance have not been firmly established. In truth, each family has its unique story, problems, and effects on its children, and each child lives a life like no other's. Under any given set of conditions, one child may do well, another be destroyed. Serious family problems — alcoholism, divorce, criminality, a hateful relationship between husband and wife — will, of course, have an adverse impact on children. However, reasonably healthy children from reasonably normal homes also become antiachievers. While their parents cannot be assumed to be the *cause* of underachievement, they do appear to at least *contribute* to conditions in which it may thrive. Three such family patterns predominate: indifferent, rigid, and permissive parents.

Society generally recognizes indifferent parents as "bad" parents. In brief, they are so involved with their own lives as to be, or give the appearance of being, indifferent to their child's life. While the child's school grades may be important to them, the actual process of the child's life is not. Thus when he adopts psychological withdrawal as a protective strategy, his choice is reinforced and amplified by his parents' attitudes. But such parental behavior, particularly in America's child-centered and education-worshipping culture, is quite rare.

Far more typical are the parents who care deeply about their child's life, but express their concern through inappropriately rigid child-rearing practices. With quite inflexible standards as to what constitutes success, these parents are constantly critical of their child's behavior, which naturally tends to diverge from the goals they have set for him. The child, then, comes to feel that everything he does is wrong, that whatever he attempts will be considered a failure. Again, it is safer to quit trying. Though he may still get failing grades, he is at least not responsible, for he has not tried to be successful. A necessary distance is thus created between his parents' negative evaluations and the way he feels about himself.

The permissive parent is unfortunately becoming quite common. This parent does not raise his child in the conventional sense, so much as sharing living quarters and income with him. The motivations for such behavior are varied: partly a reaction to the stringency with which children were raised 30-50 years ago, partly reaction to the deprivation many parents felt in their youths, and partly the highest libertarian desire to allow children to grow as individuals. The antistringency reaction leaves children to do whatever they want; the post-Depression reaction allows them to have whatever they want; the misapplication of the libertarian ethic allows them to be whatever they want and offers them license under the guise of freedom. All such methods are based on worthy parental desires, but all spoil children to the point that their survival in school and their success in life are jeopardized. Such parents make few specific demands on their children; the schools make many. Such parents allow the child to do what he wants; the schools do not. Such parents give the child no opportunity to learn how to act when action is difficult, to do what is hard to do, to strive on in the ways that all successful adults have had to learn. Their children give little of themselves except for pleasure and quit when work gets hard — and life is often not very pleasurable and sometimes quite difficult.

The School Environment. All schools, except the most unusual, provide an environment which is radically different from any other experienced by preschool children or even by adults. While children supposedly go to school to learn, they indeed go to school to *live.* "Learning," in the usual sense, is an occasional and erratic occurrence; but the school environment does influence every pupil all day. What is learned above all in school is how to adapt to that environment, and it is the environmental aspects of the child's school experience, not the occasional flash of insight or the hard-won knowledge of how to do math, which have had the most important impact on the antiachiever. All children must adapt in some way to the work situation, with its constant evaluation, competition, and limited channels for protest.

In attending school, children are introduced to their first "work" situation. For the first time, a significant part of their lives revolves around an external and relatively distant authority which tells them what to do and keeps them at the job. In the primary grades, of course, this work often goes under the guise of play. But in all except the most chaotically libertarian schools, there is no doubt about who is in charge: the teachers are there to say what is to be done, and the children are there to do it. And despite the lip service paid to the need for each child to be treated as an individual, the usual school atmosphere is accepted both tacitly and philosophically by most concerned intellectuals. Schoolwork is considered important by society, whether or not the pupils consider it so, and must be taken seriously. Thus the emphasis on individual achievement is actually secondary: what matters is that children take a serious attitude toward their work.

Classwork is based on the assumption that everyone will at least try to cooperate with the common endeavor selected by the teacher. This assumption is enforced at considerable cost to all children; upon entering class, they must inhibit their impulses and natural desires and either focus their attention on the common activity or at least remain silent. The self-discipline required is tiresome, and the subject matter is generally less interesting than any more immediate and more emotional concerns. Of course the students supposedly have the personal goal of getting an education, but this, like the adult goal of "getting ahead," is so vague that it hardly qualifies as a goal at all. In general, the real needs and goals of the student are expected to keep him at his work but are irrelevant to the decision of what work is to be done or which goals are worked toward.

While in school, children are required to work within an atmosphere of all-pervasive and constant evaluation. They must face evaluation every day by other students, by each teacher, and by themselves, on not only their academic work, but also on their behavior and general character traits as well. To be in class, then, is to be on the spot; whatever work the child does, whatever actions he takes, whatever thoughts he admits to having, will be evaluated — and much of it perhaps negatively. Every item of behavior is measured on the scale of "good" and "bad." Except that it turns them into showoffs, this situation may not be destructive for those who are really good at schoolwork; at least they can gain a feeling of power and efficacy. As a result, as John Holt points out in *How Children Fail*, even primary school kids have already become obsessed with who is "smart" and who is "dumb," with finding the "right" answer, with trying to guess "what the teacher wants." These are good survival strategies, but they are also underlying causes of antiachievement.

As a consequence, children in school are in constant low-key competition with each other. Most teachers attempt to downplay this competition, but it is deeply rooted in the school environment. All the children in a class generally work at the same tasks, a situation which invites comparison, voiced or internal, between those who do it well and those who do it poorly. There are rarely more than four or five good scholars in a class. The rest risk ridicule when they speak, in addition to the "punishment" of poor grades for what they write. Other traditional means of earning peer group esteem (such as team sports) have been drastically reduced by adult restriction of participation to only top competitors. Increasingly students must turn to deviant activities to establish identity.

Perhaps the most brutal difference between the work environment in schools and adult work situations is that, except in a very few cases, children have not legitimate channels to protest their treatment and cannot leave of their own volition until they are sixteen. They can only withdraw psychologically within themselves or become more or less subtly disruptive of the educational process. The strategy of reducing personal concern and involvement to a point where neither success nor failure in coping is sharply felt is a major cause of underachievement. Many children, some quite bright, choose the short-range benefits of withdrawing into silence. When they work, their effort is a token offered to avoid outright failure; they do not invest themselves in that work, do not try to learn, do not bring themselves to the environment of evaluation and competition. What has not been risked cannot be found lacking; it is, quite simply, safer to quit trying.

Still others seek to win approval from their classmates through disruptive protest "games." The easiest is to be "against"; it almost doesn't matter what is being protested so long as the rebellion is outspoken to the point of requiring adult attention. Even the achievers who work hard at the tasks schools set for them play at this role. Thus, the child who is unsuccessful at schoolwork and who feels that the ordinary rewards of meeting school expectations are worthless can gain adult recognition and his peers' esteem merely by giving vent to his feelings.

If, from a mistaken desire to be "understanding," the adult takes the child's complaints seriously, many pupils will switch effortlessly to a second game. The essence of this game is a dogged insistence that the teacher is responsible for suggesting alternative, and presumably more worthwhile, classroom projects. Then begins round upon round of "You tell me what I'm to do, and I'll refuse (forget, be unable) to do it." It's a very satisfying game: the adult will keep it going indefinitely and thus offer endless opportunities to score points.

A third, closely related strategy is the power game. The antiachiever treats the class as a purely social occasion whose function is to provide not only a ready-made opponent in the form of the teacher, but a group of willing spectators. Faced with a student who simply will *not* cooperate, the teacher has no choice but to become involved. The class typically reacts with glee; the power game is much more interesting than the interrupted classwork. The student wins the game every time: the teacher is distracted from the common endeavor he has chosen and is forced to pay attention to the child's disruption. At best, he can silence the child or expel him from the class. The former leaves the door open for another round of play, the latter is considered a distinguished accomplishment, particularly if the teacher loses his temper in the process.

ASSISTING THE ANTIACHIEVER

Whether from the need to maintain immature dependence, the need to be extraordinary, or the need to avoid failure, the antiachiever is trapped — and trapped he will remain without therapeutic intervention. What then can be done to break the antiachievement cycle? The average public or private school counseling staff carries too heavy a caseload and is too closely associated in pupils' minds with the overall school environment to be able to play much of a direct therapeutic role in aiding the older antiachiever with ingrained failure patterns. (Counseling of such students requires a very heavy time commitment.) However, the guidance counselor and school administrator can take a number of very constructive steps to assist students with current and potential underachievement problems: identification, early preventive/remedial programming, and referral of students with serious antiachievement problems to appropriate sources.

Detection of antiachievement tendencies should be a key action target for guidance counselors, school administrators, and teachers. At relatively advanced stages, students with serious achievement problems can be identified readily by simultaneous evaluation of academic achievement and classroom behavior patterns. Comparisons of intelligence/aptitude test scores with school grades over an extended period can show startling patterns: in a recent Thirteenth Year class of high school graduates, students averaged in the eighty-third percentile in IQ and in the twenty-third percentile in overall class standing in high school. However, classroom behavior patterns should be carefully scrutinized for all students — with review of past history as well as current teachers' comments. (Use of a checklist of symptomatic behaviors can be helpful in ensuring appropriate attention to withdrawal and dependency factors.) Otherwise children with very high intelligence and serious anti-achievement problems can be overlooked since academic symptoms can be masked by extraordinary ability.

Standard psychological tests now available do not serve as adequate indicators of potential differences in achievement. However, several agencies have psycho-sociological instruments which make it possible to identify potential antiachievers as early as the third grade. One such sociological questionnaire has been developed by Carol Griffin, Director of Pupil Personnel Services in Quincy, Massachusetts. The Thirteenth Year also has devised an evaluation system which enables diagnosis of antiachievement syndromes.

Preventive/Remedial Programming. We urge school boards, administrators, guidance counselors, teachers, parents, and all others concerned about the antiachievement problem to work toward immediate institution of preventive/remedial programs for improvement of the school environment. Further generations of anti-achievers can be anticipated unless the school environment becomes a less threatening work situation — that is, provides a warmer, more human, and more reality-oriented atmosphere. As educators, we believe that children deserve at least as good work conditions as adults. Yet industry is far ahead of the schools in its treatment of workers. After the adverse impact of depersonalization in factories and other mass employment institutions was proved by consultants' studies, most major employers instituted human relations programs which vastly increased employee morale and productivity simply by more careful "engineering" of social factors. Certainly programs with similar intent should and can be introduced into our schools to aid children — who are far more vulnerable to stress — to learn to achieve more happily. While longitudinal studies of the impact of a healthier atmosphere on achievement can be helpful in justifying the very small additional expense, there is no need for lengthy research. Moreover, significant improvement can be achieved without adding more teachers or aides. The immediate goal should simply be to train teachers — via brief workshop courses and seminars — to respond more humanly to students in stress situations.

This approach has already been demonstrated to be successful in several schools in California. Teachers trained in Dr. William Glasser's reality therapy* method have helped potential antiachievers become more responsible in their behavior by switching from an "objective," "professional" classroom stance to a more personally oriented relationship to their pupils. Under this approach, the teacher develops a direct personal relationship with the disturbed child through such strategies as warm, positive personal comments and physical contact. Then firmly — but not punitively — the teacher rejects irresponsible behavior, asks *personally* for improvement, and teaches better ways of behaving by various techniques. Not only do substantial improvements in behavior and achievement result, but the teacher no longer has to waste large blocks of time on disciplinary problems.

Another area where preventive programs should be developed is special parent education — both for students in child care programs and for current parents. Overly permissive and rigid parenthood patterns, particularly, can be ameliorated by introducing realistic material on children's needs and what parents can expect in the various developmental stages.

Referral Sources. Unfortunately very few remedial programs have been specifically addressed to the needs of the antiachiever so it is difficult for the guidance counselor to find appropriate referral resources. However, over the next few years, more resources should become available locally. A basic component of all such programs can be expected to be individual and/or group counseling, with associated "courses" which provide key informational inputs and opportunities for learning by experience.

One currently successful resource is The Thirteenth Year, which offers a unique program designed to help antiachieving adolescents gain insight, self-confidence, and the skills needed to cope with life as a developmental process. The program was designed specifically for those adolescents (drop-outs as well as high school graduates) who have been unable to actualize themselves and whose underachievement is therefore likely to continue. Our efforts have shown

---

Reality Therapy, A New Approach to Psychiatry. New York: Harper & Row, 1965.

that these students can be helped — but not simply by a more caring environment, a shift in demands, or intensified tutorial aid. Any remedial program which ignores the cyclical relationship of belief and behavior in reinforcing and prolonging the individual's failure to achieve will be ineffective.

Accordingly, The Thirteenth Year program focuses first on the underachiever's psychological state, his self-concept, and second on the mechanics of self-actualizing vs self-destructive behavior. All other concerns must wait upon changes in these basics. Initially, we deal with one essential issue — the individual's perception of his problem — and one question: what is he doing to help himself? Sympathy or help would, at this point, merely reinforce the antiachiever's conviction of his own inability to help himself. Personal failure is extremely painful so most of our students want to be helped, but the simple fact is that they cannot be until they are attempting to help themselves. The first steps must be theirs; if teachers/counselors provide the direction at this point, then the basic lesson, that they can help themselves (indeed, that only they can help themselves), will never be learned.

As the student begins to move, we then introduce a new focus on goal setting. Antiachievers tend to set goals which they cannot meet; if occasionally not guided, their efforts would lead to virtually assured failure, which would in turn push them toward regression into psychological withdrawal. They are often vague as to what their real goals are, and effort expended toward, say, a parental goal will not prove to be self-actualizing. Moreover, they need practice in formulating their life situations in such ways that the obstacles to, and hence tactics for, goal-achievement become clear.

The third and final stage of treatment is to give the student the opportunity to improve whatever academic skills he feels are lacking and to test his skills in an environment beyond The Thirteenth Year. Each student makes his own individual decision in these areas — his goals must remain his own. For therapeutic reasons, we require all students to become significantly involved in some activity beyond our walls, but we restrict staff involvement to providing guidance and back-up support. While problem-centered psychological discussions continue, the individual is all but on his own

233

as he decides what work to do and how to accomplish it. A lesser degree of freedom would heighten the chance of a return to failure when the end of the program abruptly removes our support.

This process takes time — at least two full school terms of intensive work for most of our students and longer for others. Techniques include individual and group counseling and special "classes" which utilize innovative techniques to help students understand their needs and human roles, achieve better interpersonal communications, increase their creativity and flexibility, and develop sounder goals and study habits. The physical environment is quite informal, and the relatively large staff relates to students on an I-you basis, with no pretensions of omniscience. Maximum school size to sustain therapeutic quality has been found to be 60–70 students, divided into groups with 10–12 members. Our experience indicates that it would be difficult to duplicate this kind of operation within the public school structure because of the required size limitations, staffing patterns, and overall environment.

Among the other types of referral resources available to guidance counselors is psychotherapy. Generally, except where certain serious neurotic symptoms indicate otherwise, traditional psychotherapy is not recommended as a sole means of aiding antiachievers because it is too problem centered and does not provide these young people with the kinds of constructive inputs which they need to create better operating modes. Increasing their awareness of underlying problems tends merely to "adjust" these "patients" to antiachievement by providing further justifications for antisocial behavior. With its heavy concentration on past experiences, Freudian technique, for example, does not provide the kinds of insights into normal mature adult life required to build the discrete realizable goals which are basic to sound motivation.

Of all the psychotherapeutic methodologies currently available, Reality Therapy, adapted by the Thirteenth Year staff, appears to offer the most promise for antiachievers. Dr. Glasser considers reality denial a major factor in neurosis and emphasizes the need for patients to accept the reality of the world around them. His therapeutic approach centers on "the need to love and be loved and the need to feel that we are worthwhile to ourselves and to others." He considers it desirable to ignore the past and concentrate on learning to fulfill these needs by continued involvement with people and acquiring responsibility. The therapist is trained to become personally involved with his patient, to reject unrealistic behavior while still accepting the patient, and to teach the patient better ways to fulfill his needs. Reality Therapy can be used in both group and individual sessions and by both psychiatrists and counselors — with the major difference a matter of intensity, according to Dr. Glasser.

THE HOPEFUL FUTURE

The future of the antiachiever used to appear bleak: without means of intervention, he was locked into an immobilizing cycle of self-destructive beliefs and behaviors, and many of our brightest young people, who *could be* our most productive, still will play only marginal roles throughout their lives because they will remain bound to this deadly cycle. Fortunately, however, the new techniques and resources available to guidance counselors, school administrators, and teachers will enable many to cope with this challenge. By identifying current and potential antiachievers, by introducing preventive/remedial approaches, and by referring those antiachievers with the most serious symptoms to appropriate referral sources — such as The Thirteenth Year — these educators will break the antiachievement cycle not only for individual students, but throughout the systems in which they are employed. A relatively small investment of time and resources can give your community a leadership position in this literally life-saving movement.

A rationale and blueprint for what could be the most powerful movement for the reform of secondary education in our time. Inspired by the walkabout of a native Australian boy — the six-month endurance test that precedes his acceptance into adult society — it outlines the requirements of a similar transition to adulthood in post-industrial civilization.

Walkabout: Searching for the Right Passage from Childhood and School

MAURICE GIBBONS
Professor of Education

Simon Fraser University,
Burnaby, British Columbia

A year ago I saw an Australian film called *Walkabout** which was so provocative — and evocative — I am still rerunning scenes from it in my mind. In the movie, two children escape into the desert-like wilderness of the outback when their father, driven mad by failure in business, attempts to kill them. Within hours they are

---

*Now available in book form. James Vance Marshall. *Walkabout*. New York: William Morrow, 1971, and G. Belmont Tower Books, paper.

exhausted, lost, and helpless. Inappropriately dressed in private school uniforms, unable to find food or protection from the blazing heat, and with no hope of finding their way back, they seem certain to die. At the last moment they are found and cared for by a young aborigine, a native Australian boy on his walkabout, a six-month-long endurance test during which he must survive alone in the wilderness and return to his tribe as an adult, or die in the attempt. In contrast to the city children, he moves through the forbidding wilderness as if it were part of his village. He survives not only with skill but with grace and pride as well, whether stalking kangaroo in a beautiful but deadly ballet, seeking out the subtle signs of direction, or merely standing watch. He not only endures, he merges with the land, and he enjoys. When they arrive at the edge of civilization, the aborigine offers — in a ritual dance — to share his life with the white girl and boy he has befriended, but they finally leave him and the outback to return home. The closing scenes show them immersed again in the conventions of suburban life, but dreaming of their adventure, their fragment of a walk-about.

The movie is a haunting work of art. It is also a haunting comment on education. What I find most provocative is the stark contrast between the aborigine's walkabout experience and the test of an adolescent's readiness for adulthood in our own society. The young native faces a severe but extremely appropriate trial, one in which he must demonstrate the knowledge and skills necessary to make him a contributor to the tribe rather than a drain on its meager resources. By contrast, the young North American is faced with written examinations that test skills very far removed from the actual experience he will have in real life. He writes; he does not act. He solves familiar theoretical problems; he does not apply what he knows in strange but real situations. He is under direction in a protected environment to the end; he does not go out into the world to demonstrate that he is prepared to survive in, and contribute to, our society. His preparation is primarily for the mastery of content and skills in the disciplines and has little to do with reaching maturity, achieving adulthood, or developing fully as a person.

The isolation involved in the walkabout is also in sharp contrast to experience in our school system. In an extended period of solitude at a crucial stage of his development, the aborigine is confronted with a challenge not only to his competence, but also to his inner or spiritual resources. For his Western counterpart, however, school is always a crowd experience. Seldom separated from his class, friends, or family, he has little opportunity to confront his anxieties, explore his inner resources, and come to terms with the world and his future in it. Certainly, he receives little or no training in how to deal with such issues. There are other contrasts, too, at least between the Australian boy and the urban children in the movie: his heightened sensory perception, instinct, and intuition, senses which seem numbed in them; his genuine, open, and emphathic response toward them in saving their lives, and their inability to finally overcome their suspicious and defensive self-interest to save his. And above all there is his love and respect for the land even as he takes from it what he needs; and the willful destruction of animals and landscape which he observes in disbelief during his brushes with civilization.

CONTRAST TO GRADUATION CEREMONIES

Imagine for a moment two children, a young native looking ahead to his walkabout and a young North American looking ahead to grade 12 as the culminating experiences of all their basic preparation for adult life. The young native can clearly see that his life will depend on the skills he is learning and that after the walkabout his survival and his place in the community will depend upon them, too. What meaning and relevance such a goal must give to learning! What a contrast if he were preparing to write a test on survival techniques in the outback or the history of aboriginal weaponry. The native's Western counterpart looks forward to such abstractions as subjects and tests sucked dry of the richness of experience, in the end having little to do directly with anything critical or even significant that he anticipates being involved in as an adult — except the pursuit of more formal education. And yet, is it not clear that what will matter to him — and to his community — is not his test-writing ability or even what he knows about, but what he feels, what he stands for, what he can do and will do, and what he is becoming as a person? And if the clear performative goal of the walkabout makes learning more significant, think of the effect it must have on the attitude and performance of the young person's parents and instructors, knowing that their skill and devotion will also be put to the ultimate test when the boy goes out on his own. What an effect such accountability could have on our concept of schooling and on parents' involvement in it!

For another moment, imagine these same two children reaching the ceremonies which culminate their basic preparation and celebrate their successful passage from childhood to adulthood, from school student to work and responsible community membership. When the aborigine returns, his readiness and worth have been clearly demonstrated to him and to his tribe. They need him. He is their hope for the future. It is a moment worth celebrating. What, I wonder, would an alien humanoid conclude about adulthood in our society if he had to make his deductions from a graduation ceremony announcing students' maturity: speeches, a parade of candidates — with readings from their yearbook descriptions — a formal dinner, expensive clothes and cars, graduates over here, adults over there, all-night parties, occasional drunkenness and sexual experiences or flirtation with it, and spray-painting "Grad '74" on a bridge or building. For many it is a memorable occasion — a pageant for parents, a good time for the students. But what is the message in this celebration at this most important moment of school life and in this most important shared community experience? What values does it promote? What is it saying about 12 years of school experience? The achievement of what goals is being celebrated? What is it teaching about adulthood? How is it contributing to a sense of community? What pleasures and sources of challenge and fulfillment does it encourage the young to pursue? And if our alien humanoid could look into the students' deepest thoughts, what would he conclude about their sense of readiness to live full and independent lives, to direct their own growth, to contribute to society, and to deal with the issues that confront us as a world — perhaps a universe — citizenry? I think his unprejudiced conclusions would horrify us.

CHALLENGING MODEL FOR OUR SOCIETY

In my opinion, the walkabout could be a very useful model to guide us in redesigning our own rites of passage. It provides a powerful focus during training, a challenging demonstration of necessary competence, a profound maturing experience, and an enrichment of community life. By comparison, preparation and trial in our society are incomplete, abstract, and impersonal; and graduation is little more than a party celebrating the end of school. I am not concluding that our students should be sent into the desert, the wilderness, or the Arctic for six months — even though military service, Outward Bound, and such organizations as the Boy Scouts do feature wilderness living and survival training. What is appropriate for a primitive subsistence society is not likely appropriate for one as complex and technically sophisticated as ours. But the walkabout is a useful analogy, a way of making the familiar strange so we can examine our practices with fresh eyes. And it raises the question I find fascinating: *What would an appropriate and challenging walkabout for students in our society be like?* Let me restate the problem more specifically. What sensibilities, knowledge, attitudes, and competencies are necessary for a full and productive adult life? What kinds of experience will have the power to focus our children's energy on achieving these goals? And what kind of performance will demonstrate to the student, the school, and the community that the goals have been achieved?

The walkabout model suggests that our solution to this problem must measure up to a number of criteria. First of all, it should be experiential and the experience should be real rather than simulated; not knowledge about aerodynamics and aircraft, not passing the Link-trainer test, but the experience of solo flight in which the mastery of relevant abstract knowledge and skills is manifest in the performance. Second, it should be a challenge which extends the capacities of the student as fully as possible, urging him to consider every limitation he perceives in himself as a barrier to be broken through; not a goal which is easily accessible, such as playing an instrument he already plays competently, but a risky goal which calls for a major extension of his talent, such as earning a chair in the junior symphony or a gig at a reputable discotheque. Third, it should be a challenge the student chooses for himself. As

Margaret Mead has often pointed out — in *Growing Up in Samoa,* for instance — the major challenge for young people in our society is making decisions. In primitive societies there are few choices; in technological societies like ours there is a bewildering array of alternatives in lifestyle, work, politics, possessions, recreation, dress, relationships, environment, and so on. Success in our lives depends on the ability to make appropriate choices. Yet, in most schools, students make few decisions of any importance and receive no training in decision making or in the implementation and reassessment cycle which constitutes the basic growth pattern. Too often, graduation cuts them loose to muddle through for themselves. In this walkabout model, teachers and parents may help, but in the Rogerian style — by facilitating the student's decision making, not by making the decisions for him. The test of the walkabout, and of life, is not what he can do under a teacher's direction, but what the teacher has enabled him to decide and to do on his own.

In addition, the trial should be an important learning experience in itself. It should involve not only the demonstration of the student's knowledge, skill, and achievement, but also a significant confrontation with himself: his awareness, his adaptability to situations, his competence, and his nature as a person. Finally, the trial and ceremony should be appropriate, appropriate not as a test of the schooling which has gone before, but as a transition from school learning to the life which will follow afterwards. And the completion of the walkabout should bring together parents, teachers, friends, and others to share the moment with him, to confirm his achievement, and to consolidate the spirit of community in which he is a member. Keeping these features of the walkabout analogy in mind, let us now ask the question, What might a graduation ceremony in this mode be like in a North American high school?

EXAMPLES OF "WALKABOUT" GRADUATIONS

The time is September. The place, a school classroom somewhere in the Pacific Northwest. Margaret, a student who has just finished grade 12, is making a multimedia presentation to a number of relatives, over 20 of her classmates, several friends from other schools, some teachers, the mayor, and two reporters she worked with during the year. Watching intently are a number of younger students already thinking about their own walkabouts. Margaret has been thinking about this moment since grade 8 and working on her activities seriously since the night the principal met with all the grade 10 students and their parents to outline and discuss the challenges. Afterwards she and her mother sat up talking about her plans until early morning. She is beginning with the first category, *Adventure*, which involves a challenge to her daring and endurance. The film and slides Margaret is showing trace her trip through the Rockies following the path of Lewis and Clark in their exploration of the Northwest. Her own journal and maps are on display along with a number of objects — arrowheads and the like — which she found enroute. The names of her five companions — she is required to cooperate with a team in at least one, but no more than two, of the five categories — are on display. In one corner of the room she has arranged a set of bedroom furniture — a loft-desk-library module, a rocking chair, and a coffee-table treasure-chest — designed, built, and decorated as her work in the *Creative-Aesthetic* field. On the walls are photographs and charts showing pollution rates of local industries which she recorded during the summer and used in a report to the Community Council. The three newspaper articles about the resulting campaign against pollution-law violators, and her part in it, are also displayed to give proof that she has completed the third category, *Community Service*.

Margaret, like many of the other students, engaged in *Logical Inquiry* which related closely to her practical work. Her question was, What structural design and composition has the best ratios of strength, ease of construction, and economy of materials? Using charts of the various designs and ratios, she describes her research and the simple experiment she developed to test her findings, and she demonstrates the effectiveness of the preferred design by performing pressure tests on several models built from the same material. After answering a few questions from a builder in the crowd, she shows how the problem grew out of her studies in architecture for the *Practical-Vocational* category. Passing her sketch books around and several summer-cabin designs she drew up, she goes on to describe her visits to a number of architects for assistance, then unveils a model of the summer camp she designed for her family and helped them build on their Pacific Coast property. Slides of the cabin under construction complete her presentation. A teacher asks why she is not performing any of the skills she developed, as the challenge requires, and she answers that her committee waived that requirement because the activities she chose all occurred in the field.

As Margaret's friends and relatives gathered around to congratulate her, down the hall Ken is beginning his presentation with a report on his two-month *Adventure* alone in a remote village in France where he took a laboring job and lived with a French family in which no one spoke English. The idea arose during a discussion of his proposal to travel when the teacher on his committee asked him to think of a more daring challenge than sight-seeing in a foreign country. A professor in modern languages has been invited by the school to attend the presentations, converse with him in French, and comment on his mastery. Later, with his own guitar accompaniment, Ken will sing a medley of three folk songs which he has composed himself. Then, to meet the requirements of the *Community Service* category, he plans to report on the summer-care program which he initiated and ran, without pay, for pre-school children in the community. The director of the local Child Health and Welfare Service will comment upon the program. Finally, Ken will turn to the car engine which stands, partially disassembled, on a bench at the back of the room. His *Logical Inquiry* into the problem, "What ways can the power output of an engine be most economically increased?" is summarized in a brief paper to be handed out and illustrated with modifications he has made on the display engine with the help of a local mechanic and a shop teacher. He will conclude his presentation by reassembling the engine as quickly as he can.

FIVE COMPONENTS OF MODEL

If we entered any room anywhere in the school, similar presentations would be under way; students displaying all kinds of alternatives they selected to meet the five basic challenges:

1. *Adventure*: a challenge to the student's daring, endurance, and skill in an unfamiliar environment.

2. *Creativity*: a challenge to explore, cultivate, and express his own imagination in some aesthetically pleasing form.

3. *Service*: a challenge to identify a human need for assistance and provide it; to express caring without expectation of reward.

4. *Practical Skill*: a challenge to explore a utilitarian activity, to learn the knowledge and skills necessary to work in that field, and to produce something of use.

5. *Logical Inquiry*: a challenge to explore one's curiosity, to formulate a question or problem of personal importance, and to pursue an answer or solution systematically and, wherever appropriate, by investigation.

We would learn about such *Adventures* as a two-week solo on the high river living off the land, parachute drops, rock climbing expeditions, mapping underground caves, an exchange with a Russian student, kayaking a grade three river to the ocean, scuba-diving exploits, sailing ventures, solo airplane and glider flights, ski-touring across glaciers, a month-long expedition on the Pacific Crest trail, and some forms of self-exploratory, meditative, or spiritual adventures.

We would see such *Aesthetic* works as fashion shows of the students' own creations, sculpture and painting, jewelry, tooled leather purses, anthologies of poetry, a humor magazine, plays written and directed by the author, a one-man mime show, political cartoons, a Japanese garden featuring a number of home-cultivated bonsai trees, rugs made of home-dyed fibers, illuminated manuscripts, gourmet foods, computer art, a rock-group and a string quartet, a car-body design and paint job, original films, a stand-up comic's art, tapes of natural-sound music, and a display of blown-glass creatures.

In the *Service* category students would be reporting on volunteer work with the old, ill, infirm, and retarded; a series of closed-circuit television hookups enabling children immobilized in the hospital to communicate with each other, a sports program for the handicapped, a Young Brother program for the retarded, local Nader's Raiders kinds of studies and reports, construction of playgrounds, hiking trails and landscaped parks, cleanups of eyesore lots, surveys of community needs and opinions, collecting abandoned cars to sell as scrap in order to support deprived families abroad, shopping and other trips for shut-ins, and a hot-meals-on-wheels program for pensioners.

In the *Practical* realm we might see demonstrations of finely honed secretarial skills, ocean-floor plant studies, inventions and new designs of many kinds, the products of new small businesses, a conservation program to save a locally endangered species, stock market trend analyses and estimates, boats designed and built for sale, a course taught by computer-assisted instruction, small farms or sections of farms developed and managed, a travel guidebook for high school students, a six-inch telescope with hand-ground lenses and a display of photographs taken through it, a repair service for gas furnaces and other home appliances, and a collection of movie reviews written for the local suburban newspaper.

And we would hear about *Logical Inquiries* into such questions as, How does a starfish bring about the regeneration of a lost arm? What does one experience when meditating that he doesn't experience just sitting with his eyes closed? What is the most effective technique in teaching a dog obedience? How do they navigate in space? Does faith-healing work, and if so, how? How many anomalies, such as the ancient Babylonian battery, are there in our history and how can they be explained? What folk and native arts and crafts have developed in this area? What are the 10 most important questions man asks but can't answer? What is insanity — where is the line that separates it from sanity? and, What natural means can I use to protect my crops most effectively from disease and insects? All day long such presentations occur throughout the school, each student with his own place and time, each demonstrating his unique accomplishment, each with an opportunity to be successful in his own way.

At the end of the day the families, their children, and their friends meet to celebrate this moment. The celebration takes a variety of forms: picnics, dinner at a restaurant, meals at home — some cooked by the graduating students — and buffets which all guests help to provide. In some instances two or three families join together. The ceremonies are equally varied, according to taste and imagination; some are religious, some raucous, some quite quietly together. In each the student is the center of the occasion. Parents and guests respond to the graduate's presentation. Teachers drop by to add their comments. And the student talks about his plans for the future. Some may find ways to announce the young person's entry into a new stage of independence and responsibility, helping him to clarify and pursue his next life goal. To conclude, there may be a school or community celebration to which all are invited for music, singing, and dancing. The only formal event would be a presentation of bound volumes of the student's reports on their accomplishments to the principal and mayor for the school and the community libraries. My own preference would be to include, also, some ritual experience of the family being together at the moment of its coming apart, or some shared experience of life's mystery; perhaps a midnight walk or coming together to watch the dawn — the world beginning again, beginning still.

BASIC PRINCIPLES AND FLEXIBLE IMPLEMENTATION

Far-fetched? I don't think so. It is true that Margaret and Ken appear to be exceptional students. So many colleagues identified them as atypical that I almost added a Charlie and Lucy of much more modest accomplishment. But it seems to me that our expectations are conditioned by student performance in courses. In fact, we have no idea what they may be capable of when the same energy and ingenuity that has gone into our system for teaching them subjects is transformed into a system for supporting their own development of their own potential. How far they can and will go along any particular path they choose may be limited, over the years, only by their ability to conceive of it as possible and our ability to confirm it. Besides, we are concerned here as much with depth as with range, as much with the quality of the students' experience as with the manifest products of their effort. One experience of true caring for another without expectation of reward, one experience of breaking through the confines of one's own believed limitations, one mystery unraveled, are the seeds of all later commitment and growth, and are worth cultivating with everything at our disposal. The purpose is not just to stimulate an impressive array of accomplishments, but to enable students to find out who

246

they are by finding out what they can do, and to confirm the importance of that most essential human work.

Nor is it far-fetched to think of schools adopting a program to accomplish these ends. The concept is flexible. Any school or community may adapt this proposal to its own circumstances by choosing different categories of achievement, different plans for preparation in school time, a different manner of demonstrating accomplishment, and a different kind of ceremony. The basic principles — personal challenge, individual and group decision making, self-direction in the pursuit of goals, real-world significance in activity, and community involvement at all stages of preparation and conclusion — can be accomplished in a variety of ways. It is true that a decade ago such a proposal was unthinkable. The importance of grades and the singular pattern of schooling for achieving them were so general it appeared impossible and impractical to break out of the system. Since the educational troubles of the sixties, with the rise of a responsible radicalism and the appearance of a number of technological and humanistic alternatives, many schools have successfully broken from old patterns to search for forms of education more appropriate for our times.

Some innovators, however, have merely put old content into new programs — for instance, by translating courses into assignment sheets and letting the student work through them at his own pace. Some changes — in the freest of free schools, for example — eliminate all content and directive instruction, relying instead on the student's discovery of his own program. Unfortunately, such laissez-faire aproaches too often create a leadership and authority vacuum in the classroom, one that students are unable to fill. The approach suggested here reflects what many innovative teachers and administrators have pointed out to me: that real change does involve new freedom for students, but that independence must be combined with a vivid personal goal and a framework within which the student can pursue it. If we remove the structure of subjects, disciplines, courses, lessons, texts, and tests, it is essential that we develop superstructures which will support the student's efforts to create a structure of his own. Autonomy, like maturity, is not a gift but an accomplishment of youth, and a difficult one to attain. This walkabout proposal describes one possible superstructure. For students who are already developing elements of their own programs — in open area elementary schools and interdisciplinary walkabout humanities programs, for example — an appropriate walkabout would provide a clear, long-term goal and open the way for the school and community to develop a support structure as the student's need for assistance in pursuing his goal intensifies.

Preparation for the walkabout challenge can be provided in various degrees of intensity, depending upon how committed the school staff is to creating a curriculum which focuses upon personal development.

1. It can be an extracurricular activity in which all planning and work is done during out-of-school time.

2. It can be one element of the curriculum which is included in the schedule like a course, giving students time for planning, consultation, and training.

3. It can be the core of the grade 12 program, one in which all teaching and activity is devoted to preparing for trial.

4. It can be the goal around which a whole new curriculum is designed for the school, or for a school-within-the-school staffed by interested teachers for interested students.

If the school is junior secondary — this concept can readily be adapted to elementary schooling, too — students and parents should be notified of the graduation trial upon entry in grade 8, perhaps by a single announcement with an accompanying descriptive brochure. Trial committees — including the student, the parents, and a teacher — should be organized for meetings, likely as early as grade 9, to guide the student's explorations of possible challenges, so that serious planning and the preparation of formal proposals can begin in grade 10. To make the nature of the walkabout vivid, the committee should involve students in a series of "Experience Weeks" during which they would be out of school pursuing activities, first of the school's design and later of their own designs, as trial runs.

During these early years the student could also benefit from association with "big brothers" in the school, older students in more advanced stages of preparation who can help their younger colleagues with considerable benefits for themselves as well. The committee would also be responsible for helping the student make his own choices and find the resources and training necessary to accomplish them; and by their interest, they would also help the student to develop confidence in his decisions and commitment to his own goals. A survey of student plans during any of the senior years would give the staff the information necessary to plan the most useful possible training, which could be offered in mini-courses — one day each week, for instance — or in a semester or a year-long curriculum devoted to preparation for trial.

If students were required to write a two-page report on each challenge, a collection of these reports could provide an accumulating resource for younger candidates as well as a permanent "hall of accomplishment" for graduates. In such ways the walkabout challenge could also become a real focus for training in such basic skills as speaking, writing, and use of the media. These are only a few of the ways this proposal can be implemented and integrated with other aspects of school life.

OVERCOMING POTENTIAL PROBLEMS

But colleagues and parents with whom I have discussed the idea raise a number of problems potential in the walkabout challenge. What about the inequality that exists between students who have great resources for such walkabout activities at home and students who have few resources at their disposal? What about the risks involved for students on their own in the city and the wilderness? What if competition among students to outdo each other drives them to traumatic extremes or failure? On the other hand, what if students don't want to be bothered? How can we account for differences in ability; that is, how can we distinguish the apparently modest accomplishment that is a severe challenge for one student from the apparently grand accomplishment which is actually a modest challenge for another? These are not fantasy what-ifs, but the real concerns of those who want to anticipate and eliminate as many liabilities as possible. They deserve consideration.

Such questions point to basic issues; motivation, risk control, support, and assessment. In each case resolution depends upon close communication and cooperation among students, parents, teachers, and other members of the community. Students will be motivated by the personal challenge, but it will be essential for all the adults to confirm the importance of these challenges by their interest, concern, and involvement. Counseling by the parent/teacher committees will be essential to help students to clarify their personal goals and to help them decide on activities which stretch, but do not threaten to break, their spirit. But, since this walkabout is a growth experience, I must emphasize that appropriate counseling must help the student to clarify *his* goals and should not be advice giving or demand making. Failure, except where health and safety are seriously threatened, can also be a growth experience for persons who have accepted responsibility for their decisions and actions.

When risk is involved, as in the *Adventure Challenge*, communication and cooperation between home and school will be extremely important. The risk and liability must clearly be the student's, accepted as such by him and his family. But the adults should then help the student to eliminate all unnecessary dangers from the adventure and to develop the knowledge and skills which will make him the master of the dangerous situation he is planning to enter. If his challenge involves scuba diving, for instance, they should be sure that his equipment is adequate, that he has received professional training and certification for free diving, and that he has arranged for a skilled companion to accompany him. The adult committee can also be of assistance in helping students to arrange for necessary resources, such as scuba-diving equipment, in order to equalize the support each of them has available. However, the student with too many readily available resources is as much a problem as the student with too few — in terms of this proposal, at least. A more appropriate solution to the support issue would make the acquisition of resources the student's responsibility, no matter how much was available to him from parents — earning money for equipment and courses, scrounging materials, finding economical ways to travel — so that any achievement is more clearly and completely his own.

A spirit of competition among students attempting to outdo each other could easily emerge. Of course, competition is already a driving force in schooling. The difference is that there is only one kind of contest and one way to win in school competition, and the basic finishing order is quite clearly established after 12 years — usually, after the first year. In the walkabout experience proposed here each student chooses goals and activities which are important to him. Each will be different. Comparison will be difficult and somewhat pointless, particularly if the adult/student committees maintain focus on the student's personal growth through challenging himself rather than others. Everyone can be successful. To be an appropriate part of this learning/growing experience, any assessment must be the student's own judgment of the quality and importance of what he has done. The responses of many people during trial will provide participants with feedback on their progress, as will the audience at their final presentations and the guests at the evening ceremonies. Marks, grades — any comparative evaluation — would be disastrous. The competition is with one's self, not others. The pride is in the confirmation of competence, not superiority. The satisfaction is in the recognition by others of what one has proven to one's self: "I can accomplish. I can become. And therefore I can look forward with hope and anticipation." In these ways the issues of motivation, risk, support, and assessment can be converted from potential problems to beneficial elements of the program.

If there are problems to overcome, the effort required will be repaid by a number of benefits for the student and for the school. The school — any concerned adult — can have no higher aspiration for young people than assisting them to develop a profound sense of their own worth and identity. To reach this state, the young must find their way through the stormy clouds of self-doubt until they win the higher ground of confidence where greater clarity is possible. Getting there requires autonomy, initiative, and industry; three aspects of competence essential in the quest for identity — personal accomplishments which cannot be given or demanded, only nurtured. I believe the trial described here provides a framework for nurturing such development. The individual can clarify his own values and his goals. He can make decisions about his own directions and efforts. He can explore his personal resources by testing them in action. Curiosity, inquiry, and imagination will take on new significance. He will see the uniqueness of his emerging accomplishments and abilities gain greater recognition than his adaptation to the norms of school and peer behavior. The student can learn to work intimately with a small group on a real and significant task, and can learn from them how his contributions are perceived. With goals clearly in mind, he will be encouraged to initiate his plans and see them through to fulfillment even though obstacles challenge his resourcefulness. And having reached these goals, he may take justifiable pride in the competencies he has developed as well as the things he has achieved. In schools where students are directed, dependent, and ultimately have no personal rights, such an opportunity to earn respect and dignity on their own terms would be a significant advance. Most important, the student will not have begun to clarify his life goals through these challenges, he will have experienced the cycle by which life goals are pursued. His graduation can thereby be transformed from a school ceremony marking the end of one self-contained stage to a community celebration marking his transition to an independent, responsible life. It can be a celebration of a new stage in the flow of his becoming a person. The school also seems likely to reap a number of benefits from the walkabout challenge program: a boost to school spirit; an opportunity to establish a new, more facilitative relationship between staff and students; a new, focus for cooperation with parents and the rest of the community; a constant source of information about what is important to students — and parents; a means of motivating and focusing learning for everyone, particularly younger, beginning students; a constant reminder of the relationship between education and living; and a device for transforming the nature of schooling to combine freedom and responsibility, independence and clearly directed effort. And most important, it will enable us to communicate to our younger generation how important their growth and accomplishment is to us. In fact, the success of this concept depends on that communication.

I am interested in the walkabout challenge because it promises what I most want for my own children. No one can give life meaning for them, but there are a number of ways we can help them to give life meaning for themselves. Central to that meaning is their sense of who they are in the scheme of things and their confidence that, no matter what the future holds, they can decide and act, that they can develop skills to be justifiably proud of, that they can cross the most barren outback with a certain grace and find even in simple moments a profound joy. I hope that by exploring what they can do and feel they will come to know themselves better, and with that knowledge that they will move through today with contentment and will look forward to tomorrow with anticipation. I think a challenging walkabout designed for our time and place can contribute to that kind of growth.

About
the
Contributors*

EDITOR
Monroe D. Cohen is Director of Publications and Editor of *Childhood Education* for the Association for Childhood Education International.

AUTHORS
Marjorie Blaufarb is the managing Editor of *Update* and the staff liaison to the Task Force on Equal Opportunity and Human Rights of the American Alliance for Health, Physical Education, and Recreation.

Wayne C. Booth is Professor of English at the University of Detroit and author of *The Rhetoric of Fiction* (Chicago: University of Chicago Press, 1961).

Marguerite Brydegaard is Professor of Education at San Diego State University, San Diego, California.

*The professional affiliations and other personal data cited are given for the dates of original publication.

Fred G. Burke is Commissioner of Education for the State of Rhode Island and Providence Plantations.

James E. Calkins is Assistant Superintendent, Staples High School, Westport, Connecticut.

Karl W. Deutsch is Professor of Government, Faculty of Arts and Sciences, Harvard University, Cambridge, Massachusetts.

Mario D. Fantini is Dean of Education and Professor at the State University College, New Paltz, New York.

Maurice Gibbons is Professor of Education, Simon Fraser University, Burnaby, British Columbia, Canada.

Nat Hentoff frequently comments on educational and civil liberties issues in leading magazines. He is the author of *Our Children Are Dying* (New York: Viking Press, 1967) and other books, is a former Guggenheim Fellow in Education, and is a member of the Board of Directors of the New York Civil Liberties Union.

Harlan Hoffa is Head, Department of Art Education, Pennsylvania State University, University Park, Pennsylvania.

James E. Inskeep, Jr. is Professor of Education at San Diego State University, San Diego, California.

Peter E. Kane is Professor of Speech at the State University College, Brockport, New York.

Jean Karl is Vice-president and Editor of Children's Books, Atheneum Publishers.

Judith F. Krug is Director of the Office for Intellectual Freedom of the American Library Association and Executive Director of the Freedom to Read Foundation.

Ruth McGaffey is Associate Professor of Communications and Chairperson of the Communications Department at the University of Wisconsin at Milwaukee.

Charles H. Rathbone is Assistant Professor of Education and Chairman, Elementary Master of Arts Teaching Program, at Oberlin College in Ohio. Recently, he edited *Open Education: The Informal Classroom* (New York: Citation Press, 1971).

Marian Ronan is a Graduate Student in Elementary Education at the University of Pennsylvania.

Donald P. Saunders is Professor of Education, Department of Educational Development and Associate Director of the Center for Human Resource Research at the Ohio State University, Columbus.

Stanley R. Sherman is Co-founder and Director of In-service Training Program of the Center for Alternative Education in Boston, Massachusetts.

Moshe Smilansky is Professor of Educational Sciences at the University of Tel Aviv, Israel.

Alan Sostek is Co-founder and Clinical Director of the Center for Alternative Education in Boston, Massachusetts.

Thomas L. Tedford is Professor of Drama and Speech at the University of North Carolina at Greensboro. He was Chairman of the Commission on Freedom of Speech of the Speech Communication Association.

William H. Van Hoose is Professor and Chairman of the Department of Counselor Education at the University of Virginia.

Asahel D. Woodruff is Professor of Psychology at the University of Utah, Salt Lake City.

David Zuckerman is Co-director of the Center for Alternative Education in Boston, Massachusetts.